P9-EMM-294

J. David Lichtenthal, MBA, PhD
Editor

Fundamentals of Business Marketing Education
A Guide for University-Level Faculty and Policymakers

Pre-publication
REVIEWS,
COMMENTARIES,
EVALUATIONS . . .

"**I**f business-to-business marketing is the most overlooked area of marketing research, business-to-business marketing education is Cinderella, requiring an extensive search before the value is found. In one volume David Lichtenthal solves this problem by bringing together some of the world's leading business-to-business scholars to provide an informed and informative text that will be essential reading for the reflective marketing educator.

The chapters go beyond simply providing classroom tips; they discuss and identify the challenges facing all business-to-business researchers who wish to see their field prosper and grow. This is possible only if new scholars can be attracted to the field and their work can be regarded as valuable not just to students but to the marketing discipline as a whole.

The backbone of the volume is a series of commentaries that examine the issues facing business-to-business educators at every level. The commentaries provide significant insights that will force teachers to reflect on what they do and how they may change in the future. Collectively, this compilation is a manifesto for the development of business-to-business education for the next decade."

Dr. Damien McLoughlin
Senior Lecturer in Marketing,
Smurfit Business School,
Dublin, Ireland

More pre-publication
REVIEWS, COMMENTARIES, EVALUATIONS . . .

"**M**ost business is business-to-business business. Yet in most of our marketing courses the *consumer* marketing context is the focus. Business marketing presents different challenges, such as the role of business and personal relationships within and between firms and the role of technology. This book brings together key thinkers and thinking regarding the nature of and issues involved in business marketing education of all kinds, including undergraduate, masters, executive, and doctoral programs. The interaction between research, teaching, and practice is central to the debate and the authors offer various perspectives and suggestions for future development. Although adopting mainly a North American focus, it includes insightful commentary from academics elsewhere in the world.

Business education and training is key to developing and sustaining a nation's and a firm's competitiveness. This book is a useful resource for business faculties, universities, and government, and will help guide the development of education policy."

Professor Ian F. Wilkinson, PhD
School of Marketing,
University of New South Wales,
Sydney, Australia

"**F**undamentals of Business Marketing Education* is a compact collection of the studies and ideas that have been exchanged between the field's thought leaders. It's a resource to consult when teaching doctoral students, MBAs, un-

dergraduates, or executives. This book provides a critical starting point for identifying key constituents and topics, finding the apt pedagogy for the audience, and examining the most popular cases. The perspectives are global and the objectives include rigor and relevance in both instruction and development of the field."

F. Robert Dwyer, PhD
Co-author of *Business Marketing: Connecting Strategy, Relationships, and Learning;*
Joseph S. Stern Professor of Marketing,
University of Cincinnati

"**F**undamentals of Business Marketing Education* is an in-depth and thought-provoking treatment of an important topic, filling a void in business marketing education literature. The book covers business marketing education at undergraduate, masters, doctorate, and executive levels, and contains a wealth of ideas that will both inform and spark debate. With insightful chapters and commentaries written by acknowledged experts, this book will be a very valuable resource to anyone involved in business marketing education."

Jan B. Heide, PhD
Irwin Maier Chair in Marketing,
School of Business,
University of Wisconsin–Madison

Fundamentals of Business Marketing Education

A Guide for University-Level Faculty and Policymakers

BEST BUSINESS BOOKS
Foundation Series in Business Marketing
J. David Lichtenthal, MBA, PhD
Editor

Fundamentals of Business Marketing Research by David A. Reid
and Richard E. Plank

*Fundamentals of Business Marketing Education: A Guide for University-
Level Faculty and Policymakers* edited by J. David Lichtenthal

Fundamentals of Business Marketing Education
A Guide for University-Level Faculty and Policymakers

J. David Lichtenthal, MBA, PhD
Editor

Best Business Books®
An Imprint of The Haworth Press, Inc.
New York • London • Oxford

Published by

Best Business Books®, an imprint of The Haworth Press, Inc., 10 Alice Street, Binghamton, NY 13904-1580.

This book is a compilation of articles that appeared previously in the *Journal of Business-to-Business Marketing,* 5(1/2) (1998): 1-164 and 9(4) (2002): 27-126, published by The Haworth Press, Inc.

Cover design by Jennifer M. Gaska.

Library of Congress Cataloging-in-Publication Data

Fundamentals of business marketing education : a guide for university-level faculty and policy-makers / J. David Lichtenthal, editor.
       p. cm.
    "This book is a compilation of articles that appeared previously in the Journal of business-to-business marketing."
    Includes bibliographical references and index.
    ISBN 0-7890-0121-7 (case : alk. paper)—ISBN 0-7890-0132-2 (soft : alk. paper)
    1. Industrial marketing. 2. Industrial marketing—Management. 3. Industrial marketing—Study and teaching (Higher) 4. Business education—Curricula. I. Lichtenthal, David. II. Journal of business-to-business.

HF5415.1263.F857 2004
658.8'0071'1—dc22

                                                                                                            2003016230

CONTENTS

About the Editor   xiii

Contributors   xv

Series Preface   xvii

**Introduction. Business-to-Business Marketing Education
in the Twenty-First Century**   1
J. David Lichtenthal

The Impetus for This Topic   1
Purpose and Content   2
Closing Remarks   5

PART I: DOCTORAL PROGRAMS

**Doctoral Programs in Business-to-Business Marketing:
Status and Prospects**   9
Erwin Danneels
Gary L. Lilien

Introduction   9
PhD In Business: A Look Back   10
Data Collection   13
Analysis   17
    Program Characteristic Differences   19
    Admission Criteria   19
    Courses and Tracks   22
    Relevance and Preparation for Teaching   26
    Character of Programs with Emphasis
       in Business-to-Business   28
    Deficiencies in Faculty Applicants in Business-
       to-Business   31
    Placements   32
Discussion   34
    For Business Schools   36
       School Recommendation 1: Recruit Actively
          and Nontraditionally   36

School Recommendation 2: Internships, Sabbaticals,
    and Postdocs   36
School Recommendation 3: Rethink Reward
    Systems   36
   For Prospective PhDs (and Recent Graduates)   37
Candidate Recommendation 1: Partner Early
    and Often   37
Candidate Recommendation 2: Focus on Real
    Problems   37
Candidate Recommendation 3: Consider Industry
    Employment   37
  Conclusions   37

**Challenges for Business-to-Business Doctoral Programs:
A Commentary**   **41**
   Grahame R. Dowling

Topics Addressed: Doctoral Research, Its Impact,
  About Applied Research

**A Program of Action for Business-to-Business Doctoral
Programs: A Reply to Commentary**   **47**
   Erwin Danneels
   Gary L. Lilien

Topics Addressed: Business Marketing Context, Rigor
  versus Relevance, Academic Reward Systems

PART II: EXECUTIVE EDUCATION PROGRAMS

The Pedagogy of Executive Education in Business Markets   **51**
   Narakesari Narayandas
   V. Kasturi Rangan
   Gerald Zaltman

Introduction   51
Emergence of a Conceptual Structure in Business
  Marketing Education   52
Toward a Contextual Emphasis: Executive Education
    in the 1990s   56
Pedagogical Methods and Objectives   57
   Traditional Executive Programs   57
   Customized Executive Education   59
   Action Learning   60
   The Role of Technology   63

Design Principles for Future Executive Education
    in Business Marketing 64
        The Paradox of Current Knowledge 66
        Metaphors As Discovery Tools 67
        Linking Explicit with Implicit Knowledge 68
        Anomaly Detection 68
    Appendix: Tools for Delivery 70
        Lectures and Case Discussions 70
        The Role of Simulations 71

Business Marketing Executive Education:
A Commentary **75**
    Elizabeth J. Wilson

Topical Trends in Business Marketing Executive Education 75
Delivery of Business Marketing Executive Education 76
Approximating Action Learning in the EMBA Classroom 78

Executive Education in Business Markets:
A Reply to Commentary **81**
    Narakesari Narayandas
    V. Kasturi Rangan
    Gerald Zaltman

Topics Addressed: Conceptual Structure in Business
    Marketing Education, Pedagogical Methods
    and Objectives, Action Learning, Role of Technology,
    Future Education in Business Marketing

PART III: MASTER'S PROGRAMS

Master's-Level Education in Business Marketing: *Quo*
Vadis? **87**
    James A. Narus
    James C. Anderson

Methodology 89
    Research Procedure 89
    Research Analyses 93
Results 94
Discussion 95
    Promoting Growth in Business Marketing Education 97

Reducing the Shortage of Master's-Level Teaching
    Materials   100
Building a Business Marketing Educators' Network   102
Conclusion   103

**Master's-Level Business Marketing Education:
A Commentary**   **105**
   Earl D. Honeycutt Jr.

Introduction   105
Discussion   105
Suggestions for Future Research   106
Concluding Thoughts   107

**Making Business Marketing More Prominent in Master's
Programs: A Reply to Commentary**   **109**
   James A. Narus
   James C. Anderson

Topics Addressed: Expanding the Scope of Business-
to-Business Education, Areas for Further Research,
Experience in Business Marketing

PART IV: UNDERGRADUATE PROGRAMS

**Business Marketing Education: A Distinctive Role
in the Undergraduate Curriculum**   **115**
   Michael D. Hutt
   Thomas W. Speh

Place in the Curriculum   116
Directions in Business Marketing Practice   117
   Strategic Trends in Purchasing   118
   Relationship Marketing   121
   High-Technology Markets   123
   Cross-Functional Connections   125
   Fast-Paced Product Development   127
Central Themes and Knowledge Areas   129
   Business Market Characteristics   129
   Organizational Buying Behavior   129
   Evaluating Market Opportunity   130
   Relationship Marketing   130
   Marketing's Cross-Functional Relationships   131
   Managing and Integrating Strategy Variables   132

Course Design 133
   Skill Development 133
   A Two-Course Sequence 134
Conclusions 135

Business Marketing Education's Distinctive Role in the Undergraduate Curriculum: A Commentary 139
Gul Butaney

Strategic Trends in Purchasing and Supplier Relations
   Management 140
Relationship Marketing 142
High-Technology Product Marketing 144
Faster, Better, and Friendlier Product Development 146
Cross-Functional Integration 147
Concluding Summary 148

Linking Content to Practice in the Business Marketing Course: A Reply to Commentary 151
Michael D. Hutt
Thomas W. Speh

Strategic Trends in Purchasing 151
Relationship Marketing 152
High-Technology Product Marketing 153
Faster, Better, and Friendlier Product Development 153
Cross-Functional Integration 153
A Concluding Note 154

PART V: ALTERNATIVE TECHNOLOGIES

Technology in the Classroom: Teaching Business Marketing in the Twenty-First Century 159
Richard P. Vlosky
David T. Wilson

Introduction 159
Why Use Technology in the Classroom? 160
Advanced Technology Classrooms 162
Integrated Software 163
The Internet and Marketing Education 164
The World Wide Web 165

Challenges and Success   167
Summary   168

Technology in the Business Marketing Classroom:
A Commentary   **171**
    Carlos M. Rodriguez

Topics Addressed: Student Learning Styles,
    Critical Thinking Capability, Instructional Technology

Technology and Learning in the Classroom:
A Reply to Commentary   **175**
    Richard P. Vlosky
    David T. Wilson

Topics Addressed: New versus Traditional Approaches,
    Educational Processes

PART VI: BUSINESS MARKETING TEXTBOOKS

Business-to-Business Marketing Textbooks:
A Comparative Review   **181**
    Klaus Backhaus
    Katrin Muehlfeld
    Diana Okoye

Introduction   181
The Selection of Textbooks for Comparison   182
Criteria and Methodology   183
    Basic Capabilities   185
    Skills   185
    Knowledge   186
    Understanding   190
    Applications   193
    Analysis, Synthesis, and Evaluation 194
Results   194
Formal Structure   194
    Textbook Group 1   194
    Textbook Groups 2 and 3   195
Approach   196
    Textbook Group 1   196
    Textbook Group 2   197
    Textbook Group 3   198
Breadth of Thematic Portrayal and Inclusion
    of Current Themes   199

Textbook Group 1   199
Textbook Group 2   200
Textbook Group 3   201
Depth of Thematic Treatment   202
Textbook Groups 1 and 2   202
Textbook Group 3   202
Comprehensibility of the Texts   203
Visual Comprehensibility   203
Link Between Theory and Practice   205
Developing More Complex Capabilities   208
Conclusions   210
Objective 1: Knowledge   210
Objective 2: Contribution to the Development
    of Cognitive Capabilities   214
Limitations and Directions for Future Research   214

**Comparative Review of Business-to-Business
Marketing Textbooks: A Commentary**   **223**
    Gul Butaney

About the Taxonomy   224
Enhancement of the Criteria and Their Application   225
Concluding Summary   230

**Comparative Review of Business-to-Business Marketing
Textbooks: A Commentary**   **233**
    Michael D. Hutt
    Thomas W. Speh

The Positioning of the Texts   234
Building a Foundation   235
Business Market Characteristics   235
The Purchasing Organization   235
Organizational Buying Behavior   236
Hurdles for a Transaction-Types Perspective   236
Developing a Relationship Marketing Perspective   237
Relationship Strategies   237
E-Commerce Tools   238
Supply Chain Management   238
Hurdles for a Transaction-Types Perspective   238

Capturing Strategic Marketing Content   239
    Hurdles for a Transaction-Types Perspective   239
Conclusions   240

**Comparative Review of Business-to-Business Marketing
Textbooks: A Commentary**   **243**
    James A. Narus

Crafting a Business Marketing Textbook   243
Criticisms of the Research   249
    Where Are the Validity Test Results?   249
    What Methodology Did the Authors Actually Use?   253
    Do the Research, Data, and Findings Support
    Their Conclusions?   255

**Comparative Review of Business-to-Business
Marketing Textbooks: A Commentary**   **259**
    Richard E. Plank

    Topics Addressed: Education As a Process, Changes
    in Business Marketing Practice, Standardization
    and Synchronization

**Business-to-Business Marketing Textbooks:
Replies to Commentaries**   **267**
    Klaus Backhaus
    Katrin Muehlfeld
    Diana Okoye

Introduction   267
Reply to Professor Butaney's Comments   268
Reply to the Comments of Professors Hutt and Speh   269
Reply to Professor Narus's Comments   271
Reply to Professor Plank's Comments   275
Some Thoughts on Future Developments of Business-
to-Business Marketing Textbooks   276

PART VII: BOOK REVIEW

**Review of *Cabell's Directory of Publishing Opportunities
in Marketing***   **283**
    J. David Lichtenthal

Index   **287**

ABOUT THE EDITOR

J. David Lichtenthal, MBA, PhD, is Professor of Marketing at Zicklin School of Business, Baruch College, The City University of New York, and a research associate with the Institute for the Study of Business Markets at Penn State. Dr. Lichtenthal has been frequently published in the *Journal of Business Research, Industrial Marketing Management, Journal of Personal Selling and Sales Management, Advances in Business Marketing and Purchasing, Journal of Contingencies Crisis Management, Research in Marketing, Journal of Business & Industrial Marketing,* and *Journal of Relationship Marketing.* The 1990 Editor for the first AMA Educator's Conference devoted to industrial marketing, he was a founding Editorial Board Member and former Book Review Editor for the *Journal of Business-to-Business Marketing.* He serves on three other editorial boards. He also has four years of corporate marketing and market research experience with a leading manufacturer of consumable office supplies.

CONTRIBUTORS

James C. Anderson is William L. Ford Distinguished Professor of Marketing and Wholesale Distribution and Professor of Behavioral Science in Management, J. L. Kellogg Graduate School of Management, Northwestern University; e-mail: <jc-anderson@kellogg.northwestern.edu>.

Klaus Backhaus is Professor of Marketing and Director of the Institute of Business-to-Business Marketing, Marketing Centre, University of Muenster, Germany; e-mail: <backhaus@wiwi.uni-muenster.de>.

Gul Butaney is Professor of Marketing, Bentley College, Waltham, Massachusetts; e-mail: <gbutaney@Bentley.edu>.

Erwin Danneels is Associate Professor, Worcester Polytechnic Institute; e-mail: <erwin@wpi.edu>.

Grahame R. Dowling is affiliated with the Australian Graduate School of Management, Marketing Department, University of New South Wales, Sydney, Australia; e-mail: grahamed@agsm.edu.au>.

Earl D. Honeycutt Jr. is Professor of Marketing, Old Dominion University, Norfolk, Virginia; e-mail: <ehonecu@odu.edu>.

Michael D. Hutt is Ford Motor Company Professor of Marketing, Department of Marketing, College of Business, Arizona State University, Tempe, Arizona; e-mail: <michael.hutt@asu.edu>.

Gary L. Lilien is Distinguished Research Professor of Management Science, Institute for the Study of Business Markets, Smeal College of Business Administration, Pennsylvania State University at University Park; e-mail: <g51@psu.edu>.

Katrin Muehlfeld is a PhD student in Marketing and Assistant Researcher, Institute of Business-to-Business Marketing, Marketing Centre, University of Muenster, Germany; e-mail: <03kamu@wiwi.uni-muenster.de>.

Narakesari Narayandas is Associate Professor, Harvard University; e-mail: <nnarayandas@hbs.edu>.

James A. Narus is Professor of Marketing, Babcock Graduate School of Management, Wake Forest University, Charlotte, North Carolina; e-mail: <jim.narus@mba.wfu.edu>.

Diana Okoye is a graduate in Business Administration, University of Muenster, Germany; e-mail: <dokoye@hotmail.com>.

Richard E. Plank is Professor of Marketing, Haworth College of Business, Western Michigan University, Kalamazoo, MI; e-mail: <Richard.plank@wmich.edu>.

V. Kasturi Rangan is Eliot I. Snider and Family Professor of Business Administration, Harvard University; e-mail: <vrangan@hbs.edu>.

Carlos M. Rodriguez is affiliated with the Department of Marketing, Johns Hopkins University (e-mail: rodri-c@jhuvms.hcf.jhu.edu).

Thomas W. Speh is James Evans Reese Distinguished Professor of Distribution, Miami University, Oxford, Ohio.

Richard P. Vlosky is Associate Professor, Forest Products Marketing, Louisiana Forest Products Laboratory, Louisiana State University Agricultural Center, Baton Rouge, Louisiana.

David T. Wilson is Alvin H. Clemens Professor Emeritus of Entrepreneurial Studies, The Smeal College of Business Administration, Pennsylvania State University, University Park; e-mail: <dtw@psu.edu>.

Elizabeth J. Wilson is Professor of Marketing, Suffolk University, Boston, Massachusetts; e-mail: <ewilson55@Comcast.net>.

Gerald Zaltman is Joseph C. Wilson Professor of Business Administration, Harvard University; e-mail: <gzaltman@hbs.edu>.

Series Preface

It is a pleasure to announce the establishment of the Foundation Series in Business Marketing. This book series fills a critical void in business-to-business marketing knowledge especially when no resources currently available address the needs of business marketing practitioners and academics looking for breadth and depth of coverage on various issues of research, practice, and education. Books published in this series will foster our understanding of business marketing phenomena and managerial practice around the globe. These books will focus exclusively on topics in business marketing combining impeccable relevance with rigor—and thus aid in cutting-edge knowledge development.

The following are the inaugural two books[1]:

- *Fundamentals of Business Marketing Research:* A comprehensive look at the literature of the business marketing area over the past twenty-five years. All areas under the general model of business marketing are examined in depth with an eye toward future research and implications for business marketing practice.
- *Fundamentals of Business Marketing Education:* An in-depth examination of business marketing education at all levels of university instruction (undergraduate, graduate, executive, MBA, and doctoral studies). Issues covered include course content, pedagogy, and policy. An informative discussion on the nature and content of business marketing textbooks is also included.

These two books provide unprecedented point-of-use access for those individuals who want to do research, enhance managerial practice, and/or teach in the various business marketing areas. These volumes were intentionally created to provide a *unique* resource guide to be used by both business marketing research professionals and business marketing educators.[2] It is my hope that these and subsequent books will provide increased access for all scholars and practitioners of business marketing.

J. David Lichtenthal, Series Editor
Zicklin School of Business, Baruch College
City University of New York

NOTES

1. Only these two inaugural books on basics of business marketing research and business marketing education will be anthology based from the *Journal of Business-to-Business Marketing.* All subsequent works will be original, "first time ever" publications.

2. Both books may be useful *across* branches of the marketing discipline (e.g., although the comprehensive research volume is targeted at researchers/practitioners, a broad-minded individual may very well find the discussion in the education volume about marketing textbooks very useful. Likewise, a business teaching professional or practitioner may find content about models of business marketing management that are examined in the research volume easy to tweak for managerial or classroom purposes.

Introduction

Business-to-Business Marketing Education in the Twenty-First Century

J. David Lichtenthal

THE IMPETUS FOR THIS TOPIC

Several forces prompt the desirability of fostering ongoing international discussion on this very important subject. The social and economic forces impacting higher education are affecting the nature of the institutions themselves and the content of the curriculum more than ever. The value of business education and its contribution to society are coming under greater scrutiny with more frequency. We must continually derive and reaffirm the enduring uniqueness and importance of business marketing education. Philosophically, one must view student training as the creation of an "industrial product," with some of its historical connotation. All of our research and teaching activities are antecedent activities, ultimately leading to providing a service input into business and consumer product service firms alike. This recognition requires our active mediation of the confluence of forces that make up corporate and academic interests in healthy tension. For academicians, there must be a *constant interplay on the circle* linking research, teaching, and interaction with business world phenomena. Research keeps our skills and knowledge levels fresh. This in turn means that teaching allows our doctrines and dogmas to be disseminated to the unindoctrinated while being progressively challenged by questions, insights, and query stemming from naive inquiry. In like manner, business phenomena inform our thinking, writing, and speaking as we in turn provide tools, perspectives, and insights to enhance corporate performance and societal well-being. The resulting exchange of ideas provides for evolutionary or sometimes dynamic changes and interaction in articulating business marketing theory, methods, and practice.

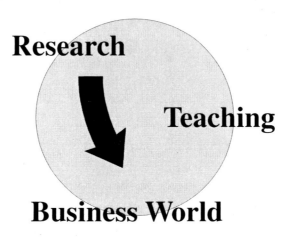

PURPOSE AND CONTENT

The purpose of this book is to provide thoughtful substantive papers that address the real concerns of consequence that face most university-level business marketing educators. This book provides a discussion of topics for formulating policy and developing curriculum.

Contained herein are seven parts. Parts I through IV address each level of instruction—doctoral studies, executive education, master's level programs, and undergraduate studies. Part V focuses on the impact of alternative technologies in delivering business-to-business marketing education. Part VI presents a comparative review of business-to-business marketing textbooks, and Part VII reviews one particular text, *Cabell's Directory of Publishing Opportunities in Marketing*. In addition to the comprehensive papers that begin each part, Parts I through VI also include commentaries by noted scholars as well as rejoinders by the authors.

We start with doctoral study. By its very nature, the graduates of this educational process can become the major emissaries to the discipline in toto. Danneels and Lilien start the debate by examining doctoral programs. There are very few programs worldwide that have the faculty qualified and interested in grooming business-to-business doctoral students. These authors also note the continuing need for bringing relevance and rigor to this high-level training process. In his commentary, Dowling notes the early use of what we now call participant-observer discovery modes for identifying often fuzzy real-world business problems. In suggesting a basis for doctoral training, he reaffirms the need for contemporary use tied to interdisciplinary multimethod approaches for business marketing problem formulation and resolution. Danneels and Lilien respond by pointing out that tenure and promotion systems reward rigor over relevance and we need not diametrically oppose the two.

Narayandas, Rangan, and Zaltman look at the substance and process of executive education for business-to-business markets. They note that rapid change in technology, time to market, and global competition created demand for business marketing training to gain unique structure and content. Furthermore, three broad program formats have emerged: action learning, custom education, and general education. They note that academic institutions have delivered high-quality conceptual and contextual knowledge. Innovative developments must now augment this and couple delivery methods to ways of orchestrating the cultural climate for effecting change. Wilson, in her commentary, supplements Narayandas et al., stating that the relationship paradigm is paramount for all supplier-customer relations no matter where in the value chain. Pedagogically, she calls for action learning where students get to apply various conceptual and methodological tools to their company's situation. Key is experiential learning and change-effecting exercises. Narayandas et al., in their reply, agree while suggesting that relationship marketing is not everything. It is a pervading aspect across the value chain at the customer, distributor, and vendor interfaces. An implication is the need for managers to develop cross-functional and interfirm coordination skills and perspectives.

Narus and Anderson conduct an exploratory study among the top fifty programs characterizing the state of master's-level education in business marketing. Approximately 1,700 students took master's-level courses during the 1996-1997 academic year, with thirty-eight universities offering forty-eight sections. The authors note there is a shortage of master's-level teaching material, especially cases. Furthermore, those academics actively involved in business marketing education were difficult to identify despite the relatively small number of industrial marketing scholars. There remains a need for increased business-to-business networking opportunities. Honeycutt, in his commentary, expands upon the need for making business-to-business marketing education more mainstream in MBA programs and in introductory courses as well. Also highlighted is the need for better business-to-business career counseling and corporate liaison work. Anderson and Narus reply, noting that demand for business-to-business graduates is on the rise, especially concerning consulting. They also note the need for more graduate-level texts and reading material. Now, many faculty have to rely on gathering all resources, which may inhibit the frequency of business-to-business course offerings.

Hutt and Speh note the unique contribution of business-to-business in the undergraduate curriculum concerning organizational buying, cross-functional processes, and leading edge marketing practice. They suggest critical course content, design, and implementation strategies. Butaney, in his commentary, supplements curriculum recommendations by noting trends in topics such as the strategic importance of purchasing, supply chain management, and global sourcing. The philosophical importance of taking a relational marketing approach is noted. In addition, there is need for faster, better, more friendly product development processes. Hutt and Speh agree with Butaney's supplementation of topics. They make specific pedagogical recommendations for implementation.

Vlosky and Wilson assess the impact of changing technology for classroom teaching. The development and use of interactive multimedia education is on the rise given the growing investment by many universities in the hardware and software necessary to support this form of instruction. Still ahead, helping the faculty and students to foster a deeper comfort level and understanding of the role these media can play in enhancing learning about business marketing. Rodriguez, in his commentary, makes several important observations. He notes the need for congruence between student learning styles and technological educational strategy. Instructional technology should blend with a process that starts from concrete experience which induces reflective observation and thinking. Alternative technologies should build on traditional instructional objectives and activities used in the classroom. Vlosky and Wilson reply, agreeing that learning styles are pivotal. The burden of learning still rests with the students, for it is their individual choice. The newer technologies may yet play an important role by fostering autonomous discovery learning.

CLOSING REMARKS

Robust relations are required with relevant market segments served. This must come about if we are to develop philosophies, curricula, and appropriate goals. Otherwise, the courses, their orientations, domains of study, pedagogy, and skill development will continue to come up "short" for the career development of those we ultimately serve.

A stronger university-business profession relationship is more important today than any other time in the prior fifty years. Higher education in business must help ensure viable programs, at least in part, by obtaining and sustaining university interest and resources to support programs and their execution. By addressing legitimate demands from corporations (without succumbing to excessive corporatization) it is, perhaps, the only way to ensure that values and norms of academic training remain viable.

PART I:
DOCTORAL PROGRAMS

Doctoral Programs in Business-to-Business Marketing: Status and Prospects

Erwin Danneels
Gary L. Lilien

INTRODUCTION

Marketing is the study of exchange relationships. PhD programs in marketing are primarily designed to train academics to create knowledge about exchange relationships through research and to disseminate that knowledge to practitioners through teaching.

The financial value of business-to-business transactions in the United States in 1995 was over $6 trillion, over twice that of consumer transactions (Slater 1996), yet the focus of the bulk of research and teaching in marketing focuses on the consumer marketplace. Penn State's Institute for the Study of Business Markets (ISBM) was founded in 1983 to help direct more academic attention to the problems and research opportunities available in the business marketplace. Since its founding, the ISBM has dedicated programs and resources to stimulate the development of the careers of marketing scholars interested in the business marketplace, including considerable resources devoted to encourage and support PhDs. We undertook this investigation to better understand the status and prospects for PhD education in business markets.

The paper proceeds as follows. In the next section, we present a historical perspective, providing background for an empirical study. Next we describe the survey and provide some descriptive statistics. In the following section we analyze the survey data that suggest some

The authors thank Anant Balakrishnan, David Lichtenthal, Ken Lusht, and Arvind Rangaswamy for their suggestions, and Annmarie Garganes for assistance with data input.

9

clear weaknesses both in the input (applicants) to the programs and the training that the programs provide. We discuss the implications of these findings for improvements both in the recruiting for PhD programs as well as program contents. Finally, we sum up and suggest the need for ongoing study in this area. We will use the terms *business marketing* and *business-to-business marketing* synonymously in this chapter.

PhD IN BUSINESS: A LOOK BACK

A book edited by Byrt (1989) describes the historical development of business schools from a global perspective. In most countries outside the United States, there appears to have been little research or academic development in business prior to the World War II period. Definitions are fuzzy here; business or commerce often began to grow within faculties of economics or law, which had much earlier beginnings. However, with the possible exception of France and its Grands Ecoles, started with the foundation of the Ecole des Hautes Etudes Commerciales (HEC) in 1881, it appears that the oldest and deepest roots of academic business education were in the United States. We will take a U.S.-centric perspective here, noting that our data will have some global implications.

The earliest business schools in the United States were founded around the turn of the century: The Wharton School (1881), the University of Chicago (1898), New York University (1900), and the Harvard Business School (1908). These early developments were followed by the rapid addition of business school programs in public universities during the period shortly after World War I. That proliferation led Leon Marshall (1928) from the University of Chicago to critique the quality of the programs that were developing. He was concerned that rapid growth was not accompanied by academic rigor.

The economic boom following World War II led to an accompanying increase in the demand for business education. That demand created a second surge in the supply of such programs, exacerbating the situation that Marshall noted. Both the academic and business communities became concerned about the problem, with several results.

First the AACSB (American Assembly of Collegiate Schools of Business), although founded in 1926, truly began to exercise influence in the 1950s through its accreditation process. By 1958, eighty-five schools had joined and a number of others were actively seeking the membership and approval that AACSB accreditation afforded.

The AACSB sponsored several studies (Kozelka 1954; Arden House Report 1956), designed to guide the standards for accreditation. These studies highlighted the need for further study and signaled the need for rigorous research within the framework of business schools, paving the way for the foundation reports.

The publication of the foundation reports (Pierson 1959, sponsored by the Carnegie Foundation; Gordon and Howell 1959, sponsored by the Ford Foundation) had perhaps the greatest impact on the development of U.S. business schools of any events in this century. They outlined the evolution of business education in the United States and the changes that would be needed to insert academic rigor into those programs. The Gordon and Howell report in particular stresses the need to link business research and education to three underlying disciplines: economics, behavioral science, and applied mathematics. The reports make numerous recommendations about research rigor and the need for such rigor in business school programs if they are to achieve scientific acceptance. They highlight the need for release time for faculty research and stress that fundamental, rigorous research be part of the PhD educational process. To sum up, Gordon and Howell recommend:

> There is a critical need to develop in the business schools a more stimulating intellectual atmosphere and to generate within their faculties more probing questions and to engage in more significant research (p. 377.) . . . Most thoughtful observers are agreed that the research performance of the business schools has so far been unsatisfactory. (p. 389)

Pierson echoed these sentiments and the two reports changed the hiring practices, the reward systems, and the instructional programs around the country. Scholars with PhDs in disciplines other than business (economics, psychology, operations research, engineering, statistics, mathematics, and the like) were hired by business schools and encouraged to keep "rigorous" research links with their underlying disciplines. Universities answered the call for action that the foundation reports sent, but not all were happy with the results.

In 1988, the AACSB released the Porter-McKibben report, which documented the impact, both positive and negative, of the foundation reports. On the positive side, Porter and McKibben note, business school faculty were clearly producing large quantities of research valued by their academic colleagues, both in business and in underlying core disciplines. On the negative side, they cite concerns that too much basic (abstract? irrelevant?) research was being produced and more applied research was needed. It is interesting to note that this need for more applied research is echoed by faculty, deans, and provosts at the reports' most research-oriented (category I) schools, who state by a factor of more than two to one that business school research should become more applied (p. 172). They also cite overemphasis on research quantity versus quality and too much focus on the academic audience as the target for the research. The report points out that at that time, the overriding concern of business school deans was to improve their research output, while the business community was concerned about the relevance and practical nature of the education that business schools were providing. The report also notes a concern about the lack of supply of high-quality job applicants (new PhDs?), a point that we will return to later.

Since the Porter-McKibben report, the discussion has continued. The Dallas Conference (1992) provided a lively forum for debate on critical issues of doctoral education. Several of the key concerns raised at the conference were as follows:

Doctoral education lacks relevance to business concerns. (p. 17)

Today's training of doctoral students is one-dimensional; its exclusive attention to research produces graduates unprepared for teaching, the activity in which they will spend most of their careers. (p. 18)

Business schools continue to be at a competitive disadvantage with other academic departments in vying for faculty appointments, doctoral students and research recognition. (p. 21)

Much of the recent discussion has surrounded the need to become more customer-oriented, viewing students as the primary customers. Leavitt (1993) and West (1991, 1992) criticized business schools for a lack of preparation for teaching.

Dulek and Fielden (1992) blame the "better business schools" who have created an escalation game by putting narrow research output (relevant or not) at the top of their priority list, above teaching and responsiveness to students' needs. They admit that their call will not be heard as it will be seen as a request to return to the low-status days of the prefoundation report era. Alutto (1993) criticizes business schools for not employing an interdisciplinary approach to business problems.

May (1994) points out some other shortcomings of existing programs: that while folks have been paying lip service to the need for internationalization, there is little happening in PhD programs to make this come to pass. He sees no likelihood of a major change in program structure in the next fifteen to twenty years without major intervention. Madansky (1994), in an interesting twist, argues that the role of the PhD program is to ensure that candidates have mastered a body of knowledge and are trained to add to that body of knowledge. He argues that the hiring institution has the onus of ensuring that future research will be relevant and that the newly hired PhD gets training in imparting the material he or she has learned.

So it appears that the pendulum has swung to the other side. The background for our study is an environment that before the 1960s was seen as low in scientific merit, producing little research of consequence. The production of such research, as a necessary ingredient for status with universities, got much of the focus of developments during the 1960s, 1970s, and 1980s. The 1990s have seen pressure in the opposite direction, calling for high-quality PhDs who can produce good and practical research and who understand and can relate to key constituencies (students and the business community). Much of the discussion of doctoral programs has been conducted without solid data about the current status of doctoral education (Graduate Management Admission Council 1992). This paper takes stock of the current situation of doctoral programs in marketing, focusing especially on the nature of doctoral education in business-to-business marketing.

DATA COLLECTION

We developed and administered a two-part mail survey to generate the data for this research. The first part of the survey asked for data about marketing PhD programs and the second asked for input into research priorities of the ISBM. We report only on the analysis of the first part of the survey here. That survey asked about program characteristics, coursework, perceived deficiencies in current training methods, mechanisms for addressing those deficiencies, placements of recent PhDs, and satisfaction with those placements. We included a cover letter with the survey, explaining the purpose of the study and a reply envelope (postage paid for U.S. respondents). Respondents also had the option to fax their responses.

The population we were interested in consists of all doctoral programs in marketing. We derived our sampling frame from two sources: we used the academic database from the ISBM and selected those universities that we believed had PhD programs. We integrated that list with the information we found in the *Wiley Guide for Marketing Faculty* (Hasselback 1995). Whenever we had any doubt about whether a university had a PhD program, we included that university in our sample. We also included as many PhD programs outside North America as we could locate; although (as we will see) those programs are structured quite differently from U.S. programs, the increasing focus on internationalization of PhD programs makes their inclusion quite appropriate (May 1994).

We executed two waves of mailings. The first wave, sent late November 1996, went to 107 U.S. and seventy-two non-U.S. institutions, for a total of 179. It yielded only sixteen usable responses by mid-December; some surveys were returned, notifying us of the absence of such a program, but with reaction to the ISBM priorities. We sent another wave to nonrespondents in mid-December, with a more personal, urgent request for response. The second wave went to eighty-eight U.S. and fifty non-U.S. institutions. After three months, we received usable data on forty-one doctoral programs from all over the world, for an overall response rate of 23 percent (Box 1 gives a list of the responding institutions). This response rate is biased downward since we may have included institutions without a doctoral program in our sampling frame. The diversity of the schools suggests that the population is extremely heterogeneous; nonetheless a comparison of the responses from the first wave with those from the second wave revealed no apparent response biases.

Table 1 describes our sample. We achieved a spread of countries, and we believe that these schools are a representative sample of the

BOX 1. List of Responding Schools

Aarhus School of Business (Denmark)
University of Arizona
Arizona State University
Australian Graduate School of Management*
University of California, Irvine
Catholic University of Leuven (Belgium)*
Chung Nam National University (South Korea)*
University of Cincinnati
Columbia University
Copenhagen Business School (Denmark)*
Erasmus University (Holland)
University of Florida
Florida State University
Georgia State University*
University of Illinois, Champaign
University of Innsbruck (Austria)
University of Liege (Belgium)
University of Linz (Austria)*
London Business School*
Louisiana State University
Massachusetts Institute of Technology
University of Muenster (Germany)*
Nanyang Business School (Singapore)
University of Nebraska
New Mexico State University
University of North Carolina, Chapel Hill
University of North Texas
Northwestern University
Norwegian School of Economics and Business Administration
University of Oregon
University of Otago (New Zealand)
Penn State University
University of Pennsylvania
Purdue University*
University of South Carolina
University of Southern California
University of Texas, Austin*
University of Western Ontario*
University of Wisconsin, Madison
University of Wollongong (Australia)
Yale University

*We classified this school as having an emphasis on business-to-business marketing (25 percent or more of faculty and students are involved in this field).

TABLE 1. Description of the Respondents ($n = 41$)

	Absolute Number	Percentage
School Type		
Top-Tier Research Schools	6	14.6
Research-Intensive Schools	13	31.7
Teaching-Intensive Schools	22	53.7
Country		
United States/Canada	26	63.4
Europe	10	24.4
Asia	2	4.9
Australia/New Zealand	3	7.3
Respondent Position		
Instructor	1	2.4
Assistant Professor	6	14.6
Associate Professor	8	19.5
Full Professor	26	63.4
Doctoral Program Advisor	3	7.3
Department Chair	15	36.6
Business-to-Business Involvement		
Indicated at least some involvement in business-to-business area	25	62.5

major producers of doctoral degrees in marketing. We directed the survey either to a faculty member that we knew had some business marketing interest or to the faculty chair if we could not identify such a faculty member. Our respondents are spread over the various faculty ranks and include 37 percent department chairs. Nearly two-thirds (63 percent) of the respondents indicated interest in business marketing.

In consultation with several faculty colleagues, we attempted to classify the respondent schools and the schools of placement into four categories: top-tier research school, research-intensive school, teaching school with some research, and predominantly teaching school. After several rounds of independent classification and reconciliation, we found that we had only four schools in the fourth category for responding schools. Therefore, we collapsed the third and fourth categories into a single category, "teaching-intensive schools," for classifying responding institutions. For classifying schools of placement we maintained our original four groups.

We content analyzed answers to the open-ended questions as follows. First we transcribed all of the answers to the open-ended questions. Then we developed a coding scheme and coded each of the answers. We then included these codes with the response data.

ANALYSIS

Table 2 describes some key characteristics of the programs. Note that the average number of faculty indicating interest in business marketing in the responding institutions is 2.1. This number is likely to overstate the universe average, given that our sample was selected at least partially to favor such interest. We calculated a proportional interest in business-to-business among faculty by dividing the number of faculty specializing in business-to-business by the total number of faculty (both expressed as FTE, or full-time equivalents). We find that, on average, 19 percent of the faculty have a particular interest in business-to-business. We also find that programs on average have two students with a particular interest in this area, or proportionally 23 percent of the students (calculated similarly). Both faculty and student interest in business-to-business show a wide range across the various programs as the minimum and the maximum columns in Table 2 indicate.

We are interested in how training philosophies vary across doctoral programs. Casual observation suggests that some doctoral programs focus much more on breadth of training, while others concentrate on depth. We asked the respondents to assess the relative breadth versus depth of training in their doctoral program both for substantive areas and methodology on a scale from 1 (depth dominates) to 7 (breadth dominates). On average, programs rate themselves in the middle on both methodological and substantive dimensions of training, although there is substantial diversity across programs. We also asked respondents to indicate the relative emphasis on teaching versus research in their doctoral training on a seven-point scale ranging from 1 (research dominates) to 7 (teaching dominates). Most programs emphasize research, but, again, there is considerable diversity.

TABLE 2. Description of Responding Programs ($n = 41$)*

	Mean	Standard Deviation	Minimum	Maximum
Number of Marketing Faculty (FTEs)	11.6	6.2	2	32
Number of Faculty Specializing in Business-to-Business (FTEs)	2.1	1.9	0	9
Number of PhD Students Taken in per Year	2.6	0.9	0.5	4
Number of PhD Students (all years)	8.9	4.2	0	20
Number of PhD Students with Interest in Business-to-Business	2	1.5	0	6
Years to Complete PhD (on average)	4.2	0.7	3	6
Doctoral Student to Faculty Ratio	0.95	0	5	0.77
Proportional Faculty Emphasis on Business-to-Business	19%	15%	0%	59%
Proportional Student Emphasis on Business-to-Business	23%	17%	0%	75%
Breadth in Training in Methods	3.8	1.3	2	7
Breadth in Training in Substantive Areas	3.7	1	1	5
Relative Emphasis on Teaching	2.3	1	1	5

*If a respondent indicated a range in response to any of the questions, we used the midpoint of that range.

Program Characteristic Differences

Table 3 shows some striking differences in program characteristics by geography and by type of school. Programs outside North America place a higher emphasis on teaching in their doctoral training and also report a higher involvement in the business-to-business area among students as well as faculty.

The self-rating of the respondents provides some validation for our classification of schools. The top-tier research schools identify themselves unanimously with the extreme of the scale (research dominates), whereas the research-intensive and teaching-intensive schools place themselves more toward the teaching end of the continuum.

Although the top-tier research schools on average employ more faculty in total than any of the other categories, they report only one faculty member specializing in the business-to-business area, less than half reported in the other categories. They also report much less student interest in this area. The same finding is evident from the proportional faculty and student interest in business-to-business.

Admission Criteria

We asked for the general prerequisites for marketing PhD program applicants (Table 4). About half of the programs consider prior work experience desirable while the other did not consider it critical, and only one program required prior experience. Just over half of the programs require an MBA or equivalent degree. Sixty-one percent of the programs do not require any prior marketing coursework. In an open-ended question we asked respondents to indicate other prerequisites. Respondents indicated up to three items. Almost half of the respondents said that the applicant's GMAT score was important. Another 27 percent suggested that the results of previous study were important, and 24 percent mentioned the research interests of the faculty, especially in regard to fit with faculty areas of interest:

> We have no faculty who do experimental work or focus strictly on consumer behavior issues. We seldom admit anyone who mentions a strong interest in these areas, since there are no faculty to support them.

TABLE 3. Program Differences by Region and School Type ($n = 41$)*

Program Characteristics	North America	Outside North America	Top-Tier Research Schools	Research-Intensive Schools	Teaching-Intensive Schools
Number of Marketing Faculty (FTEs)	12.5	10.2	13.5	12.2	10.8
Number of Faculty Specializing in Business-to-Business (FTEs)	2	2.3	1	2.1	2.5
Number of PhD Students Taken in per Year	2.8	2.2	2.7	2.6	2.5
Number of PhD Students (all years)	10.5	6.1	9.8	9.6	8.3
Number of PhD Students with Interest in Business-to-Business	2	2.1	0.8	2.1	2.3
Doctoral Student to Faculty Ratio	0.9	1.1	0.7	0.9	1.1
Years to Complete PhD (on average)	4.4	4	4.3	4.2	4.1
Proportional Faculty Emphasis on Business-to-Business	16%	24%	7%	19%	22%
Proportional Student Emphasis on Business-to-Business	19%	32%	6%	23%	29%
Relative Emphasis on Teaching	2	2.7	1	2.2	2.7

*If a respondent indicated a range in response to any of the questions, we used the midpoint of that range.

TABLE 4. Prerequisites for Marketing PhD Applicants by Region and School Type ($n = 41$)*

Prerequisites	Overall %	North America	Outside North America	Top-Tier Research Schools	Research-Intensive Schools	Teaching-Intensive Schools
MBA (or equivalent)						
Required	53.7	38.5	80	0	38.5	77.3
Prior Work Experience						
Required	2.4	3.8	0	0	7.7	0
Desirable	51.2	65.4	26.7	50	53.8	50
Not Critical	46.3	30.8	73.3	50	38.5	50
Prior Marketing Courses						
Required	39	19.2	73.3	0	23.1	59.1
Other Admission Criteria (Mentioned in open question—multiple responses possible)						
GMAT	46.3	69.2	6.7	–	–	–
GPA/Grades	26.8	19.2	40	–	–	–
Research Area/Interests	24.4	19.2	33.3	–	–	–
Recommendations	7.3	–	–	–	–	–
Master's Degree	7.3	–	–	–	–	–
Are Prerequisites Different for Applications with Interest in Business-to-Business?						
Not different	89.7					
Business experience	7.7					
Feel for technicality	2.6					

*Comparisons omitted if some cells have four or fewer observations.

A number of respondents indicated that their evaluation of each candidate is "holistic," judged on a case-by-case basis, and that no one criterion is applied rigidly.

In answer to the question if any of their prerequisites were different for applicants with a specific interest in the business-to-business area, the answer was generally "no," with only one respondent answering in the affirmative:

> I think it is inappropriate for people who have no experience to start their research activities in Business to Business.

However, a few respondents indicated that while the same prerequisites were applied to all, business-to-business marketing had a special nature:

> Motivation is most important and a "feel" for technicality.

> Perhaps experience should be emphasized more for Business to Business.

> It would be amazing if anyone had an interest in this area, but no relevant experience.

Table 4 displays some striking differences in prerequisites by region and school type. (We report comparisons only where there are at least five observations per cell.) In particular, none of the top-tier research schools require an MBA (or equivalent), while 77 percent of the teaching-intensive schools do and 80 percent of the schools outside North America do. Top-tier research schools require no prior marketing courses, while 59 percent of the teaching-intensive schools do, and 73 percent of the schools outside North America do.

Only 27 percent of the schools outside North America report that work experience is desirable, compared with 65 percent of the North American schools. The schools outside North America rarely use GMAT scores and rely more heavily on grades and research area interests.

Courses and Tracks

We asked respondents which courses they required of all students in their program. We provided a list of courses and allowed the respondents to add to the list. Table 5 gives the results (with the added

TABLE 5. Required Courses and Tracks by Region and School Type ($n = 41$)*

Required Courses**	Overall %	North America	Outside North America	Top-Tier Research Schools	Research-Intensive Schools	Teaching-Intensive Schools
Marketing Models (M)	51.2	65.4	26.7	66.7	76.9	31.8
Marketing Channels (S)	14.6	–	–	–	–	–
Marketing Management (S)	46.3	53.8	33.3	16.7	76.9	36.4
Statistics (any graduate course) (M)	70.7	88.5	40	83.3	92.3	54.5
Econometrics (M)	26.8	30.8	20	50	30.8	18.2
Consumer Behavior (S)	65.9	80.8	40	66.7	84.6	54.5
Business-to-Business Marketing (S)	9.8	–	–	–	–	–
Research Methods (in Marketing) (M)	78	88.5	60	83.3	100	63.6
Psychology (any graduate course) (F)	17.1	–	–	–	–	–
Sociology (any graduate course) (F)	7.3	–	–	–	–	–
Philosophy of Science (F)	36.6	34.6	40	0	53.8	36.4
Preparation for Teaching (F)	17.1	–	–	–	–	–
Organization Theory (F)	9.8	–	–	–	–	–
Microeconomics (F)	31.7	38.5	20	66.7	46.2	13.6
Proseminar/Colloquium (added) (F)	12.2	–	–	–	–	–
Marketing Theory (added) (S)	22	–	–	–	–	–

TABLE 5 (continued)

Required Courses**	Overall %	North America	Outside North America	Top-Tier Research Schools	Research-Intensive Schools	Teaching-Intensive Schools
Game Theory/Choice Models (added) (M)	7.3	–	–	–	–	–
Measurement (added) (M)	4.9	–	–	–	–	–
No courses required	17.1	3.8	40	0	0	31.8
Relative Coursework Emphasis						
Number of Methods Courses	2.4	2.9	1.5	3.2	3	1.8
Number of Substantive Courses	1.6	2	0.9	1	2.6	1.4
Number of Foundational Courses	1	1.2	0.8	1	1.3	0.9
Number of Required Courses	5	6	3.2	5.2	6.5	4.1
Relative Emphasis on Methods	51%	51%	51%	62%	48%	49%
Relative Emphasis on Substance	30%	32%	26%	19%	33%	32%
Relative Emphasis on Foundation	19%	17%	23%	19%	18%	19%
Tracks in the Program						
Programs with Tracks	19.5	–	–	–	–	–
Programs with a Business-to-Business Track	2.4	–	–	–	–	–

*Comparisons omitted if course is required in fewer than ten programs.
**(M) Methods course, (S) Substance course, (F) Foundation course

24

courses indicated). More than half the programs require statistics, marketing models, and consumer behavior, only about 10 percent of all programs require a course in business-to-business marketing, and 17 percent of the schools (mostly non–North American) require no coursework at all. The programs without required courses operate in an apprenticeship format, with the doctoral program designed by the advisor and student around their joint interests:

> We have no required courses. We design course programs on an individual basis.

> We don't have courses. Ph.D. is by thesis. Students read in relevant areas.

> None, however, we have a "mentoring" model where faculty members work closely with students in designing a customized curriculum.

We classified courses into three areas of doctoral study: methods, substance, and foundation disciplines. For methods, we included marketing models, statistics, econometrics, research methods, measurement, game theory/choice models; for substance, marketing channels, marketing management, marketing theory, consumer behavior, business-to-business marketing, microeconomics; for courses in the foundation disciplines, psychology, sociology, philosophy of science, organization theory, and microeconomics.

We summed the number of required courses in each of these areas and calculated the relative coursework emphasis in each program by dividing the number of methods, substance, and foundation courses, respectively, by the total number of required courses. The results are displayed in Table 5. On average, programs require five courses, half of which are in methods. All of the schools that do not require any coursework are in the teaching-intensive category. We report comparisons for individual courses only if ten or more programs offer the course. Programs outside North America require only half the number of courses (about three) that North American schools do (six); 40 percent of non–North American schools require no coursework at all. The top-tier schools place more emphasis on methods, and less on substantive courses, whereas the other two types of schools emphasize these areas equally. We also noted a positive, significant correlation (0.32) between the number of required courses and the number of years reported that it takes to graduate from the program!

We asked respondents which courses they recommended for students with an interest in the business-to-business area. Respondents suggested up to three courses (Table 6), with organization theory, relationships/alliances, and negotiation/sales the most frequently mentioned.

Only about 20 percent of respondents report distinct tracks within their program:

> The program is completely individualized to the student's interests.
>
> Tracking is informal only.
>
> We allow for individual design of course programs. Worked out together with supervisor.

Only one out of the forty-one programs in our sample reports a formal track for business-to-business marketing (University of Nebraska). Even though some programs have a significant number of doctoral students interested in business-to-business, they do not appear to develop specific programs for those students with such an interest:

> Our program does not have the scale to consistently offer Ph.D. level business-to-business courses. We are reasonably comfortable with the customized approach, even though it is particularly labor-intensive.
>
> As presently structured, the program can serve the needs of a student with Business Marketing interests. The student can pursue this specialty in research projects tied to the required marketing seminars as well as through a research assistantship. Corporate access and funding are available for dissertation research and students have the opportunity to teach electives, like Business Marketing, if they wish.

Relevance and Preparation for Teaching

We asked respondents if and how their programs try to bring relevance to their students' research, and what preparation for teaching their programs provide.

TABLE 6. Recommended Courses for Business-to-Business Students (*n* = 18)

Recommended Courses for Business-to-Business Students (multiple responses possible)	Percentage
Strategy	11.1
Organizational Theory	33.3
I/O Economics	16.6
Relationships/Alliances	33.3
Channels	16.6
Game Theory	5.5
Technology/Innovations	5.5
Qualitative Research Methods	11.1
Negotiation/Sales	27.7
Microeconomics	11.1

Respondents mentioned four ways of bringing relevance to student research (Table 7), the most popular of which was the use of industry sponsors who provide research funding and access to their data. One-quarter of our respondents reported no efforts to encourage relevance. The following are typical comments:

> A major criterion for dissertation research is potential managerial relevance. [Our] positioning is very much at the theory/application interface.

> Nothing explicit. Most of our students come with practical experience. Rigor is a bigger problem than irrelevance.

> Often get funding through a corporate funded research center that values practical research. Many students do interviews with practitioners in the early part of their data collection.

Respondents reported three ways to help prepare PhD students to be teachers (Table 8): working as a teaching assistant (grading, class design), having PhD students participate in teaching workshops, and actually teaching a class. Almost half the programs give PhD students opportunities to actually teach classes. The following are typical comments:

We insist everyone teach on their own, and we attempt to monitor performance.

Seminar in teaching methods. Each student teaches several undergraduate courses before they graduate.

Our students all teach, we have a teaching effectiveness program, which includes workshops several times a year.

In some cases, students are prohibited from teaching.

The University of California prohibits Ph.D. students from teaching.

Ph.D. students are not allowed to give seminars or classes on their own in Germany!

Character of Programs with Emphasis in Business-to-Business

It is not surprising that students and faculty with interests in business marketing find themselves in the same programs: the correlation

TABLE 7. Ways of Bringing Relevance to Doctoral Student Research ($n = 32$)

Approach Taken	Percentage
Nothing/not much done	25.0
Field methods	12.5
Industry sponsors/data access	31.3
Practitioner teaching/speakers	12.5
Research problem relevance	18.8

TABLE 8. Preparation for Teaching ($n = 37$)

Approach Taken (multiple responses possible)	Percentage
None/very little	17.1
TA (grading, class design)	26.8
Workshops	31.7
Teach class	46.3

between the proportion of business to business students and the proportion of business-to-business faculty is 0.7. We defined programs with an emphasis in business-to-business as programs that have both a minimum of 25 percent of the faculty and 25 percent of their doctoral students interested in business-to-business. Eleven schools in our sample (26.8 percent) classify as such. We indicated these schools with an asterisk in our list of respondents (Box 1).

Table 9 compares schools with a high emphasis on business-to-business with their counterparts with a low emphasis on this area. Programs with emphasis on business-to-business have, on average, smaller faculties and a higher student-to-faculty ratio. Business-to-business intensive programs place greater emphasis on substance and foundation courses, and somewhat less on methods courses. We listed individual courses only if they were required by ten or more of the original forty-one schools in our sample (with the exception of the course in business-to-business marketing). The only noticeable difference between these programs in terms of individual courses required is that business-to-business-intensive programs more often require econometrics and microeconomics than the other programs.

None of the programs with emphasis on business-to-business are located in the top tier of schools. About one-third of them are at research-intensive schools, but two-thirds are at teaching-intensive schools. They are also more prevalent outside North America. Both types of programs are as likely to require an MBA as a prerequisite, and business-to-business-intensive programs place less emphasis on prior work experience than programs low in business-to-business faculty and students. This pattern holds even when controlling for region (North America versus non–North America). On the other hand, programs with a business-to-business emphasis more often require prior marketing courses.

We expected that business-to-business-intensive programs might do more to encourage relevance in research than other programs. Because the frequency counts for each separate way of encouraging relevance in doctoral student research (see Table 7: field methods, industry sponsors/data access, practitioner teaching/speakers, research problem relevance) were too small, we took any of these answers as an indication of some effort to bring relevance to doctoral research. We found that 90 percent of all respondents from programs with an emphasis on business-to-business indicated some effort to encourage

TABLE 9. Character of Programs with Emphasis in Business-to-Business ($n = 41$)

	Low Emphasis on Business-to-Business	High Emphasis on Business-to-Business
Program Characteristics		
Number of Marketing Faculty (FTEs)	12.4	9.7
Number of Faculty Specializing in Business-to-Business (FTEs)	1.6	3.7
Number of PhD Students Taken in per Year	2.5	2.7
Number of PhD Students (all years)	9.1	8.4
Number of PhD Students with Interest in Business-to-Business	1.5	3.4
Doctoral Student to Faculty Ratio	0.84	1.26
Years to Complete PhD (on average)	4.2	4.3
Proportional Student Emphasis on Business-to-Business	17%	40%
Proportional Faculty Emphasis on Business-to-Business	12%	38%
Region		
North America	73%	36%
Outside North America	27%	64%
School Type		
Top-Tier Research Schools	20%	0%
Research-Intensive Schools	30%	36%
Teaching-Intensive Schools	50%	64%
MBA		
Required	54%	55%
Prior Work Experience		
Required	0%	9% (n =1)
Desirable	63%	18%
Not critical	37%	73%
Prior Marketing Courses		
Required	30%	64%
Required Courses		
Marketing Models	53%	46%
Marketing Management	43%	55%
Statistics (any graduate course)	70%	73%

Econometrics	23%	36%
Consumer Behavior	67%	64%
Business-to-Business Marketing	3% (*n* = 1)	27% (*n* = 3)
Research Methods	80%	73%
Philosophy of Science	37%	36%
Microeconomics	27%	43%
Relative Coursework Emphasis		
Number of Methods Courses	2.4	2.4
Number of Substantive Courses	1.5	1.9
Number of Foundational Courses	0.9	1.4
Number of Required Courses	4.8	5.6
Relative Emphasis on Methods	53%	43%
Relative Emphasis on Substance	30%	29%
Relative Emphasis on Foundation	18%	22%
Bring Relevance to Student Research	68%	90%

relevance, compared to 68 percent for those without business-to-business emphasis.

Deficiencies in Faculty Applicants in Business-to-Business

We asked respondents what deficiencies they have noted in faculty job applicants in the business-to-business area. Since we specifically referred to applicants in the business-to-business area, many respondents did not respond to this question, except to note that they have not hired in this area. The fourteen respondents noted three main deficiencies: poor methodological skills, poor conceptual/analytical skills, and lack of a practitioner perspective (Table 10). The following quotes represent these concerns:

> Unaware of profitability and other operational business constraints.

> Those whom we interviewed seem to lack methodological foundation. They are not terribly strong in data analysis, experimental design, etc.

> Lack of ability to conceptualize marketing problems at an abstract, theoretical level.

TABLE 10. Deficiencies in Job Applicants in Business-to-Business Area ($n = 14$)

Deficiencies (multiple responses possible)	Percentage
Methodological/conceptual skills	50.0
Analytical skills	28.6
Lack of practitioner perspective	35.7

Placements

We asked respondents to report the placements of their three most recent graduates. Table 11 relates placements to the type of school of origin. The school where the faculty candidate graduates has a strong relationship to placement, with graduates more likely to stay at the same tier or to descend than to ascend. The likelihood of placement in industry is inversely related to the research emphasis of the school.

About half (48.6 percent) of the respondents report that they were not satisfied with their placements. The satisfaction rate increases with increasing research emphasis of the school, as shown in Table 11. Based on the respondents' comments, it seems that most programs would like to place their students at more research-intensive schools, or at least achieve parity between their own school and the school of placement, as exemplified by these statements:

> More top ranked academic placements.

> Would like to do better, e.g., other Big Ten Schools.

We noted a difference between the North American and non–North American schools in the tendency of the latter to retain their graduates and to place more of their students in industry:

> Most of our doctoral students do not choose an academic career, but I would prefer them doing so.

Many non–North American schools also seem to place graduates within the same country:

> It would be nice to have more international appointments. The lack is more due to personal commitments than lack of quality.

TABLE 11. Placements by School of Origin

School of Origin	Number of Placements	Placement (*n* = 38)					Proportion Satisfied with Placements (%) (*n* = 35)
		Top-Tier Research Schools (%)	Research-Intensive Schools (%)	Teaching Schools with Some Research (%)	Teaching Schools (%)	Industry (%)	
Top-Tier Research Schools	15	40	26.7	20	13.3	0	66.7
Research-Intensive Schools	36	5.6	33.3	33.3	19.4	8.3	54.5
Teaching-Intensive Schools	48	2.1	6.3	29.2	43.8	18.7	44.4

DISCUSSION

In the Porter-McKibben report, in the Dallas conference (and later commentary), as well as in our survey results, some issues critical to (business) marketing doctoral education emerge.

It is clear that PhD programs in marketing and in business in general are feeling the same pressure that enterprises all over the world are feeling. They are being asked to be all things to all constituencies. Faculty who emerge from these programs are being asked to do high-quality research that is both rigorous and relevant, to be excellent teachers, as well as to carry a substantial service load at their institutions.

While it is healthy and important to stress the need to improve on all these fronts, junior scholars are limited in terms of time and skills. The ideal business marketing researcher would be sophisticated methodologically, have a multidisciplinary background, and draw on extensive industry experience. However, in practice, both faculty members and the schools that train them must make some compromises when reaching for this ideal.

It appears that top-tier research schools, not surprisingly, place the highest weight on research quality. But they struggle with the rigor-relevance debate and seem to be unsure how to face it. The overall dissatisfaction with the relevance of most of the academic research in marketing is putting increasing pressure on business school faculties worldwide. It is clear that relevance will play a more important role in coming years; the mechanisms for facilitating that relevance have not been finely tuned at this point.

The foundation reports recommended hiring from outside the discipline. With their lack of MBA or similar program prerequisites, many top-tier institutions embrace this idea in PhD admissions. The schools that are dissatisfied with their placements (output) should perhaps look at the quality of their input. We will return to this later, but it is not evident that a strong background in business (through an MBA, for example) necessarily provides the best background to make research contributions in the area.

While these issues are critical to marketing in general, business marketing presents particular challenges. We have argued that the business marketing area is highly relevant and important, and yet we find that it is underrepresented in academia, both in terms of faculty and PhD students, particularly at the top-tier schools. We speculate about some reasons for this. The operations of business markets are not overt, often taking place out of sight of casual observers. Without some job experience, it is difficult for a researcher to have a sufficient understanding of the operation of those markets to conceptualize problems appropriately. In addition, academics may have an insufficient understanding of technology to appreciate how value is created in market transactions. Hence, business marketing academic researchers often do research that is deemed irrelevant by those who actually work in the field. In fact, technically oriented practitioners may not even talk to naive academics who cannot communicate in their language.

The survey revealed that job applicants in business marketing have a reputation for poor conceptual and methodological skills. If true, it may be because strong quantitative methodologists are drawn to areas where greater quantities of data can easily be collected. There are fewer (although larger economic value) transactions in the business marketplace and many of those transactions do not take place through public channels such as supermarkets where bar code scanners readily collect such data. Hence, many good quantitative methodologists may be drawn away from doing research in business marketing, while few highly skilled qualitative researchers to date have exploited the research opportunities that this area provides.

What are schools doing about the situation? Generally they opt to self-clone. Top-tier institutions focus primarily on research and stress methodology. Individuals from those institutions rarely go into business marketing for the reasons that we have noted. Teaching-intensive schools stress substantive issues over fundamental research training in their PhD programs. Individuals graduating from those institutions may therefore lack the conceptual and methodological skills to become top-quality researchers.

So what can individuals and schools do to improve the situation to increase the proportion of marketing PhDs focusing on business marketing and be sure that such individuals are close to the Pareto frontier of quality in substantive knowledge, conceptual skills, and methodological training? We make a few suggestions here in order to provoke further discussion, and hopefully some action.

For Business Schools

School Recommendation 1:
Recruit Actively and Nontraditionally

The lack of "quality" PhD student prospects will not cure itself. The individuals who can become good business marketing scholars may not be inclined toward the field. Therefore, active recruitment is important. Sociologists and anthropologists are ideal candidates to do qualitative work in business marketing. Engineers and those specializing in the hard sciences can bring technical and methodological skills to the table. Many of these people will need to be courted to get them to consider entering a marketing PhD program. And joint PhD programs with technical departments (similar to MDs/PhDs for medical researchers) might be an exciting and viable option for some.

School Recommendation 2:
Internships, Sabbaticals, and Postdocs

Internships, sabbaticals, and Postdocs may help (aspiring) scholars to become knowledgeable in business marketing. We feel that industry internships during PhD programs as well as postdoctoral appointments and sabbatical leaves in industry should be actively considered and encouraged as part of legitimate doctoral training. A number of the ISBM sponsoring institutions have expressed interest in such programs and are awaiting nominations from academia.

School Recommendation 3:
Rethink Reward Systems

Too many schools count publications as surrogates for research quality. Schools must signal to junior scholars that they will reward small sample studies with the longer lead time that primary data collection demands. Business researchers must navigate the relevance-rigor frontier and need metrics for relevance that are appropriate for business marketing. Some academic departments have enacted practitioner advisory boards. Getting such boards involved in the faculty review process, even in an advisory capacity, could provide a more balanced reward system. A changed reward system should evaluate research on its merit and not on its volume.

For Prospective PhDs (and Recent Graduates)

Candidate Recommendation 1:
Partner Early and Often

Because the mixture of conceptual, methodological, and substantive skills is difficult to find in one individual, business marketing scholars should be encouraged to form research partnerships early in their careers. For example, industry internships should be used to generate research sites. Broaden the structure of your coursework and your PhD committee: consider having members from science and engineering as well as statistics and economics on those committees. Consider doing collaborative research during the PhD program with folks in other business functions (operations and logistics, in particular) as well as in the sciences and technology areas.

Candidate Recommendation 2:
Focus on Real Problems

Both the academic and practitioner communities in business marketing are intolerant of research on toy problems. Convenience samples of purchasing agents and laboratory studies with undergraduates or MBAs as surrogate organizational buyers have little credibility. Ask a good research question and do the research the right way, which may not be the easy way. The reward will be in the long run.

Candidate Recommendation 3:
Consider Industry Employment

PhDs in marketing have traditionally focused on academic appointments as the focus of their educational programs. In the engineering disciplines, however, it is common for the bulk of graduates to get their first jobs in industry. Increasing industry appointments for business marketing PhDs may force more relevance into doctoral training and close the relevance-rigor gap.

CONCLUSIONS

In this paper we have attempted to understand where PhD programs in business marketing are today and how they can be improved. We looked at those programs within the historical context of PhD education in business in general and marketing programs in particular.

Not surprisingly, we have identified many deficiencies and challenges for marketing PhD programs in general and for business marketing PhDs in particular. For the latter, the need for relevance and substantive understanding of problem areas combines with the often inaccessible nature of the marketplaces to provide substantial research challenges.

PhD education in business is based on the premise that active, high-quality research in a discipline is a necessary ingredient for high-quality teaching at a university level. We strongly concur and most of our recommendations focus around mechanisms for enhancing such research.

There is no single solution here. Schools have been making and must continue to make critical trade-offs, although schools should make their positions clear:

> Unless doctoral programs can identify the specific types of business schools that would provide the most supportive environments (niches) for their graduates, they are destined to contribute to frictions between producers and users of the products of doctoral education. . . . We can no longer act as though all schools of business have identical missions and operational values, nor can we continue to assume that all doctoral programs are, or should be, very similar. (Alutto, pp. 40, 42)

On a positive note, many of the criticisms leveled at business schools about their lack of concern with relevance appear to be misguided. Business schools are deeply concerned about their constituencies and the needs of the business community in particular. And they are modifying their programs in response. Those modifications are taking place slower than some might want, but academia has both the luxury and responsibility to take a more careful, longer-term perspective. We hope that some schools and prospective business marketing scholars decide to make some of the changes we have suggested, and to do what is important to do and not just what is expedient.

REFERENCES

Alutto, Joseph A. (1993). "Whither Doctoral Business Education? An Exploration of Program Models." *Selections* 9(3), 37-43.

Arden House Report (1956). *Faculty Requirements and Standards in Collegiate Schools of Business*. Minneapolis: American Association of Collegiate Schools of Business.

Byrt, William (Ed.) (1989). *Management Education: An International Survey*. New York: Routledge.

Dulek, Ronald E. and John S. Fielden (1992). "Why Fight the System: The Non-Choice Facing Beleaguered Business Faculties." *Business Horizons* 35(5), 13-19.

Gordon, Robert A. and James E. Howell (1959). *Higher Education for Business*. New York: Columbia University Press.

Graduate Management Admission Council (1992). "Current Issues in Business Doctoral Education: A Report on the Dallas Invitational Conference." *Selections* 9(1), 10-26.

Hasselback, James R. (1995). *The Wiley Guide to Marketing Faculty*. New York: Wiley.

Kozelka, R. (1954). *Professional Education for Business*. Minneapolis: American Association of Collegiate Schools of Business.

Leavitt, Harold (1993). "The Business School and the Doctorate." *Selections* 9(2), 12-21.

Madansky, Albert (1994). "Fine Tuning the Business School Doctorate: Who Should Do It?" *Selections* 11(1), 4-7.

Marshall, Leon C. (Ed.) (1928). *The Collegiate School of Business*. Chicago: University of Chicago Press.

May, Robert G. (1994). "Internationalizing Business Doctoral Education: Bringing Down the Barriers." *Selections* 11(1), 1-3.

Pierson, F.C. (1959). *The Education of American Businessmen*. New York: McGraw-Hill.

Porter, Lyman W. and Lawrence E. McKibben (1988). *Management Education and Development: Drift or Thrust into the 21st Century*. New York: McGraw-Hill.

Slater, Courtenay M. (1996). *Business Statistics of the United States*. Lanham, MD: Bernan Press.

West, Richard (1991). "A Response to Harold Leavitt's Article: Good Diagnosis, Bad Prescription." *Selections* 8(1), 17-22.

West, Richard W. (1992). "Doctoral Education in Business: Improving the Teacher of Our Teachers." *Selections* 9(1), 27-31.

Challenges for Business-to-Business Doctoral Programs: A Commentary

Grahame R. Dowling

The preceding paper by Danneels and Lilien makes a valuable contribution to our understanding of doctoral training in business-to-business marketing—its origins and the current state of development. The following comments are presented to build on some of the points made by these authors. They are designed to generate more discussion on this topic.

The first paragraph of the paper captures one of the key features of business-to-business marketing, namely, the study of exchange relationships. Given this focus, it is surprising to me that very few doctoral programs are organized around this principle. For example, while the courses in Table 5 *may* include some topics on exchange such as contracting, transaction cost economics, and agency theory, there seems little in here that focuses directly on the issues and problems which business marketers face when they do business with another firm. While economists have studied this topic for many years (e.g., Williamson), marketers seem slow to build on this theoretical work. Table 6's recommended courses such as Channels, I/O Economics, Relationships/Alliances, Game Theory and Negotiation suggest some progress but still no integrative course that would help managers to answer such a basic question as, "How do we write a 'good' contract with our ad agency?" (Devinney and Dowling 1997).

This brings me to the thorny question of doctoral research. There are (at least) two issues here. First, what topics and research methods should doctoral students focus on in order to position their research within the business-to-business domain? Second, should their research have direct relevance to business concerns?

If, as Danneels and Lilien suggest, the core concepts of business-to-business marketing are those of exchange and relationships, then a business-to-business doctoral thesis should either focus on these topics, or it should offer some new insights into these phenomena. These are easy criteria to stipulate, but in many cases they are difficult for a student to meet. For example, the very nature of a relationship suggests that a longitudinal research methodology is really necessary. Cross-sectional data are at best a compromise. Yet for students who have limited resources for data collection and who want to graduate within a reasonable time frame, cross-sectional data are often their preferred source of evidence. In essence, many business-to-business doctoral programs pose to students a dilemma—do a longitudinal study, but with few resources.

As to research that will impact practitioners, the best outcome is rigor (as evidenced by technically sound research) and relevance (as evidenced by its application in business-to-business situations). How can a doctoral student/program capture both outcomes? From the student's perspective the best strategy I have seen was outlined by Professor John Little of MIT at a marketing science conference some years ago. He said that many of his research papers were motivated by talking to business managers and finding out what problems they were trying to solve. His experience as an academic allowed him to ground these sometimes fuzzy problems in one or more academic disciplines and thus draw on the work of others to further conceptualize the problem and work toward a solution. Many of his marketing colleagues at MIT seem to follow a similar strategy. Some of the fruits of this approach have been published in *Management Science*—a journal in which most of us would be proud to publish.

Contrast the Little–MIT strategy with the typical approach of many doctoral candidates. First, they start with an exhaustive literature review. Then, after much photocopying, reading, confusion, and winnowing of the ideas they have found, a thesis topic is beaten (with the help of their supervisors) into shape. Once the thesis is written and published it may be "discovered" by industry. If the newly minted doctor goes into industry, the chances are somewhat higher.

The approach just described is almost the antithesis of Little's successful strategy. Little, however, was by no means the first scholar to use this strategy. He followed in the footsteps of the early economists, people such as John Maynard Keynes, Karl Marx, David Ricardo, and Adam Smith. These men were all intrigued by what they saw around them and much of their work was designed to answer the pressing questions of their day (Ormerod 1994).

How can business schools (academics and doctoral programs) facilitate this type of outcome? Fostering industry linkages is a good place to start, but it will not have the big academic payoffs for students and their supervisors if they cannot get their work published in the top journals. Here, journal editors and editorial boards come into play. They need to be more sympathetic to the practical problems of doing business-to-business research, and the motivation of studies from a real-world as well as an academic discipline basis. The mandatory "managerial implications" section at the end of many articles is really just tokenism. Also, the requirement of many journals for the literature review section to outweigh the "why this topic is interesting" section, can misdirect researchers and frighten away practitioner-readers.

Another way to foster "applied" research is for academics, and in particular university performance-appraisal committees, to reward good applied research as much as good basic research. To see what I mean here, take a moment to list what you think that your colleagues would consider to be the top five marketing journals.

_____

_____

_____

_____

_____

The following journals are frequent candidates for this list: *Journal of Marketing, Journal of Marketing Research, Journal of Consumer*

Research, Marketing Science, Management Science, International Journal for Research in Marketing, and the *Journal of Retailing.* Occasionally, the *Harvard Business Review (HBR)* might sneak onto the list, but "real academics" certainly would not publish their best work in here, would they? Well, maybe they should try, because *HBR* is arguably the single most influential source of management ideas for practitioners, that is, most of the people involved in business-to-business marketing. If *HBR* is thought to be unacceptable, then some of the other outlets for this type of research, such as the *California Management Review, Sloan Management Review, Interfaces,* or *Long Range Planning,* may be acceptable.

The quickest way to get applied journals into the marketing top ten is for performance-appraisal committees to (1) include some of these journals in the premier journal category (hence the top ten rather that the top five), and (2) weight a publication in these outlets equally with the more traditional academic journals. There is little use in asking untenured faculty to do applied research if "what counts" is publications in the traditional academic journals that practitioners have learned to avoid. We need to follow the advice of human resource people who have observed over the years that employees tend to do what is *inspected,* in preference to what is expected.

One final observation about applied research is worth noting. Students of business and executives returning to university for short courses like seeing it being used as the basis for the ideas presented in the classroom. Up go the teaching ratings.

The following points summarize the previous discussion. First, from the evidence presented by Danneels and Lilien, many doctoral programs need some integrative and customized coursework that focuses directly on the essential aspects of business-to-business marketing. (My assumption here is that exchange relationships are one [or the] core element of this discipline.) Second, we need to generate resources to help students and other academics do longitudinal research. Third, research needs to be *grounded* in both the academic literature and the "real world" of practice. Fourth, arguably, the fastest way to change the way business-to-business marketing evolves is to start by explicitly stating what are the desirable outcomes, and then critically evaluating the current performance-appraisal schemes that are used to shape the behavior of both students and faculty.

REFERENCES

Devinney, T. M. and G. R. Dowling (1997). "Paying the Piper Differently to Play a Better Tune: Understanding and Resolving Advertiser-Agency Conflicts." Australian Graduate School of Management, Working Paper.

Ormerod, P. (1994). *The Death of Economics*. London: Faber and Faber.

Williamson, O. E. (1975). *Markets and Hierarchies: Analysis and Antitrust Implications*. New York: The Free Press.

A Program of Action for Business-to-Business Doctoral Programs: A Reply to Commentary

Erwin Danneels
Gary L. Lilien

PhD programs clearly need more business marketing content. The best way to address this deficiency is for all of us to produce research that is sufficiently rigorous and relevant so it must be incorporated in PhD studies. That material should focus on the key characteristics—extended value chains, long-term relationships, heterogeneous customer groups, often with a few powerful and knowledgeable buyers, multiple decision makers with associated agency problems—that make business markets different.

We agree that rigor and relevance need not be at odds. The researcher (including the doctoral student) in search of relevance should not have difficulty identifying topics for study. Good business marketing research should be grounded in practice. Little's approach to problem-finding is to be commended but is exceedingly rare in academia. We need more good listeners: dissertation advisors and PhD students who can listen to practitioners and hear what they mean (not necessarily what they say) about the (researchable) issues that challenge their practice.

Dowling points out that real business marketing problems are often fuzzy and require an interdisciplinary and multimethod attack. And that is problematic even for seasoned researchers, not to mention new scholars. Beyond the intellectual challenges, new scholars face time and cost constraints, especially if they conduct the longitudinal research Professor Dowling calls for. Rarely can a PhD student both conceptualize and execute longitudinal research and finish a PhD program in a reasonable time. We need partnerships between businesses and academics to identify those topics worth tracking. Penn

State's ISBM was developed to provide the infrastructure and resources to execute such studies and awaits the emergence of rigorous and relevant research proposals.

Finally, Dowling underlines our concern about the misalignment between the academic reward system and problem-oriented research. New measurements and reward systems are needed. Our promotion and tenure systems currently reward research rigor much more than research relevance. Until "impact" (on practice, on other disciplines, on students, on organizational performance) becomes a recognized and measurable part of the promotion and tenure process in academia, business marketing research will continue to miss the mark and fall far short of its potential. We hope that our readers have the energy and discipline to help align the reward and measurement system to do what is best rather than what is easy to execute and measure.

PART II:
EXECUTIVE EDUCATION PROGRAMS

The Pedagogy of Executive Education in Business Markets

Narakesari Narayandas
V. Kasturi Rangan
Gerald Zaltman

INTRODUCTION

As businesses entering the twenty-first century adjust to the demands of a global economy, the need to develop new, more effective ways to compete looms larger than ever before (Vicere, Taylor, and Freeman 1994). There is a growing recognition in corporate America and other markets throughout the world that knowledge, the result of learning, and competence in technological and managerial skills are key competitive advantages—perhaps the only sustainable advantages a firm can have (Lorange 1994). It comes as no surprise that corporate training budgets have ballooned to around $45 billion to $55 billion annually (Greco 1997; Nohria and Berkeley 1994). *Business Week* estimates that approximately $12 billion of this amount is devoted to executive education. However, not all of this is being delivered through university settings. In fact, only about a quarter of this total is delivered by academic institutions, with the rest coming from consultants and training firms (Fulmer and Vicere 1996). According to Meister (1994), corporate universities, that is, non-university-affiliated in-house education and training departments of large corporations, tripled from about 400 a decade ago to more than 1,000 by 1996.

This shift toward alternatives to universities as sources for executive education is a result of a growing number of corporations that see current university-based programs as ineffective (Vicere, Taylor, and Freeman 1993). The good news is that it is still not too late for universities to respond. Ready, Vicere, and White (1993) found a growing desire on the part of the corporate community for academics to have a stronger link to the challenges and realities of today's workplace. Academic institutions with carefully crafted strategies that focus on leveraging their core competencies, coupled with a fierce dedication to quality, teaching excellence, innovation, and measured market responsiveness will not only survive but are likely to flourish in partnership with the corporate community (Vicere, Taylor, and Freeman 1993).

In this paper, we focus on executive education specifically in business marketing. Our purpose is not to pinpoint its size—we know it is big—but rather to understand its evolution and trajectory in terms of content and process. It is our belief that in order to be successful, academic and consulting institutions need to go beyond the development of concepts and their contextual application to providing the architecture that will enable the change that corporations (the customers) are looking for. Addressing this additional objective requires not only innovative development and delivery of substance but also developing and orchestrating the cultural climate for effecting change. By and large, universities and academic institutions know how to do the former; they have a lot to learn regarding the latter. Consulting companies usually force the latter, but very few are capable of harnessing the energies and knowledge of a company's managers to conceptualize the change. The need is for a happy combination of both, and that is our challenge. While the executive education market is big and getting bigger, there is the danger that business schools might miss this opportunity unless they make fundamental changes in the design, delivery, and management of executive education programs (Lorange 1994).

We present our rationale in the next three sections. We first trace the evolution of the substance of business marketing education, underscoring the current trends. We then examine the pedagogical methods used by educational programs to address the identified trends. In the concluding section we discuss what we see as the missing piece in business education—the architecture for effecting change.

EMERGENCE OF A CONCEPTUAL STRUCTURE IN BUSINESS MARKETING EDUCATION

In the 1960s and 1970s, business marketing education primarily centered around training professionals, mainly "engineers," to think like "marketers." The sales function did the bulk of the marketing, with most of the people hired into the sales function having technical backgrounds. Business marketing's challenge was to influence sales personnel, mostly technical people, to think commercially.

Meanwhile, on the consumer marketing side of the discipline, there was a sweeping movement toward the marketing concept, which was defined dramatically differently from the selling concept. Fundamentally, marketing started with the customer's needs and wants, and sales with the preconfigured product from the factory. Influenced by that wave, business marketers attempted to better understand their customers' buying behaviors. Thus, concepts of organization buying behavior (OBB) (Webster and Wind 1972) and its complement, industrial procurement and purchasing (Corey 1978), became popular executive education topics in the late 1970s. As a direct offshoot of the OBB focus, customer segmentation ideas became more refined. Thus, ideas such as benefit segmentation were added to the industrial manager's toolbox in the early 1980s.

These ideas began to coalesce around the concept of industrial marketing strategy (Corey 1978; Webster 1984), which became a hot topic of executive education programs. Not surprisingly, this trend was coincidental with the rise of corporate strategy as an important management discipline (concepts such as strategic business unit analysis and product portfolio models that became important inputs into the strategic plans of large corporations). This was indeed the heyday of conceptual thinking and many business schools mounted executive programs taught by scholars expounding elegant principles.

Toward the late 1980s and early 1990s, three trends profoundly changed the field of business marketing. First was the rise of high-technology businesses. Technology entrepreneurs brought products and services to the business-to-business domain that no longer fit the narrow definition of "industrial" products. Telecommunications, information, and computing technology changed the face of many industrial products. Software and intelligence became a big part of the equation. Under the new environment, upgrades rather than maintenance (and services) became an important product factor. A business had a lot to gain by developing relationships with customers rather than managing transactions. Consequently, customer acquisition and retention strategies began to pervade executive education. But now, armed with financial tools, the calculation of the net present value of a customer took on more bite. Customer value measurement and management gained in popularity (Gale 1994; Slywotzky 1996). Along with this rediscovery of the customer concept, account management, especially as it relates to large accounts, gained significant attention.

Second, because of the winds of change brought by the technology revolution, companies in mature businesses revamped their product development processes to refashion their product line. "Time to market" became a key competitive weapon. Meanwhile, the recession of the early 1980s and the rise of Japan as the third power (Europe being the other) forced a near universal commitment to reengineering and cost containment. Because of their engineering orientation, business-to-business firms were quick to adopt ideas of total quality management, and the notion of cross-functional teams to drive new product development became widely practiced. Thus, stage-gate type new product development efforts (Cooper 1993) began to include a lot more parallel processing.

And last, in the 1990s, businesses were becoming global, especially with the fast-growing economies of Asia offering direct markets for infrastructure-related products and services in industries such as telecommunication, information technology, and power. In addition, the growth in consumer spending in these markets created demand for intermediate products, especially for machinery and chemicals. Since most of these technologies were owned by Western companies (and Japan), there was a natural migration of these businesses worldwide eastward and southward. Such globalization, of course, brought unique challenges of its own. Most large customers expected their suppliers to provide a coordinated sales and service effort at various locations around the globe. This forced a certain standardization and centralization of key marketing functions such as pricing. Yet, at the same time, because the regulations and regional politics were so different, business marketers had to hone their local adaptation skills. Managing global customers was now a very important aspect of business marketing strategy.

So by the early 1990s, a somewhat circumspect field had exploded with managers seeking cutting-edge knowledge that went beyond the traditional bounds of marketing. New ideas on customer loyalty management, new product development processes, order cycle management, and global account management got added to the ever-expanding thirst among business-to-business marketing practitioners. High-tech marketing consultant Regis McKenna wrote:

> In the 1990s, the critical dimensions of the company—including all of the attributes that together define how the company does business—are ultimately the functions of marketing. That is why marketing is everyone's job, why marketing is everything, and everything is marketing.

The executive landscape had also begun to look much more varied, with backgrounds other than engineering or technology being just as common, further complicating the role and task of the educator. Moreover, business marketers were looking for connections to general management in addition to function-specific knowledge. Box 2 provides a brief overview of the substantive trends in business marketing education.

BOX 2. Changes in Emphasis:
Business Marketing Executive Education

1970s	*1980s*	*1990s*
Sales Management	Marketing Management	Customer Value Management
Focusing on Training Engineers	Understanding the Marketing Mix	Creating, Delivering, and Capturing Customer Value
Negotiations	Linking Marketing Effort to Sales Effort	High-Technology Marketing
Industrial Buyer Behavior	Benefit Segmentation	New Product Development
Procurement Strategy	Marketing Strategy	Supplier Base Reduction and Supplier Tiering
	Strategic Business Unit Analysis	Managing the Global Customer
		Global Account Management
		Managing in the Interactive World of the Internet

Toward a Contextual Emphasis: Executive Education in the 1990s

The trend toward conceptualization that started in the 1970s and strengthened in the 1980s was blended into corporations' needs for customized applications in the 1990s, where the dominating trend was for making the concepts relevant in the context of one's work environment.

There has been a clear shift from a pursuit of knowledge for the sake of erudition to knowledge for the sake of action. Gone are the days when firms would send people to one-off courses "almost as an inoculation that would ward off management failure" for fifteen years or so (Arkin 1996). Now firms want education and training that will help them re-create their businesses on an ongoing basis (White et al. 1994). This trend is strengthened by the fact that business managers are increasingly well equipped with the frameworks to quickly absorb knowledge because of their own formal business (MBA) training in the essentials of management. What managers seem to want is a better understanding of how to apply these concepts in the best possible way in their environments, and help in creating the right climate for the planned changes. The contextual application of the content has therefore become critical along with a focus on creating the right environment that will facilitate and support change. In fact, the very notion of "understanding" means that a manager has the ability to apply standard or formal knowledge in a novel context. It is one thing to know, in principle, how to assess the lifetime value of a customer; it is another thing to make that assessment when the customer has become a very different entity.

In the past, corporate education played a reactive role in sustaining firm performance (White, Pierce, and Rush 1994). In this approach, firms defined the necessary skills, knowledge, and attitudes required by personnel and arranged for training in areas where a gap was identified. Usually, the answers were found in standard, off-the-shelf programs. Once the people were trained, the job was done. Now, the focus is more on developing customized programs (Hequet 1992) that (1) keep in mind the targeted firm's needs in its industry environment and (2) focus on continuously anticipating training needs over time while developing programs that proactively fill potential gaps in skills and capabilities (Boyatzis, Cowen, and Kolb 1995), rather than trying to fill gaps in the needs of the present. To achieve this, firms have pushed toward developing in-house, on-the-job training that lets employees learn in the environment that they work in. They want executive education programs to be focused on how the participants can use their learning on the job rather than accumulating concepts for knowledge's sake (Noel and Charan 1992).

Other changes have taken place as well. Executive education programs are more cross-functional than the departmental or compartmentalized approach of the past. Last but not least, the global nature of the business in most industries has led to a demand for a global rather than a North American perspective. Box 3 provides a summary of some of these trends.

PEDAGOGICAL METHODS AND OBJECTIVES

In keeping with changes that drive a more contextual emphasis from a purely conceptual one, pedagogical methods to deliver business education have also broadened from traditional open-enrollment programs (i.e., managers from different businesses in the same class) to customized programs and action learning exercises, where managers from the same business or company get together to solve a common problem. In this section, we discuss key aspects of three regularly used program architectures and the role of technology in enhancing their effectiveness and efficiency.

Traditional Executive Programs

Traditional executive programs include focused programs that are built around a topic such as sales force management, new product development, etc., and general programs that provide a broad coverage of several topics in the field of business marketing.

Focused programs are usually of three- to six-day duration. General programs are longer, up to two weeks in length. These programs are traditionally offered by academic institutions or by the training arm of large corporations, often with assistance from academics. The purpose is to expose a cross-section of practitioners to recent thinking in the field and to ensure that some of the evergreen classics, such as "segmentation," "value pricing," etc., are duly covered.

BOX 3. The Changing Face of Executive Education

Unique Events	➡ Lifelong Learning
Standard Off-the-Shelf	➡ Customized to Specific Needs
Reactive—Fill Gaps for Today	➡ Proactive—Train for Tomorrow's Needs
Acquiring Knowledge	➡ Action Orientation
Listen and Learn	➡ Ask, Interact, and Learn
Individual Focus	➡ Team Focus
Functional Silo Approach	➡ Interfunctional Emphasis
Domestic Focus	➡ Global Emphasis

These programs provide managers considerable opportunity to learn laterally from one another as they share their experiences of how a particular concept was applied in their respective organizations. This is possible mainly because of the heterogeneous backgrounds of the participants from a wide variety of firms in a wide variety of industries. Such an exchange is very useful in catalyzing participant thinking for possible in-house adaptations.

A more recent trend, especially at educational institutions, has been to blend classroom and field learning. The program is delivered in two or three modules with executives going back to their work environments during the in-between time that could vary from a month or two to almost a year in some cases. The in-class program may not be particularly customized and may rely on the "lateral learning" advantages of an open enrollment course. But at the end of each module, participants are assisted in fashioning a project that they would attempt to conceptualize, organize, and implement over the course of the three modules.

The advantage of this model is that the analytical and implementation parts are integrated by design. Over the life of the program, participants have a chance to adjust their plans based on the feedback from the implementation. These staged programs work well when teaching material is sequenced from analyses to implementation.

Customized Executive Education

An organization that sees the need for change (e.g., market orientation), or simply the need for higher sensitivity toward a certain set of issues (e.g., relationship with distribution partners), may seek an educational institution or a group of educators to help focus its managers through a customized education program.

As part of the educational program, some stimuli, such as business cases, may be customized to closely reflect the host company's business situation. It is important to note that it might not be necessary or even desirable to structure a large chunk of the program with company-specific material. In fact, by using outside-company material, especially of firms in similar situations, the educational experience is vastly enhanced. Senior management may not be that sanguine to believe that solutions to complex problems could be worked out in two weeks. Rather, the purpose is to open up the host company's managers to out-of-the-box thinking. This is best achieved by a compare-and-contrast of several similar situations, both within and outside the industry. Lectures and discussions on relevant topics of interest to the host company could also add considerably to the value of the program.

A customized executive education program is usually only as successful as the commitment shown by senior management to the program, and the openness and willingness they show in capturing ideas that come out of the program for further exploration and action. If senior leaders do not seize the initiative in structuring in-house forums, task forces, and follow-on mechanisms to sustain the momentum of the educational program, a lot of well-directed energy could be wasted and middle management may end up being even more frustrated and demotivated than before the program. These programs also invariably involve a close working relationship with the host company's senior managers, including the design of the course syllabus. The outcome of the discussion, however, should reflect the true and open sentiments of the group.

In one specific case, which one of the authors of this paper spearheaded, a large high-technology company with a diverse range of analytical instruments and high-value-added supplies used a customized executive education forum as a process to identify and prioritize key issues it faced. The up-front research and cases provided a frame for top management to hone in on issues and problems. The CEO and all members of the company's executive committee along with all senior managers participated in every session of the one-week program. The trainer's role was to surface and elaborate on the several issues faced. Not surprisingly, at least half of them were "systems and process" related, and only about half "substance" related. Much of this was possible only because of the open-mindedness and humility of the senior management. The trainer's responsibility had been to maintain a balance whereby the key decision makers could approach the realignment constructively and objectively. The company then undertook a major realignment and reorganization task over the next year after the executive program was concluded.

Action Learning

The ultimate test of a program's impact is the ability to observe and measure significant change (Fulmer and Vicere 1996). In action learning, a small set of senior managers from a host company typically initiate work with a team of educators to clarify and refine a set of problems or issues of primary focus. Once identified, the educators and host company's senior management usually prioritize and select a cluster of topics to lead off the action learning exercise. Through a mixture of case discussions around company-specific issues and lectures jointly offered by educators and managers, a large cross section of appropriate middle managers is exposed to the problems and challenges. This is usually a quick, one-to-three-day event.

The initial follow-on action learning workshops could take a couple of days but are usually the starting point of a longer process. In action learning, experiential learning through spirited dialogue with peers and faculty can promote new ways to solve daily management challenges, as well as build strategies for the future (Rasmusson 1997). The educator's role here is very tricky. One has to maintain a sense of objectivity, listen carefully, and encourage broad participation, yet not take away attention from the core issues that the group has been assembled to address and solve.

After this problem *socialization* has been achieved, the next step in action learning involves the structuring of internal task forces to attack the problem pieces. The educator's role is to ensure a creative process without necessarily having to participate in the substantive discussions. For example, the task force should be carefully composed to ensure that it has necessary breadth and depth of knowledge to create solution paths to ensure continuity of the work outside the task force. This will invariably suggest someone who has (or is likely to have) some responsibility and accountability for the potential action steps.

Ensuring transition steps to consolidate and advance the deliberations from the task force is a very important part of action learning. The educator may have a role to play in helping the senior management integrate the various pieces into a collective blueprint. He or she may need to assist the senior management in working out a mechanism by which the resultant huge surge of thinking and action planning will get imbibed as part of the routine work of the organization. Depending on its nature and size, an action learning project cycle can vary from several months to over a year.

Consider, for example, AT&T's Leadership Development Program (Vicere 1996). This two-week residential program is designed to transform middle managers into general managers and leaders and to create change agents that could transform AT&T's culture, starting with themselves. The program is rooted in the basic philosophy that learning has not taken place unless behavior has changed and new action has been constructed. The core elements of the program include

1. precourse work where each manager documents a key challenge he or she faces and engages in a dialogue with an AT&T coach on his or her expectations from the program;
2. group process where at the outset of the program each manager shares with a small group (that he or she was assigned to) the gap between where they are and where they need to be with regard to addressing their current and future business challenges;

3. classroom discussions with business school professors, top AT&T executives, and customers that broaden the perspectives of the individuals;
4. learning circles where individuals discuss and debrief what happened during the day;
5. leadership laboratories and experiential exercises where the managers have an opportunity to work in teams to solve unique problems;
6. holistic activities including physical exercises, and
7. action plans where individual managers leave with a documented plan of what they need to do in order to address a pinpointed future challenge.

In 1986, GE implemented an action learning format that complemented changes in the company. GE's action learning places participants in a problem-solving mode. It stretches them by challenging them with the types of problems faced by business leaders who are a level or two above them. The issues are relevant and require decisions. Typically, two teams of five to seven people each work on a single project provided by a senior business development manager from one of GE's thirteen separate businesses. The problems are real and participants receive continuous feedback on their efforts. Each group is given all the information required for them to make the decisions. In addition, they are also given the opportunity to interview GE managers, customers, suppliers, analysts, and other GE employees. At the end of the program, the groups make a presentation to the business manager and his or her team that is actually faced with the exact same issue. The groups are expected to present and defend their positions or rethink their strategies. One such project required participants to develop a consumer lighting strategy for western Europe. This task was prompted by GE's acquisition of Tungsram in Hungary and Thorn Lighting in the United Kingdom; this had given GE an 18 percent share of the market from its previous 2 percent (Noel and Charan 1992).

The three broad methods of delivery discussed in this paper are not mutually exclusive approaches; they serve to underscore the difference in objectives. Many times, a hybrid combination will better serve the educational objectives. Box 4 summarizes the key distinguishing aspects of the three approaches.

BOX 4. Key Elements of Three Program Formats

Action Learning	Goal: Problem solving Emphasis: Action planning Role: Trainer plays the role of catalyst
Custom Education	Goal: Problem identification Emphasis: Awareness and analysis Role: Trainer is part facilitator and part catalyst
General Education	Goal: Continuous learning Emphasis: Reinforce existing, and introduce new, knowledge Role: Trainer is mainly facilitator

---

The three program formats illustrated in Box 4 should not be confused with the pedagogical tools such as lectures, case discussions, and simulations (these are discussed briefly in the appendix). Each program architecture should use a blend of these tools and more. For example, workshops and structural exercises are critical to the action learning format (a detailed discussion of these tools is outside the scope of this paper).

The Role of Technology

Recent technological advances have created new opportunities to enhance the effectiveness and efficiency of executive education programs. These opportunities cluster around three sets of activities: on-campus applications, off-campus applications, and distance learning (Bardach 1997).

Examples of on-campus applications include putting an existing written business case on disk so that participants can use the power of spreadsheets to analyze alternative scenarios and conduct what-if analysis. Other examples include development of simulations that can be adapted to the needs and expectations of different companies in different industries. It is not uncommon for instructors in most business schools to teach in multimedia-enabled environments where they seamlessly switch from the conventional blackboard to PowerPoint files for presentations to videos and simulation exercises, and then to live video conferences with senior executives or experts at remote sites (Bardach 1997).

Technology has also influenced off-campus communications. Executive education participants demand and expect to have the ability to communicate and share information with one another electronically from remote locations off-campus. A number of schools have begun to experiment with instruction on the Internet or via CD-ROM to provide advance readings, exercises, and information to participants.

Finally, technology has also broken down the walls of a classroom. In distance learning, traditional programs are now delivered via satellite, delayed tape broadcasting, or the Internet (Bardach 1997). These modes of instruction appear to work better for lectures dealing with technical details rather than interactive discussions of complex and nebulous management and business problems.

DESIGN PRINCIPLES FOR FUTURE EXECUTIVE EDUCATION IN BUSINESS MARKETING

In spite of the rapid growth and availability of new approaches and concepts, as is the case in other areas of management, their successful implementation in business marketing executive education has been limited. For example, Hammer and Champy (1993) write that less than a quarter of all reengineering efforts have been successful. There are several factors that need to be in place to implement changes. First and foremost, it is important for senior management to wholeheartedly support these initiatives. At GE, the Work Out program was essentially CEO Jack Welch's antidote to action paralysis. Change is hard and difficult only rarely because of lack of relevant ideas; it is mainly because of managerial resistance. Much of this is not an active defiance of turning down new approaches but instead borne out of a genuine misperception of whether change would be beneficial. New ideas are rarely shot down, but rather dissipated through a multitude of queries and delays. Fundamentally, it is a problem of the mind, and unless executive education can boldly and directly incorporate a change process as part of the user's action agenda, its ultimate benefit to the user would be questionable. In fact, a constructive approach in any program is to have executives actively monitor and share their own and others' resistance to accepting and using new ideas. An open discussion of the sources of resistance and the forms they can take can make managers not only more skilled in assessing new ideas and approaches but also more willing to accept those which are believed to be truly valuable.

Perhaps an even more fundamental requirement for effective executive education would be to provide the climate and support necessary for executives to carry their change ideas forward into their work environment. Dhebar (1995) argues the need for "spending most time on courses that hone problem-solving and process-management skills geared to the overall organization." Fundamentally, executive education is about causing change. This change may be something as focused and narrow as a specific program or it may involve broader organizational systems, processes, and people. But regardless of its scope, the hardest part of change is the "execution," not the idea. Action learning and custom executive education methods are superior alternatives on that score, but they do not have the general forum and a cross-sectional peer group of the traditional program. While the former may be better suited to execute change, the latter may have the creative edge in designing opportunities for change. We will need to learn better how to transition from substance to action in future executive education efforts. This, however, may appear to get uncomfortably close to what consultants are supposed to do. But there is a difference. Good executive education relies on the creativity and ability of participants to cause change. The trainer's role is not to solve the problem (that is usually the consultant's role); it is to provide a forum to help executives solve their own problem by providing the appropriate platform. Therefore, the design elements become critical. One has to design not only the course content but also the ambiance of the mind to enable translation into practice.

While executive education has adjusted well to customers' needs to blend conceptual knowledge with contextual reality, there is one more important component that has to be tackled before executive education programs can become truly effective—that is cultural change.

The single most important quality that distinguishes outstanding executives from those who are just very good involves their style or habits of mind. That is, it is how an executive thinks more than what or how much he or she knows or thinks about that is most critical to his or her success. Executive education programs must be concerned with helping managers understand and, as appropriate, improve upon their way of thinking. In order to do a good job, there are several issues of which program developers need to be cognizant.

The Future of Business-to-Business Executive Education

Concepts➔ Concepts + Context ➔ Concepts + Context + Cultural Change

The Paradox of Current Knowledge

Two interesting outcomes of creativity research merit attention here. The first is that essentially the same processes involved in ordinary thinking are also involved in creative thinking. The second is that the development of new ideas is shaped to a considerable extent by existing ideas. Concerning this last point, it is no surprise that early passenger railroad cars resembled stage coaches, or that when executives are asked to draw an animal found on a newly discovered planet where any conditions may be assumed that these animals are remarkably similar to those found on Earth.

The more experienced a manager or executive is, the greater the reservoir of existing knowledge. This offers, simultaneously and paradoxically, more opportunity to be creative and to be constrained. Since there are more items or building blocks of knowledge that can be combined and/or used in novel ways, there is more opportunity to develop a unique perspective, just as the larger the number of pieces in a kaleidoscope, the greater the number of potential patterns that can emerge with each subsequent twist. At the same time, the greater the experience or knowledge base, the larger the number of assumptions, decision rules, and expectations operating, especially without awareness, and hence the more structured and inhibited thinking is likely to be. This leads to a paradox marked by more opportunity to be creative and to be more constrained. The greater an executive's experience, the greater the magnitude and likelihood of this paradox. In executive education, then, it becomes especially important to map existing knowledge. By mapping existing knowledge, it becomes easier to determine which element of the paradox is most being served.

Since different executives in a program will have different experiences, even if employed by the same organization, many different and even conflicting (hopefully) assumptions, expectations, and decision rules will be surfaced. In this instance, it is important to explore such disagreements. This can be done in two ways. First, by asking, Under what conditions is each conflicting assumption likely to be correct/incorrect? This helps identify even more basic considerations that may normally be hidden from program participants. Second, it is important to ask why each of the alternative positions might always be the preferred position and to push on the boundaries of when it would not be preferred. In this way, existing knowledge can be mapped and then used creatively to fashion new knowledge.

Metaphors As Discovery Tools

Another important principle for designing executive education programs concerns the prominence of metaphors. A metaphor is the representation of one thing (a "topic" such as competition) in terms of another (a so-called "vehicle" such as the concept of war). Metaphors are essential for learning. In fact, learning is the process of acquiring and using metaphors. In the simplest case, the process of metaphor as learning is found in the use of past experience as a metaphor (vehicle) for understanding—learning about—a new experience (the so-called topic).

For example, warfare metaphors relating to competitive strategy reveal a number of useful short-term and long-term tactics and strategies to consider. They help highlight important differences between defensive, offensive, and preemptive business policies. At the same time, they tend to "hide" strategies that are more tacitly cooperative, that tend to grow a general market, and that put the best interest of the customer ahead of the worst interest of a competitor. These latter ideas are hidden by the warfare metaphors in the sense that they are less likely to be thought of at all because they are incommensurate with existing frames of reference, they are less likely to be openly suggested when they do occur to someone, and they are less likely to be considered seriously once suggested since existing insights and associated supporting evidence favor the warfare metaphors. It is then useful to try to identify the cost of having alternative strategies hidden from consideration. The hidden strategies could produce a very different posture for a firm and even a very different industry climate.

Linking Explicit with Implicit Knowledge

A general learning principle is that new knowledge is acquired only in conjunction with existing knowledge. (Here, too, we cannot provide explanation but will note that this applies even to seemingly completely novel ideas or other stimuli.) An idea will go unnoticed if it does not trigger a relevant existing mental model. This is also consistent with the observation made earlier concerning the paradox of current knowledge that being creative depends in part on what is already known.

The majority of what executives know is implicit or tacit knowledge acquired without awareness. It would be surprising were it otherwise since most of an executive's time is spent in informal rather than formal instructional settings. Formal executive education programs almost by definition stress explicit knowledge, no matter what instructional methods are used. To be learned well, explicit knowledge, such as a particular way of calculating the future value of a customer, guidelines for managing cross-functional teams, or how to establish pricing policy, should be connected with other existing knowledge, assumptions, expectations, and decision rules. This may be done by showing how an idea is an extension of an established practice, or it may simply be introduced using a familiar analogy or metaphor to help convey the new idea. Since tacit and explicit knowledge comingle, one cannot be understood without the other—a central premise of mental models is that each element within a model has meaning only in terms of other elements with which it is connected. A manager who is aware of only his or her explicit knowledge may be aware of only a few pieces of his or her mental model. Imagine trying to anticipate the image of a jigsaw puzzle when fewer than 12 percent of the pieces are available and there is no box cover. Without a fuller understanding of the tacit elements of their mental model, managers will have difficulty not only in understanding why it is (or it is not) working well but also in conveying the same to their colleagues.

Anomaly Detection

Most business problems have no clear best answer and are not routine, and therefore standard responses are unlikely to work. And it may not even be clear what the problem is—only that there is one. Ill-structured problems represent major learning situations. In fact, they demand learning, in contrast to routine problem situations that demand use of what has already been learned.

In a study done by one of the authors of this paper, a striking distinguishing characteristic among people with different levels of problem-solving skills was their treatment of anomaly and pattern seeking. Less-skilled problem solvers tended immediately to look for patterns in the problem situation that suggested solutions. They seemed to ask first, "What is there about the present that resembles what has been seen in the past?" More skilled problem solvers, on the other hand, tended first to seek out irregularity or anomaly. They seemed to ask first, "What is different about the situation that distinguishes it from what has been seen before?" Past experience was also relevant for more skilled problem solvers, but at a later point in the process. Alternatively, their past experience might have said, "Do not constrain your view of a novel situation too soon with prior perceptions and solutions."

Having established the importance of understanding mental models, we will not elaborate on techniques here. Several, such as Zaltman (1997), are available. It will suffice to say that all executive actions are the result of different bundles of connected ideas or constructs. It is important to understand what executives' mental models are. This is a requisite first step for addressing change.

Change management has to go beyond addressing managers' mental models. As work by Kotter (1996), Kanter (1983), and others reveals, there are many structural dimensions to change. While educational programs by themselves might not be enough to address such systemic issues, it is important that one of their main objectives should be to create the climate for structural change. We urge program managers to give this issue its due in their course design. Many forward-looking companies provide exactly such a forum for executives returning from executive education. The HR or training department of such organizations will reap a fortune, if the ideas from such a forum are integrated into a larger change process.

In this paper, we argue that executive education's primary role has changed from knowledge dissemination to action orientation. It is in the action required of a novel challenge brought on by a competitor's actions or a change among customers, for instance, that the true grasp of knowledge is measured. But effective action cannot come without good analyses anchored by the appropriate product/market/industry context. The power of executive education is that it creates a new knowledge frame that is generated by managers who are ultimately responsible for implementing them as well. In our opinion, universities and academic institutions are only halfway there.

APPENDIX: TOOLS FOR DELIVERY

There are several ways in which program content can be delivered in executive education. These include lectures and case discussions. In addition, technology enhancements now allow for the use of simulations as effective pedagogical tools.

Lectures and Case Discussions

Lectures are very useful when the instructor communicates knowledge or explores a new phenomenon or develops a new way of looking at things. In this mode, the instructor has the flexibility of choosing the sequence/flow of information that he or she feels is the most appropriate. What participants receive, therefore, is an understanding of the phenomenon from the instructor's point of view. This approach can miss out on the opportunity for participants to synthesize and customize knowledge in their contexts. While such a step is difficult to achieve when lecturing to a heterogeneous group of managers, in more homogenous groups (e.g., managers from the same company or industry), it is always useful to embellish the lecture with steps to adapt the ideas in the participants' own context.

Case discussions are a more interactive mode of learning. They allow for participants to learn content in a specific context and then validate this learning in other contexts as well. By properly choreographing a case (Rangan 1995), an instructor can lead students through key conceptual and decision issues in a case without necessarily prejudging the correctness of the participants' contributions. Given that a case is an instrument to stimulate inductive thinking, a healthy vigorous debate on the merits of an argument is an absolute cornerstone for a good case discussion. This does not mean that the instructor does not have a point of view; it only means that the instructor does not presuppose that his or her viewpoint is the most accurate. At the same time, a wrong analysis should not be condoned. It is better for a deliberate and systematic discussion to expose the faulty premise. In a good case discussion, the participants build frameworks inductively by taking the responsibility for putting the building blocks together. In this mode, if done correctly, participants learn the content in the right context.

The Role of Simulations

Simulations are very effective in helping business marketing executives understand specific aspects of the dynamic nature of their marketing strategy decisions. As with the case method, participants engage ideas in a manner that stimulates discussion of issues and comparison of strategies.

One very popular simulation used in business marketing programs is INDUSTRAT, developed by Professors Jean-Claude Larréché and David Weinstein. It allows executives to experience firsthand the use and value of strategic market orientation concepts. It mirrors the complexity of the industrial marketing environment, including the evolution of customer buying behavior and product technologies. Participants in the exercise actively employ ideas, analytical approaches, and marketing data to manage a firm's business. The core decisions are interactive and their effect critically depends on competitive actions. Each participant acts as a member of a management team involved in strategic marketing decisions. Each team competes against four others over a number of iterations, each representing a year in the history of the industry. Each firm starts the simulation with its own set of strengths and weaknesses. The competitive scenario, while subject to some industrywide parameters, evolves according to the interactions among the firms. Another business-to-business simulation, "Managing Customers for Profit" (Narayandas and Petersen 1997), written by one of the authors of this paper, develops concepts of customer management, exposing and training participants to notions of how customers are acquired and served, loyalty built, and mutual performance enhanced.

In general, simulations enhance learning because they have the following attributes:

1. *They are interactive.* They use multimedia (films, audio, video clips) to provide instantaneous feedback, coaching, and encouragement to users. In the customer management simulation, described previously, when the manager makes a decision to significantly cut account management expenses, there is the immediate feedback of an irate customer (on video) complaining about the lack of response from the field sales rep. Or, in another situation, when the manager makes a decision that leads to a significant drop in revenues and profitability, an audio of the CEO comes on highlighting the cash flow problem as a result of that decision. This kind of interactivity is not possible in conventional pedagogical tools such as paper-based cases where the decision making is in a static one-shot mode of analysis and action plan.
2. *They are open.* In these simulations, the manager has access to the underlying model and the assumptions made in creating the model. This allows the manager to understand the reason for a certain type of re-

sponse. The manager can then challenge the assumptions of the model and make changes accordingly to customize the simulation to his or her needs. This is especially true of the customer management simulation just described.

3. *They are nonthreatening and encourage out-of-the-box analysis.* Dynamic simulations encourage managers to test out actions that they might not otherwise risk. Many times this leads to valuable insight regarding long-term effects of certain strategic actions.

Overall, we have found that these dynamic simulations provide managers with an interactive, user-friendly learning mode that closes the gap between an intellectual understanding of business marketing concepts and the operational understanding it takes to actually do it.

REFERENCES

Bardach, Kenneth C. (1993). "Patterns and Trends in Executive Education." *Selections* 14(1), 18-25.

Boyatzis, Richard E., Scott S. Cowen, and David A. Kolb (1995). "A Learning Perspective on Executive Education." *Selections* 11(3), 47-55.

Cooper, Robert G. (1993). *Winning at New Products: Accelerating the Process from Idea to Launch,* Second Edition. Reading, MA: Addison Wesley.

Corey, E. Raymond (1978). *Procurement Management: Strategy, Organization, and Decision Making.* Boston, MA: CBI Publishing.

Dhebar, Anirudh (1995). *Rethinking Executive Education, Training and Development* 49(7), 55-57.

Fulmer, Robert M. (1997). "The Evolving Paradigm of Leadership Development." *Organizational Dynamics* 25(4), 59-72.

Fulmer, Robert M. and Albert A. Vicere (1996). "Executive Development: An Analysis of Competitive Forces." *Planning Review* 234(1), 31-36.

Gale, Bradley T. (1994). *Managing Customer Value.* New York: The Free Press.

Greco, JoAnn (1997). "Corporate Home Schooling." *Journal of Business Strategy* 18(3), 48-52.

Kanter, Rosabeth Moss (1983). *The Change Masters.* New York: Simon and Schuster.

Kotter, John P. (1996). *Leading Change.* Boston: Harvard Business School Press.

Lorange, Peter (1994). "Back to School, Executive Education in the U.S." *Chief Executive* 92(March), 36-39.

Meister, Jeanne C. (1994). "Training Workers in the Three C's." *Nations Business* 82(9), 51-53.

Narayandas, Das and Steve Petersen (1997). "Managing Customers for Profits." *Harvard Business Review* #87513, Harvard Business School, Boston, MA.

Noel, James L. and Ram Charan (1992). "GE Brings Global Thinking to Light." *Training and Development* 46(July), 28-33.

Nohria, Nitin and James D. Berkley (1994). "An Action Perspective: The Crux of the New Management." *California Management Review* 36(4), 70-92.

Rangan, V. Kasturi (1995). "Choreographing a Case Class." Case #9-595-074, Harvard Business School, Boston, MA.

Rasmusson, Erika (1997). "Should Managers Go Back to School?" *Sales and Marketing Management* 149(5), 40-41.

Ready, Douglas A., Albert A. Vicere, and Alan F. White (1993). "Executive Education: Can Universities Deliver?" *Human Resources Planning* 16(4), 1-11.

Slywotzky, Adrian J. (1996). *Value Migration.* Boston, MA: Harvard Business School Press.

Vicere, Albert A. (1996). "Executive Education: The Leading Edge." *Organizational Dynamics* 25(2), 67-81.

Vicere, Albert A., Maria W. Taylor, and Virginia T. Freeman (1994). "Executive Development in Major Corporations: A Ten Year Study." *Journal of Management Development* 13(1), 4-22.

Webster, Frederick E. (1984). *Industrial Marketing Strategy,* Second Edition. New York: John Wiley and Sons.

Webster, Frederick E. and Yoram Wind (1972). *Organization Buying Behavior.* Englewood Cliffs, NJ: Prentice-Hall.

White, Roderick, Barbara Pierce, and James C. Rush (1994). "Educating for Change." *Business Quarterly* 59(2), 53-61.

Zaltman, Gerald (1997). "Rethinking Marketing Research: Putting People Back In." *Journal of Marketing Research* (August).

Business Marketing Executive Education: A Commentary

Elizabeth J. Wilson

In the previous paper's review of the state of executive education in business markets, the authors address two basic issues: first, the evolution of topics and paradigms used in business marketing education, and second, the need for new and innovative pedagogical methods to educate managers so that they are able to effect change in their organizations. The authors contend that universities have traditionally done a good job at executive education in business markets insofar as imparting conceptual and contextual knowledge but fall down when it comes to teaching managers how to *effect change*. In other words, the university courses and programs provide good foundational knowledge but do not go far enough in terms of providing specific prescriptions for actions that lead to goal attainment (e.g., become more profitable, gain more market share, achieve higher sales volume, lower costs, reduce inventory, etc.). The method of "action learning" is introduced as a way to integrate the change component into executive education programs offered by institutions of higher learning.

TOPICAL TRENDS IN BUSINESS MARKETING EXECUTIVE EDUCATION

To begin with the first section on the evolution of the topics and paradigms studied in business marketing executive education, one additional paradigm should be added to Box 2. The recognition of the importance of the "relationship" between all parties involved in business markets is significant (Webster 1992) and affects all of the items listed in the "1990s" column. For example, to remain competitive in most markets, suppliers must provide superior customer value, i.e., maintain a productive and profitable relationship with the customer.

In essence, marketing *is* successful management of the supplier-customer relationship no matter where in the supply chain a firm happens to be (manufacturer, distributor, customer).

Sometimes relationships must be *reinvented* for firms to maintain a competitive advantage. A good example is the development of JIT II by Bose Corporation (Dixon and Porter 1994). Using a system of evergreen contracts with a few proven suppliers, Bose has shifted much of the routine purchasing and materials management chores over to the "in-plant supplier representatives." These individuals maintain a presence in the Bose corporate office to oversee orders, shipments, payments, and other routine responsibilities. This relationship allows Bose to use its purchasing employees in more value creation tasks and also lower production costs. The JIT II suppliers can offer Bose higher quantity discounts than normal because they are assured of a sufficient volume of production. Bose "wins" by getting quality products at lower prices; the supplier "wins" by having steady orders from a large customer. Furthermore, by using a few approved suppliers, Bose achieves supplier base reductions that provide further cost reductions. This concept has also been used at Bose in development of new audio products, and in managing inventory and shipping.

In short, for all the topics in the 1990s column of Box 2, the importance of the supplier-customer relationship is a key concern for managers. A rephrase of the quote of Regis McKenna that is cited in the paper might read as follows:

> In the 1990s, the critical dimensions of the company—including all of the attributes that together define how the company does business—are ultimately the functions of *the supplier-customer relationship*. That is why management of the supplier-customer relationship is everyone's job, why the supplier-customer relationship is everything, and everything is relationship management.

DELIVERY OF BUSINESS MARKETING EXECUTIVE EDUCATION

In their introduction, the authors identify a need in business marketing education programs for "a happy combination" of conceptual knowledge and actionable solutions that firms may use to effect change. University business schools are called on to make changes in the design, delivery, and management of executive education programs to achieve this goal. The dilemma is in the way executive education programs are typically delivered—a faculty member cannot offer a custom-tailored solution to each participant's specific problem; this would be consulting rather than education. Indeed, the role of the university in society is traditionally to teach students how to think rather than to have the faculty member do the thinking for them. (While many university business professors do outside consulting, this is on their own time and outside their normal university teaching duties.)

The authors introduce, in Box 4, three program formats that may help to resolve the dilemma. While most university business marketing executive education programs provide general education and some custom education when requested by corporations, action learning is a relatively novel pedagogical format. It would certainly be feasible to implement given a partnership between a host university and corporate client, assuming that the problems could be addressed with resources in terms of faculty experts. For example, strategy formulation issues facing the client corporation could be studied and solutions proposed with input/direction of faculty experts in marketing, management, finance, and other functional areas, as needed.

Getting these types of action-oriented programs in place will probably require a grassroots effort on the part of the business school. Such programs might be an incentive for a corporation to become a sponsor/contributor to the business school. The formation of such programs will probably have to begin in discussions between senior administrators of the school (the dean) and senior management of the corporation (the CEO). When corporations approach the business school regarding customized programs, the action learning approach should be suggested to ensure that the corporate client sees some tangible benefit resulting from the program.

The preceding discussion is in the context of a customized program between one organization and a business school. In most cases, though, executive education programs have participants from many organizations, with the program leader presenting information on a variety of standard business marketing topics. In this more common situation, how can we approximate action learning so that participants can effect change in their home organization? One solution from my experience teaching executive MBA (EMBA) students is offered next.

APPROXIMATING ACTION LEARNING IN THE EMBA CLASSROOM

In their description of executive education in the 1990s, the authors note that managers want conceptual knowledge *as well as* information on how to apply new concepts in their own environment. This is certainly the case with the EMBA students I have taught. To address this situation, I require students to learn the basics of conjoint analysis and complete a project based on some problem in their home organization. Since the students are from different functional areas, not all projects are about marketing-related problems; some address HR issues, finance issues, management issues, etc.

Briefly, conjoint analysis (or "tradeoff analysis") is a technique for understanding customer preference and choice (see Green and Srinivasan 1990; Green and Wind 1975; Hair et al. 1995). In teaching conjoint analysis, I make the point that understanding customers (internal or external) is crucial. During class time, there are several lectures with problem-solving demonstrations on the basics of conjoint analysis. Students are then required to design a research proposal that incorporates conjoint analysis to solve a problem in their home organization. Past marketing-related projects have been on issues such as product packaging for Novartis, customer service for Motorola, and new product development for Lucent Technologies, to name a few. Some nonmarketing projects include configuring an employee health insurance program for a large commercial construction firm and designing a supplier rating system for evaluating bids for use by engineers in a large chemical plant.

Student reactions to the project have been favorable. Many have commented that the business marketing course was one of the few where they used class material to address directly a situation at work. While not all students achieve a direct benefit from this exercise, many do. And it forces them to apply what they are learning toward their own situation, much in the way that action learning does (based on the authors' description).

In conclusion, based on my experience in teaching a two-day purchasing management program and a forty-hour EMBA course in business marketing, the authors' call for imparting problem-solving skills as well as contextual knowledge is timely. Using myself as a sample (*N*=1), this call is being heeded by university business school faculty. I devote half of any program or class to experiential learning exercises to develop skills that can be "taken home" (i.e., exercises in marketing strategy, negotiation, corporate responsibility, etc.). More evidence of this trend can be seen from the articles in an issue of the *Journal of Marketing Education;* Krishnan and Porter (1998) describe a process approach for skill development in a consumer behavior course. Moon and colleagues (1998) recognize the importance of customer value in offering MBA marketing education services.

As described by the authors, action learning will be best executed when students are all from one corporate client. However, some "change-effecting" content can, and should, be successfully integrated into courses with a diverse student audience through projects and other problem-solving, experiential learning exercises.

REFERENCES

Dixon, Lance and Anne Millen Porter (1994). *JIT II: Revolution in Buying and Selling.* Newton, MA: Cahners Publishing.

Green, Paul and V. Srinivasan (1990). "Conjoint Analysis in Marketing: New Developments with Implications for Research and Practice." *Journal of Marketing* 54(October), 3-19.

Green, Paul and Yoram Wind (1975). "New Way to Measure Consumers' Judgments." *Harvard Business Review* 53(July-August), 107-117.

Hair, Joseph F., Rolph E. Anderson, Ronald L. Tatham, and William C. Black (1995). *Multivariate Data Analysis,* Fourth Edition. Englewood Cliffs, NJ: Prentice-Hall, 556-599.

Krishnan, H. Shanker and Thomas W. Porter (1998). "A Process Approach for Developing Skills in a Consumer Behavior Course." *Journal of Marketing Education* 20(1), 24-34.

Moon, Mark A., John T. Menter, Richard C. Reizenstein, and Robert B. Woodruff (1998). "A Customer-Value-Based Approach to MBA Marketing Education." *Journal of Marketing Education* 20(1), 53-62.

Webster, Fredrick E. (1992). "The Changing Role of Marketing in the Corporation." *Journal of Marketing* 56(October), 1-17.

Executive Education in Business Markets: A Reply to Commentary

Narakesari Narayandas
V. Kasturi Rangan
Gerald Zaltman

The commentary advances our paper in two significant ways. First, it highlights the importance of the "relationship" construct that has become a central organizing theme for many business markets. Second, it points to concrete opportunities for implementing our action learning agenda. In this reply, we embellish each of those points.

There is no doubt that relationship marketing is an important conceptual thrust, and we should have included it in Box 2 of the paper. While we would not go so far as to claim that "relationship marketing is everything" (as implied by the modified Regis McKenna quote in the commentary and as referenced by us in the paper), we acknowledge its all-pervading quality across the value chain. At the customer interface, it has been shown to improve quality and process performance in addition to gaining cost reductions (Newman 1988; Trevelen 1987; Wilson, Dant, and Han 1990). At the distribution interface, it has been used to coordinate channel activities and stimulate cooperative activities among independent channel members (Weitz and Jap 1995). And, finally, at the vendor interface, it has been shown to lead to higher sales growth, lower marketing and sales costs, and higher profitability (Kalwani and Narayandas 1995).

The focus on "relationship" poses two unique challenges for executive education. First, the phenomenon demands cross-functional and interfirm coordination skills—a point that we have discussed in great detail in our paper. Second, the phenomenon requires that line managers in touch with customers, distributors, and vendors show an appreciation for the value creation possibilities of such contacts. An executive's capacity to empathize with and gain insights from customers is the single most important skill that he or she can use to direct a company's strategy (Gouillart and Sturdivant 1994). The reality is that most managers, given their current training and skills, maintain only a limited contact with their customers and suppliers, especially those in nonselling functions of the marketing organization. Executive education programs must be redesigned to address these new challenges as well. Managers need to have a broader understanding of their customers, distributors, vendors, and other parties in the supply chain.

Now for the second observation regarding the real challenge of incorporating action learning elements in "general" or "open" executive education programs: The idea of building exercises such as the one (conjoint analysis) suggested by the author of the commentary is a very good one. We ourselves use similar exercises on segmentation, distribution (audit), pricing (audit), and positioning (maps). The only reason we did not elaborate on this is that our paper focuses on executive education at the senior-management level and, as a result, addresses strategic learning opportunities. The suggestion emanating from the commentary is pitched at the middle-management level. Moreover, our concentration was on organization renewal and change, while the commentary addresses functional effectiveness. Nonetheless, the suggestion is a good one and an important one.

The big advantage (and also the challenge) of educating such middle managers is their constant return to the work environment. The executive education program content has to be relevant to their work even as it trains their minds to think expansively outside the current boundaries. It also needs to blend the strategic and conceptual elements with hands-on tools and techniques carefully and judiciously. If done well, this could be a real live laboratory, and for a change, we in marketing education who talk and write of customer feedback will have a chance to experience it firsthand.

REFERENCES

Gouillart, Francis J. and Frederick D. Sturdivant (1994). "Spend a Day in the Life of Your Customers." *Harvard Business Review* (January), Reprint 94103.

Kalwani, Manohar U. and Narakessari Narayandas (1995). "Long-Term Manufacturer-Supplier Relationships: Do They Pay Off for Supplier Firms?" *Journal of Marketing* 59(January), 1-16.

Newman, R. G. (1988). "Single Source Qualification." *Journal of Purchasing and Materials Management* 24(Summer), 10-16.

Trevelen, M. (1987). "Single Sourcing: A Management Tool for the Quality Supplier." *Journal of Purchasing and Materials Management* 23(Spring), 19-24.

Weitz, Barton A. and Sandy D. Jap (1995). "Relationship Marketing and Distribution Channels." *Journal of the Academy of Marketing Science* 23(4), 305-320.

Wilson, David T., Shirish P. Dant, and Sang-Lin Han (1990). "State-of-Practice in Industrial Buyer-Supplier Relationships." Report 6-1990. University Park, PA: Institute for the Study of Business Markets.

PART III:
MASTER'S PROGRAMS

Master's-Level Education in Business Marketing: *Quo Vadis?*

James A. Narus
James C. Anderson

The decade of the 1990s has brought considerable changes to master's-level programs in business worldwide.[1] In the United States, a record 93,437 students earned a master's-level degree in 1994; however, the rate of enrollment in programs has slowed appreciably since then (*Digest of Education Statistics 1996; The MBA Newsletter* 1997). Moreover, many universities have reengineered their programs to address such topical areas as cross-functional teams, international business, high technology, entrepreneurship, and ethics (O'Reilly 1994). In Canada, while enrollments in full-time master's programs have declined, those in executive programs have soared (*The MBA Newsletter* 1997). Responding to market trends, many Canadian schools have reduced program length to between one year and sixteen months and sought to distinguish themselves through specialization by company, by industry, or by topical area (Carpenter 1996).

In Europe, there has been an explosion in the number of universities offering master's programs. As in Canada, European programs tend to run one year in length and specialize in industries or topical areas. However, European master's programs tend to be more varied than their North American counterparts, spanning the range from professional degree programs to vocational training (McClenahen, Bredin, and Clark 1995). Furthermore, Europeans prefer "modular" programs where students intersperse periods of time in residence at

The authors gratefully acknowledge the considerable influence that Professor David T. Wilson has had on them over the years, a small reflection of which appears in our use of the Latin phrase "Whither are you going?" The authors also gratefully acknowledge the research assistance of Nicole Avril, Ellen Carr, Sandra Diaz, Robin Dodge, Laura Farrelly, and P. J. Platt.

the university with stints at work to give them the opportunity to apply what they have learned.

In Asia, with the exception of Japan, universities are chartering new master's-level programs rapidly to absorb skyrocketing demand for management degrees. The challenge these schools face is to legitimize their degrees, that is, demonstrate that they are on a par with those in North America and Europe (McClenahen, Bredin, and Clark 1995). In Japan, only a handful of master's programs exist as companies continue to prefer in-house training. When Japanese managers decide to pursue a master's degree abroad, they do so to establish global contacts and to learn about emerging practices (McClenahen, Bredin, and Clark 1995).

Although pundits and scholars have written hundreds of articles about the global changes in master's-level pedagogy, they have described next to nothing about the impact these trends are having at the functional level. For example, while we know that 678 individuals received a master's of science degree in marketing in the United States in 1994, we do not know how many received a master's degree (e.g., MBA) with a concentration in marketing *(Digest of Education Statistics 1996).*[2] *Business Week* tells us that U.S. recruiters find their best marketing graduates in these master's programs in order: Northwestern, Vanderbilt, Michigan, Harvard, Indiana, UCLA, Columbia, Wharton, Dartmouth, and Stanford (Byrne et al. 1996). And, the *Princeton Review Student Advantage* reports that the top master's programs where "students develop strong marketing skills" include Babson, Georgetown, Northwestern, Maryland, Berkeley, Thunderbird, Virginia, Wake Forest, Emory, and Arizona (Gilbert 1996). Beyond this modicum of information, little is known about master's-level education in marketing, let alone business marketing.

In response to the global changes and absence of published information, the editor of the *Journal of Business-to-Business Marketing* (JBBM) asked us to examine the state of master's-level pedagogy in business marketing. We intend to contribute to knowledge of business marketing in several ways. First, we try to estimate the number of business marketing courses universities offered in the United States. Second, through exploratory research in North America and Europe, we gain some understanding of those topics that graduate-level instructors cover in their business marketing courses, and the teaching materials (textbooks and cases) that educators commonly use in those courses. Finally, drawing on these findings and discussions with business marketing colleagues, we offer some recommendations for improving the quality of business marketing education.

METHODOLOGY

Early on in the process, we decided to conduct an exploratory survey of instructors who teach business marketing at the master's level at selected universities in North America and Europe. Immediately, we encountered difficulties due to the fact that no mailing lists of graduate business schools that offer business marketing courses or instructors who teach those courses at the master's level exist. Therefore, we had to identify and qualify potential research participants before we could send them a questionnaire to complete.

Research Procedure

We enlisted the help of three graduate assistants. They began by gathering the names of the top fifty master's programs in the United States from the *Business Week Guide to the Best MBA Programs* (1997). Then they identified seventy-five academics on the membership roster of the American Marketing Association's (AMA) Business-to-Business Marketing Special Interest Group (B2B SIG). To generate a list of graduate-level business schools in Canada and Europe, they turned to *Bricker's International Directory* (1996) and *Which MBA? A Critical Guide to the Best Business Schools Outside the United States* (1995). They identified fifty international schools in this manner.

The graduate assistants compared the universities listed on the *Business Week Guide,* the B2B SIG membership roster, and the international directories and eliminated redundancies. Thus, they reduced the number of universities considered to approximately 120. At this point, the graduate assistants telephoned the marketing departments of each of the listed universities to obtain the names, addresses, telephone and fax numbers of instructors who taught business or industrial marketing. In the process, they eliminated approximately fifty universities from consideration because these schools do not offer a course in business or industrial marketing at the master's level.

To solicit participation in our study, the graduate assistants telephoned the North American and European scholars. They read the following script:

> Greetings from [city]! We are doing a study on graduate education in business or industrial marketing, which we will publish in a special issue of the *Journal of Business-to-Business Marketing*. We need your help in this, and as an incentive to participate, we will share the results of this study with you. As an example, we will share with you the names of those cases considered to be the best for the various topics in business or industrial marketing.
>
> The survey is one page in length, and will take about five minutes of your time to complete.
>
> Will you contribute to a better understanding of graduate education in business or industrial marketing by participating in this study?
>
> Great! What method of completing the survey do you prefer: e-mail, fax, or the mail?
>
> Thank you for your assistance!

A total of forty-eight North American and fifteen European instructors agreed to participate in the study. Five scholars did not return student telephone calls. The graduate assistants e-mailed, faxed, or mailed these instructors a copy of a brief questionnaire. That questionnaire addressed the three potential research contributions we posed in the introduction. We include a copy of that questionnaire as Figure 1. Thirty-two educators from North America and six from Europe completed and returned the questionnaire for response rates of 67 percent and 40 percent, respectively. We list the participating schools in Table 12. Due to the small sample size and potential lack of representativeness, we consider this to be a *convenience sample* (Kotler 1997).

The graduate assistants report that the process was both time-consuming and difficult. Many marketing department receptionists neither knew what courses their schools offered nor what instructors taught which courses. The assistants had a difficult time reaching instructors while they were in their offices. Often, professors did not return voice mail messages. Several educators lost or misplaced questionnaires and the assistants had to send duplicates. Others told the

Questionnaire:
Study of Graduate Education in Business Marketing

1. How many sections of a master's-level course in business or industrial marketing is your department offering during the 1996-1997 academic year? What is the typical enrollment per section?

    _____ section(s) during 1996-1997
    _____ students per section during 1996-1997

2. How many sections of a master's-level course in business or industrial marketing did your department offer two years ago, during the 1994-1995 academic year? What was the typical enrollment per section?

    _____ section(s) during 1994-1995
    _____ students per section during 1994-1995

3. If there has been a change between 1994-1995 and 1996-1997, what is the explanation?

    _____
    _____
    _____

4. Is there a required textbook for this course? ____ No ____ Yes
    If "Yes," please give the title and author(s):

    _____

5. What **five topics** do you cover in this course (e.g., organizational buying behavior) that you consider to be the **most important?** [Please also attach or send a course syllabus.]

    1. _____   4. _____
    2. _____   5. _____
    3. _____

6. What do you consider to be the **five best cases** that you presently use? Please also indicate the source of the case (e.g., HBS), and the topic for which you use it.

Case name	Case source	Topic
1. _____	_____	_____
2. _____	_____	_____
3. _____	_____	_____
4. _____	_____	_____
5. _____	_____	_____

Thanks for your participation! Would you like a summary of our study results?

____ Yes ____ No

Please return the questionnaire by e-mail, fax, or mail.

FIGURE 1. Survey Questionnaire

TABLE 12. Participating Schools and Universities

School	University
North America	
Graduate School of Business	Boston University
Skaggs Institute of Retail Management	Brigham Young University
Graduate School of Industrial Administration	Carnegie Mellon University
Amos Tuck School of Business	Dartmouth College
Roberto Goizueta Business School	Emory University
School of Business	Fairfield University
Graduate School of Business Administration	Fordham University
Harvard Business School	Harvard University
Department of Business Administration	Illinois Benedictine College
Sloan School of Management	M.I.T.
J. L. Kellogg Graduate School of Management	Northwestern University
Krannert Graduate School of Management	Purdue University
Lally School of Management and Technology	Rensselaer Polytechnic Institute
Cox School of Business	Southern Methodist University
College of Business Administration	Texas A&M International University
A. B. Freeman School of Business	Tulane University
College of Business Administration	University of Akron
Haas School of Business	University of California, Berkeley
Graduate School of Business	University of Chicago
Barney School of Business and Public Administration	University of Hartford
College of Business and Management	University of Maryland
College of Management	University of Massachusetts at Boston
The Michigan Business School	University of Michigan
College of Business and Public Administration	University of Missouri, Columbia
Kenen-Flagler Business School	University of North Carolina at Chapel Hill
The Wharton School	University of Pennsylvania
Katz Graduate School of Business	University of Pittsburgh
College of Business Administration	University of Toledo
Darden Graduate School of Business Administration	University of Virginia
School of Business	University of Wisconsin at Eau Claire

Babcock Graduate School of Management	Wake Forest University
Haworth College of Business	Western Michigan University
Europe	
Institute of Marketing	Copenhagen Business School, Denmark
Rotterdam School of Management	Erasmus Universiteit, The Netherlands
School of Business	IESE, Instituto de Estudios Superiores de la Empresa, Spain
Department of Applied Economics	Katholieke Universiteit, Belgium
The Otto Beisheim Graduate School	Koblenz School of Corporate Management, Germany
London Business School	

graduate assistants by telephone that they were too busy to complete the questionnaire. Internationally, the graduate students found the differences in time zones as well as language to be major obstacles.

To gain a better estimate of the number of U.S. universities that offer business marketing courses at the master's level, the students next turned to the Internet. They visited the home page of the American Assembly of Collegiate Schools of Business (AACSB) and obtained a listing of some 335 programs in business that the AACSB has accredited. In turn, they visited the home pages of each of those 335 programs and searched for a listing of elective courses. We summarize their findings in Figure 2. Through this procedure, they were able to identify seventy U.S. universities that offer courses in business marketing, business-to-business marketing, or industrial marketing at the master's level.[3] Thus, respondents in our telephone and fax survey represent approximately 46 percent of these universities (i.e., 32/70).

Research Analyses

The six questions on our survey instrument gathered data from research participants on each of the following topics:

- the number of sections of business marketing each school offered and the number of students who enrolled in each course during the 1996-1997 school year,

- the number of sections offered and students enrolled the previous year,
- the reasons for any changes in the number of sections and students,
- the textbook, if any, that instructors required,
- the top five topics the professors covered, and
- the five best cases that educators presented during the course.

For each of the six questions, we prepared frequency counts and percentages by response categories. We created a table of cases by topic areas.

RESULTS

At the thirty-eight universities in our study, approximately 1,747 students took master's-level business marketing during the 1996-1997 school year. That was an increase of 111 students from 1994-1995. The thirty-eight universities offered forty-eight sections of business marketing in 1996-1997. Twenty-two of the thirty-eight schools provided one section of business marketing each year. During the 1996-1997 school year, four universities eliminated one section and one school deleted two sections of business marketing, while eight programs added one section. Research participants cited the availability of faculty members who were willing and able to teach the course as the predominant reason for adding or deleting sections

		Business Marketing Offered at the Master's Level		
		No	Yes	Total
Business Marketing Offered at Undergraduate Level	No	134	**26**	160
	Yes	46	**44**	90
	Total	180	**70**	250

FIGURE 2. Number of U.S. Universities That List Business Marketing As an Elective Course on Their Home Pages

(*Note:* Some eighty-five U.S. universities the AACSB has accredited do not post their elective courses on their home pages.)

of business marketing. Class sizes varied widely between four to 120 students per session.

Seventeen of the research participants do not use a textbook or casebook. Six require Hutt and Speh (1995), four Webster (1995), three Corey (1991), and three Rangan, Shapiro, and Moriarty (1995). The remaining educators use other undergraduate business marketing textbooks or casebooks.

Instructors cover a wide range of topical areas in their courses. Educators in our convenience sample cited these topics most frequently: pricing, which 39 percent of research participants mentioned; segmentation, targeting, and positioning (32 percent); channels (32 percent); marketing strategy and market entry (23 percent); new product development (23 percent); physical distribution (19 percent); and sales force management (19 percent).[4] We list all the topic areas that instructors reported in Table 13. Few instructors reported popular management issues, such as business process reengineering, value and its assessment, supply chain management, cross-functional teams, international business marketing, relationship management and business networks, high technology, negotiations, information systems, and the management of professional services, among the five most important topics they cover in their courses.

Professors rely on an extensive variety of business marketing cases. Among the cases research participants cited as the five best they used were Cumberland Metal Industries, which 30 percent of research participants mentioned; Becton Dickinson and Company (22 percent); Signode Industries (19 percent); Ingersoll-Rand (19 percent); Fabtek (13 percent); Rohm & Haas (13 percent); and Sealed Air Corporation (13 percent). In Table 14, we summarize cases by topic areas. Overall, we found that many of the cases that instructors consider as their best were over ten years old. In addition, we noted that many of these cases came from traditional and mature manufacturing industries that reflect the discipline's origin as *industrial marketing*.

DISCUSSION

Based on our exploratory research, discussions with colleagues who teach business marketing, and a review of articles on master's-

TABLE 13. Business Marketing Topical Areas

Topical Areas	% Respondents
Organizational Buying Behavior	65
Pricing	39
Segmentation, Targeting, and Positioning	32
Channels Management	32
Marketing Strategy and Market Entry	23
New Product Development	23
Physical Distribution	19
Sales Force Management	19
Marketing Communications	16
Relationship Management	16
Product and Brand Management	13
Strategic Alliances	9
Business Planning	9
High Technology Management	9
International Marketing	9
Market Research	9
Supply Chain Management	9
Personal Selling	6
Key Account Management	6
Demand Analysis	6
Marketing Mix	6
Measuring Performance	6
Negotiations	6
Opportunity Analysis	6
Purchasing Management	6
Value Assessment	6
Commoditization	3
Competitive Analysis	3
Differences Between Consumer and Industrial Marketing	3
Cost Accounting	3
Customer Service	3
Functional Integration	3
Integrated Marketing Communications	3
Interactive Marketing	3
Life Cycle Analysis	3
Loyalty, Bonding, and Commitment	3
Manufacturing and Marketing Interface	3

Marketing Implementation and Control	3
Role of Information Technology and the Internet	3
Trade Shows	3
Industrial Services	3
Sources of Competitive Advantage	3
Timing	3
Value Chain Participation	3

Note: Percentages are based on thirty-eight respondents.

level management education, we believe that three challenges and opportunities confront business marketing education at the master's level. First, significant changes are occurring in the format and structure of master's programs worldwide that will have a profound impact on the number and frequency of business marketing courses offered. Second, there is a shortage of relevant and timely master's-level teaching materials, including cases and textbooks. Third, although the academic business marketing community is relatively small, it has not created an effective mechanism or network for disseminating information on teaching topics, materials, and practices. We next evaluate each insight in detail and propose solutions.

Promoting Growth in Business Marketing Education

In our opinion, the preponderance of accelerated master's programs in Europe and Canada, and the increase in lock-step, integrated general management, and executive programs in the United States and elsewhere, poses a threat to potential growth in the number of business marketing courses. The only place that there seems to be a significant opportunity to expand the number of business marketing sections are in two-year, full-time master's programs in the United States, where most students still concentrate in one or more functional disciplines during their second year of studies. Based on our research results, however, schools that fit this latter category often find that they have no one who is willing or able to teach business marketing.

TABLE 14. Cases by Topical Area

Topical Area	Case Name	Source
Buyer Behavior	Charlestown Chemical, Inc.	HBS 9-590-024
	Dominion Motors & Controls Ltd.	HBS 9-589-115
	Gervasi Brothers, Inc.	Corey Casebook
	High-Tech versus Low-Tech Marketing	HBS 9-588-012
	The Brownie Factory	Hutt & Speh Text
Channel Management	Alloy Rods Corporation	HBS 9-586-046
	Atlas-Copco (A)	HBS 9-588-004
	Brand Pipe Company	Hutt & Speh Text
	Computervision-Japan (A)	HBS 9-591-097
	Goodyear: The Aquatred Launch	HBS 9-594-106
	Ingersoll-Rand (A)	HBS 9-589-121
	MathSoft, Inc. (A)	HBS 9-593-095
	Peripheral Products Company	HBS 9-586-124
	Pizza Hut, Inc.	HBS 9-588-011
	RCI Master Distributor	HBS 9-595-001
	S. C. Johnson & Sons, Ltd.	Ivey School 9-83-A020
	San Fabian Supply Company	HBS 9-582-104
High-Tech Marketing	California Vision Tools	*HBR* 95611
	GenRad, Inc. (A)	HBS 9-592-045
	GenRad, Inc. (B)	HBS 9-593-005
	Genzyme Corporation	HBS 9-793-120
	Kenics Corporation	HBS 9-574-036
Internet Marketing	Open Market (A)	HBS 9-195-205
Market Research	Clark Materials Handling	HBS 9-590-081
	MCI Telecommunications (C)	HBS 9-585-097
	Xerox Customer Satisfaction Program	HBS 9-594-109
Market Strategy	FedEx versus UPS	Darden School
	Howard, Shea & Chan Asset Management (A)	HBS 9-597-021
	Millipore Corporate Strategy	HBS 9-594-009
	Orbital Sciences Corporation	HBS 9-594-071
	Sunrise Medical, Inc.	HBS 9-794-069
Marketing Communications	BASF Corporate Advertising	HBS 9-593-021
	DuPont Corporate Advertising	HBS 9-593-023
	Siemens Corporate Advertising	HBS 9-593-022
Negotiations	Amicon Corporation (B)	HBS 9-579-094
	Becton Dickinson & Company: Vacutainer Systems Division	HBS 9-592-037
	Cumberland Metal Industries (A)	HBS 9-578-170
	Hi Tech Industries (A)	Corey Casebook
New Product Realization	Amicon corporation (A)	HBS 9-579-093
	MCI Vision (A)	HBS 9-594-057

	Monsanto Provita	Tuck School
	Ring Medical	HBS 9-589-046
	Rohm & Haas (A)	HBS 9-587-055
	Sealed Air Corporation	HBS 9-582-103
	Silicon Graphics, Inc.	HBS 9-695-061
Pricing	Avon Company	HBS 9-590-022
	Clark Equipment	Clarke Text
	Computron, Inc.	HBS 9-579-031
	Cumberland Metal Industries: Engineered Products Division	HBS 9-580-104
	Deere & Company	HBS 9-577-112
	DHL Worldwide Express	HBS 9-593-011
	Mason Instruments, Inc. (A)	HBS 9-587-041
	Optical Distortion, Inc. (A)	HBS 9-575-072
	Pricing Policies for New Products	*HBR* 76604
Product Line and Brand Management	Hewlett-Packard Imaging Systems	HBS 9-593-080 HBS 9-593-096
	Intel Corporation	HBS 9-581-066
	Loctite Corporation	HBS 9-596-112
	SaleSoft, Inc.	Hutt & Speh Text
	Sun Microsystems	Corey Casebook
	Titanium Industries, Inc. (A)	INSEAD
	Zantac	
Relationship Management and Strategic Alliances	BOSE Corp.: JIT II® Program (A)	HBS 9-694-001
	Cybercash, Inc.	Darden School
	Fabtek (A)	HBS 9-669-004
	General Electric Plastics	HBS 9-991-029
	General Motors' Asian Alliances	HBS 9-388-094
	The Lopez Affair	Tuck School
	Peak Electronics	HBS 9-594-006
Sales Force Management and Organization	Applicon, Inc.	HBS 9-582-010
	Becton Dickinson: Multidivisional Marketing Programs	HBS 9-594-060
	BOC Group: Ohmeda (A)	HBS 9-587-080
	Computer Devices, Inc.	HBS 9-581-146
	Duraplast, Inc.	Goizueta School
	MCI National Accounts Program	HBS 9-587-116
Segmentation, Targeting, and Positioning	Alto Chemicals Europe (A)	IMD 587-001-2
	Barco Projection Systems (A)	HBS 9-591-133
	Dell Computer Corporation	HBS 9-596-058
	Harper Chemical Company	HBS 9-590-027
	MacTec Control AB	Hutt & Speh Text
	Microsoft Corporation: Introduction of Microsoft Works	HBS 9-588-028
	Norton Group PLC (A)	HBS 9-589-013
	SAS	HBS 9-487-041
	Southwestern Ohio Steel	Hutt & Speh Text
	Signode Industries (A)	

TABLE 14 *(continued)*

Service Offerings	IBM After-Sales Service	HBS 9-693-001
	MCI Telecommunications (B)	HBS 9-582-108
	The Introduction of Microsoft	Kellogg School
	Product Support Network	

Note: Case Publishers: HBS = Harvard Business School Publishing; *HBR = Harvard Business Review;* Darden School = Darden Graduate School of Business Administration, University of Virginia; Goizueta School = Roberto Goizueta School of Business, Emory University; IMB = International Institute for Management Development (IMEDE), Lausanne, Switzerland; INSEAD = European Institute of Business Administration, Fountainebleau, France; Ivey School = Richard Ivey School of Business, University of Western Ontario; Kellogg School = J.L. Kellogg Graduate School of Management, Northwestern University; Tuck School = Amos Tuck School of Business, Dartmouth College.

There are several steps that the business marketing community can take to capitalize on the evolving format and structure of master's programs. To begin with, scholars and administrators need to rethink the role of business marketing in their school's curriculum. They need to challenge the assumption at many universities that core marketing management should be taught from the perspective of consumer product marketing. At the same time, they need to find ways to integrate key business marketing paradigms into master's students' core courses. For example, scholars might propose that student teams conduct a value assessment project or design a customer-supplier partnership program during their first year of study. Alternatively, they might convince schools to include business marketing topics such as organizational buyer behavior, interfirm negotiations, and value assessment in the first-year integrated-core curricula.

Looking to elective courses, instructors must adapt their business marketing courses into the new breed of accelerated programs. For instance, they must adapt semester-length business marketing courses into quarter, half-semester, or module formats.

Reducing the Shortage of Master's-Level Teaching Materials

Clearly, as the field of *industrial marketing* evolves into *business marketing,* scholars must rely more heavily on cases from emerging or growing industries such as professional services and high technology. Unfortunately, few scholars listed such cases as their five best in our convenience sample. Furthermore, we found few "teaching cases in print" that take place in these industries. For example, Howard, Shea and Chan Asset Management is one of the few cases we identified that explores professional services or financial services industries. And, there are not many cases such as the Introduction of Microsoft's Product Support Network that cover support services that firms use to augment their offerings.

Based on discussions with colleagues, we attribute the shortage of relevant and timely teaching cases to the fact that few major institutions, with the notable exceptions of the Harvard Business School and the Darden Graduate School, actively encourage scholars to research and write teaching cases. And, few major universities, in their quest for higher rankings, reward faculty members for producing teaching cases on a par with refereed articles that appear in the leading academic journals.

Compounding this lack of reward and encouragement is the fact that when educators do write cases, they discover that there are few outlets for publishing them. Two journals that publish cases include the *Case Research Journal,* which accepts teaching cases, and *Industrial Marketing Management,* which reports research cases. Without case journals to turn to, it is not at all surprising to us to learn that many of our colleagues have a difficult time learning about useful business marketing cases.

For scholars to research and write more timely and relevant business marketing cases, additional marketing journals, such as the *Journal of Business-to-Business Marketing,* must encourage scholars to submit case studies. Importantly, these journals should subject the cases to a blind review process and grant cases equivalent status to other forms of empirical work. The journals should publish accepted cases side by side with empirical and conceptual articles. Last, the key incentive for case writing will come when more universities accept refereed cases as valid and significant indicators of scholarly achievement in the tenure and promotion process.

In addition to the shortage of relevant and timely cases, we believe that the absence of a widely used, authoritative, and innovative master's-level textbook leads to a reluctance on the part of educators and their schools to offer a course in business marketing. Without the structure that a textbook and its support materials provide, inexperienced instructors are not likely to feel comfortable teaching the class. Based upon a review of business marketing textbooks on the market, we also observed that most take a more traditional and functional approach to business marketing. Among the topics we found frequently omitted from available business marketing textbooks were value and its assessment, business process reengineering, global marketing, working relationships and business markets, and cross-functional cooperation, along with many other contemporary issues.

Building a Business Marketing Educators' Network

The difficulties we encountered identifying schools that offer and instructors that teach business marketing point to a paradox. Although the business marketing community is relatively small, it is extremely difficult to know who are members at any one point in time and to communicate with them.[5] Clearly, the discipline must develop a mechanism for exchanging information on teaching materials, course topics, and research activities. Emerging technologies may provide a solution. For example, an organization such as the Institute for the Study of Business Markets (ISBM) might create a Web site and chat room on the Internet that enables scholars to learn about cases and to exchange their experiences in teaching those cases.

While technology may enable the rapid dissemination of business marketing information, we believe that the business marketing community as a whole must assemble to share teaching experiences face-to-face. Thus, we call for the AMA's B2B SIG, in conjunction with business marketing groups such as the ISBM, to sponsor a faculty consortium on business marketing. The purpose of the consortium would be to instruct participants on the techniques of teaching business marketing and to make them aware of extant cases and teaching materials. Those attending the sessions would also brainstorm new methods for integrating contemporary business marketing topics into accelerated master's programs and for transforming semester-length courses into shorter versions. Organizers should also use the consortium to forge a permanent network of scholars who can keep one another abreast of developments in the field.

CONCLUSION

We have examined the impact that recent and global changes in master's-level programs have had on business marketing pedagogy. Our exploratory research suggests that the number of sections of business marketing courses and student enrollments in those courses has remained steady in the past two years. We observed that the increase or decrease in the number of sections of the course offered at a university appears to be related to the availability of faculty members who are willing and interested in teaching the course. We found no widely used textbook on the subject. Similarly, we noted that a limited number of relevant and timely business marketing cases exist. Furthermore, survey respondents' best cases tend to be ten or more years old and come from more traditional, mature, and manufacturing-based industries. As for topical areas covered in business marketing courses, we found that instructors still take a functional perspective.

To rejuvenate the discipline, we offer several recommendations. First, educators must find ways to integrate business marketing paradigms into newly reengineered master's-level programs and to translate semester-length business marketing courses into shorter, accelerated versions. Second, scholars must write business marketing cases that reflect contemporary management thinking and topics. Finally, the business marketing community must develop mechanisms or networks to rapidly disseminate information about developments in the discipline.

NOTES

1. In recognition of the fact that universities offer a variety of graduate-level degrees in management, including Master's of Business Administration (MBA), Master's of Management (MM), Master's of Marketing Research (MMR), among others, we will use the more general phrase, "master's-level" degree programs.

2. The U.S. government does not track the number of students who concentrate in marketing.

3. As Figure 2 specifies, eighty-five schools do not list elective course offering on their home pages; so, additional U.S. universities may provide courses in business marketing.

4. The most frequently mentioned topic was organizational behavior (65 percent). However, to exemplify what we meant by topics, we listed organizational be-

havior on our questionnaire. We acknowledge that this "prompt" may have encouraged research participants to cite organizational behavior.

5. As an indicator of community size, we point to the fact that although approximately 3,000 college professors were members of the AMA at the time we wrote this paper, only seventy-five were members of the AMA's B2B SIG. And, those seventy-five had the option of registering for two additional SIGs.

REFERENCES

"A Record Number of MBAs Earn Degrees." (1997). *The MBA Newsletter* 6(May), 1-12.

Bickerstaffe, George (1995). *Which MBA? A Critical Guide to the World's Best Programmes,* Seventh Edition. Reading, MA: Addison-Wesley Publishing Company.

Bricker's International Directory 1997: University-Based Executive Development Programs, Twenty-Eighth Edition. Princeton, NJ: Petersons Guides.

Byrne, John A. (1997). *Business Week Guide to the Best Business Schools,* Fifth Edition. New York: McGraw-Hill, Inc.

Byrne, John A. and David Leonhardt, with Lori Bongiorno and Fred Jespersen (1996). "The Best B Schools." *Business Week* 3498(October 21), 110-122.

Carpenter, Rebecca (1996). "Forget the Ivy, Gimme an Education." *Canadian Business* 69(October), 50-57.

Corey, E. Raymond (1991). *Industrial Marketing: Cases and Concepts,* Fourth Edition. Upper Saddle River, NJ: Prentice-Hall, Inc.

Digest of Education Statistics 1996. Washington, DC: U.S. Department of Education, Office of Educational Research and Improvement, NCES 96-133.

Gilbert, Nedda (1997). *The Princeton Review Student Advantage: Guide to Business Schools,* 1997 Edition. New York: Random House, Inc.

Hutt, Michael D. and Thomas W. Speh (1995). *Business Marketing Management,* Fifth Edition. Fort Worth, TX: The Dryden Press.

Kotler, Philip (1997). *Marketing Management: Analysis, Planning, Implementation, and Control,* Ninth Edition. Upper Saddle River, NJ: Prentice-Hall, Inc.

McClenahen, John S., James Bredin, and Tanya Clark (1995). "The M.B.A.: Where in the World is it Headed?" *Industry Week* 244(May 15), 43-51.

O'Reilly, Brian (1994). "Reengineering the MBA." *Fortune* 129(January 24), 38-47.

Rangan, V. Kasturi, Benson P. Shapiro, and Rowland T. Moriarty Jr. (1995). *Business Marketing Strategy: Cases, Concepts, and Applications.* Chicago: Irwin.

Webster, Frederick E. (1995). *Industrial Marketing Strategy,* Third Edition. New York: John Wiley and Sons.

Master's-Level Business Marketing Education: A Commentary

Earl D. Honeycutt Jr.

INTRODUCTION

In the previous paper, the authors investigate an important academic area for those who teach in the business-to-business marketing area. In fact, this study makes a substantial contribution since little appears to have been written about the topic. It appears that, in addition to gathering basic factual data, the authors are seeking answers to two fundamental questions: (1) Given the perceived level of importance of business marketing, why isn't the course offered in more graduate business programs? (2) What tangible actions can be taken to raise the level of importance and value delivered by instructors of business marketing?

The purposes of this commentary are to expand upon related issues implied by the paper's findings and to provide suggestions to assist future researchers. The overall goal of these remarks is to broaden the business marketing education debate.

DISCUSSION

There is little argument that increasing numbers of students are completing their master's degrees. This is true in the United States and, even more so, in Europe and Asia. Several universities—such as Oklahoma City College and the University of Maryland—rotate U.S. professors to international locations to teach MBA classes. Other schools, such as Northeastern, use technology to broadcast classes to clusters in Australia and Asia. As the authors state, there is considerable variation between U.S. and overseas graduate programs and a number are striving to increase their reputation.

Business marketing classes are seldom mainstream in MBA programs. Graduate students who concentrate in marketing normally complete such standard courses as marketing management, strategy, new product development, and marketing research. Only when qualified faculty are available are business marketing classes offered, and this may be as an infrequent elective. Likewise, as seen in this sample, class sizes vary tremendously. It would be informative to learn the mean and median class sizes in this study, as well as whether these classes are required or elective in nature.

There remains debate about whether there should be a single textbook for graduate business marketing. For one thing, competition is healthy and, second, few areas of marketing rely upon a single textbook. Because seventeen survey respondents (45 percent) report they do not use a textbook, this may imply that a coursepack of cases and articles to support lectures and exercises is utilized. The instructors also provide a list of standard topics covered in class, such as buyer behavior, pricing, segmentation, channels, marketing strategy, etc. It is also apparent, from the responses, that such current topics as re-engineering and cross-functional teams are interspersed within the course. However, current topics such as these go out of style quickly and too often come to be viewed as fads by practitioners.

Certainly, a textbook with support materials permits less experienced instructors to teach business marketing. But is it advantageous to have a professor with little or no practical business marketing knowledge teaching a class based upon packaged teaching materials? In my opinion, an experienced professor brings significantly more to the classroom. Also, if constrained by budget and class size, faculty may have to choose between business marketing and more mainstream consumer behavior, strategy, and research classes. It is almost certain in this situation that business marketing will receive less support from faculty whose focus is consumer marketing.

SUGGESTIONS FOR FUTURE RESEARCH

This research provides the reader with some basic information about the status of business marketing classes. However, subsequent studies should consider the following suggestions for improving their methodology. First, the sample should be sufficiently large and representative of U.S. and/or European business schools. To obtain respondent compliance, it will be necessary to reach the small number of faculty who teach business marketing courses. Perhaps one way of solving this dilemma would be to use a mailing list from the AMA Sales and/or B2B Interest Groups. Second, once a more substantive sample is obtained, it would be more meaningful to investigate this complex problem by separating and analyzing graduate programs. Third, demographic data, such as university position, age, and industry experience, would help us better understand the survey respondents. That is, demographic information would greatly assist future analysis. Fourth, researchers must be careful not to inject bias by listing "organizational buying behavior" as an example for the "most important" course topic. This requires additional pretesting of the survey instrument. Finally, it is important not to mix findings with such opinions as "schools do not give credit for writing cases" and "a single textbook would improve the business marketing offerings in business schools." If these questions are directly asked of the respondents, then there will be stronger empirical support for their truth.

CONCLUDING THOUGHTS

If we return to the formative days of marketing, primary effort was placed upon distribution and consumer behavior. Business marketing has often been covered superficially in basic marketing classes, because few professors had the interest or the expertise—either practical or academic—to teach an entire business marketing class. Many marketing academicians produced in the 1970s and 1980s were consumer behaviorists and business marketers were a minority. Second, there is more information/research conducted in consumer behavior and this subject is viewed by many deans and chairs as being a more academic course to teach. Third, it is probably assumed that fewer graduates will work in business marketing and therefore the importance of this career path is downplayed in classes. In fact, recent research has documented that few college graduates seek a career in business marketing but prefer careers in advertising, marketing management, or public relations. These students reported they were not sufficiently counseled about business marketing opportunities (Honeycutt et al., 1999).

Perhaps a graduate text would improve the ability to deliver higher-quality instruction in business marketing, but unless instructors who currently teach in the area are surveyed, it is difficult to draw this conclusion. It would also be beneficial to have access to additional business marketing cases and current information about happenings in specific industries. Some of this information can be gleaned from the trade press, but more specific data are often difficult to gather. One possible way to improve the availability of business marketing information is to establish an Internet bulletin board—perhaps by the business-to-business academic group—to serve as a clearinghouse. A major hurdle that remains, however, is that, because of its proprietary nature, many industries and companies are reluctant to share specific information. This is especially true of their product failures and ethical breaches.

In conclusion, I agree with the authors that business marketing is important, is not taught at the level it should be, and that sufficient materials are not currently available. Additional research must be conducted, however, in order to answer many of the questions raised by the original paper and this commentary. The authors are to be commended for researching and establishing a benchmark for this important topic and I hope my remarks assist their future research, as well as that of others, in some small way.

REFERENCE

Honeycutt, Earl D. Jr., John B. Ford, Michael J. Swenson, and William R. Swinyard (1999). "Student Preferences for Sales Careers Around the Pacific-Rim: Implications for Industrial Marketers." *Industrial Marketing Management,* 28(1), 27-36.

Making Business Marketing More Prominent in Master's Programs: A Reply to Commentary

James A. Narus
James C. Anderson

We would like to thank Professor Honeycutt for his thoughtful comments on our paper. As he implies, we wrote this paper to begin a debate as to the scope and future of business marketing education at the master's level rather than as the final word on its current state of practice. In this reply, we add several reflections on business marketing that we have gleaned from discussions with our colleagues as well as respond to a few issues that Professor Honeycutt raises. Most important, we use our limited space to strongly urge those in the discipline to actively promote business marketing to master's-level students and educators alike.

First and foremost, we would like to point out that graduate-student employment trends demand that business schools place greater emphasis on business marketing. From 1995 to 1997, between 28 percent and 32 percent of all U.S. master's-level students took jobs with consulting firms (*HR Focus* 1996; *Management Consultant International* 1997). Not only do consultancies offer a significant number of job openings, they pay the highest starting salaries and give the largest "signing bonuses" (Morgenstern and McCaffery 1996). Pundits claim that these factors have caused applications to master's-level programs to skyrocket in recent years and have enabled business schools to overcome the enrollment crises of the late 1980s and early 1990s (Miller 1995). Furthermore, it is our observation that although management consulting firms serve clients in all industries, a disproportionately large percentage of their clients serve business markets rather than consumer markets. For these reasons, a course in business marketing should be of paramount interest to the increasing number of students who aspire to be consultants.

While consulting opportunities are blossoming, master's-level students are finding fewer jobs available in advertising agencies and brand management, the traditional employers of consumer marketing specialists. For example, experts contend that major U.S. advertising agencies have almost given up on master's-level students and now prefer to hire undergraduates (Farrell 1997). At the same time, many consumer product companies are eliminating brand management positions, downgrading the responsibilities of remaining brand managers, or replacing them with category managers (Richards 1997). Category managers spend far more time sustaining working relationships with superretailers such as Wal-Mart, Home Depot, and Safeway; managing logistics and inventory; and providing support services to resellers than brand managers ever did. We contend that students are more likely to learn requisite category management skills in a business marketing course than in a brand management course. As Professor Honeycutt urges, we believe that the discipline must actively trumpet the career opportunities and benefits of learning business marketing to master's-level students.

We provide the following responses to issues Professor Honeycutt raises. Professor Honeycutt cautions that researchers not mix research findings with opinions of the researchers. We have no problem interspersing research findings with observations of the researchers as long as the source is readily apparent to the reader, which we made a special effort to do in our paper.

One of the key points we make in the paper is that educators must expand the scope of their business marketing courses to include contemporary management topics such as business process re-engineering, working relationships and business networks, and cross-functional coordination. Unlike Professor Honeycutt, we do not believe that practitioners consider these business practices to be fads. Instead, we observe firms have used them to provide superior performance at lower cost. Firms have not abandoned these concepts and practices. Rather, they continue to use them as a foundation upon which they are building new sources of competitive advantage. In addition, regardless of whether these concepts are fads or not, our graduates must know something about them when they are asked by recruiters and future employers.

We agree that scholars must conduct further research to determine such things as the number of faculty members willing and able to teach business marketing, the type of universities that offer business marketing, and the extent to which schools give credit to faculty members for writing cases. However, we are not as sanguine about the likelihood that researchers can gather a *large* sample of respondents. Based on our telephone survey and Internet search, we doubt that more than 100 accredited U.S. universities offer business marketing at the master's level. As to Professor Honeycutt's query concerning class sizes in our sample, the median number of students per business marketing class during the 1996-1997 school year was thirty and the mean was thirty-three.

We did in fact draw upon the mailing list of the Business-to-Business Marketing Special Interest Group (B2B SIG) of the American Marketing Association. And we point out that the B2B SIG runs its own Internet Web site, the B2B Marketing Exchange (www.mba.wfu.edu/mba/b2b.htm). However, as with other Web sites, the Exchange must function with limited resources and topical materials.

Contrary to what Professor Honeycutt states, we did not and do not advocate a single textbook for business marketing. Rather, we found that nearly half of respondents to our survey did not use a textbook and observed that a widely used, authoritative and innovative textbook does not appear to exist. This void makes it more difficult and time-consuming for less-experienced faculty members to prepare new courses in business marketing. In addition, there is no standard reference source for those outside the discipline to turn to when they need to know something about business marketing.

In retrospect, we may have overstated the credit universities should afford professors for writing cases. However, we maintain that a well-written case study does make a contribution to the discipline, and that this should be acknowledged more than it has. We also emphasize that academics write far fewer business marketing cases each year than consumer product cases, and that they have not focused enough attention on professional service industries or contemporary business marketing issues.

Finally, we cannot disagree with Professor Honeycutt that professors with experience in business marketing bring significantly more to the classroom. In an ideal world, everyone who taught business marketing would have significant work experience in the discipline.

However, we find few new marketing professors who do. Thus, to grow the discipline of business marketing, we need to reach out to those marketing professors who have some interest in business marketing but who may not have experience in it. Widely known, "user-friendly" teaching materials in business marketing, and an active network of business marketing academics and practitioners to draw on will encourage and help those interested marketing professors to develop graduate courses in business marketing.

REFERENCES

"Consulting Firms Snap Up New MBAs." (1996). *HR Focus* (January), 15.

Farrell, Greg (1997). "B-School Brownout." *Adweek* 38(June 2), 29-32.

"MBA Graduates Demand Better Quality of Life." (1997). *Management Consultant International* (September), 5.

Miller, Cyndee (1995). "Return of the MBA; Enrollments Up and So Are the Salaries for Grads." *Marketing News* (July 17), 1.

Morgenstern, Marlene L. and Mary K. McCaffery (1996). "MBAs Lose in Jobs, but Gain in Pay." *Compensation and Benefits Review* (September-October), 6-7.

Richards, Amanda (1997). "Brand New Days, Brand Managers." *Marketing* (December 4), 26.

PART IV:
UNDERGRADUATE PROGRAMS

Business Marketing Education:
A Distinctive Role
in the Undergraduate Curriculum

Michael D. Hutt
Thomas W. Speh

In the face of resource constraints and pressure from constituents, business schools are revamping the curriculum and reassessing the merit of traditional course offerings. In turn, marketing departments are being challenged to build a curriculum that emphasizes the knowledge fundamentals and professional skills required for managing the marketing function in an environment characterized by increasingly complex buyer-seller relationships and continuous changes in information technology, the nature of markets, and the structure and boundaries of organizations. This challenging mission is pursued through required marketing courses and elective offerings such as business marketing.

The purpose of this paper is to examine the nature and structure of the undergraduate business marketing course and to explore the role that it assumes in the marketing curriculum. To this end, the discussion is divided into four parts. First, attention centers on the distinctive content of the course and the special insights into marketing processes that are provided. Second, several prominent trends in business practice are highlighted and linked directly to the business marketing course. Particular attention is given to recent changes that are transforming buyer-seller relationships, organizational processes, and marketing strategy patterns. Third, the central themes and knowledge areas that comprise the business marketing course are detailed. Fourth, attention turns to the role that cases and other learning tools can assume in developing the skill set of business marketing students.

PLACE IN THE CURRICULUM

The business marketing course contributes to the marketing curriculum on several counts. First, the most widely used examples in required marketing courses, such as marketing principles and marketing management or strategy, are drawn from the context of consumer packaged products. Of course, such examples are appropriate because they are nicely aligned with a student's experience as a consumer. However, a large proportion of business school graduates enter firms that have a direct hand in the business market. Indeed, business marketing and consumer goods marketing are different. Between consumer and business marketing, there are differences in the nature of markets, buying processes, buyer-seller relationships, environmental influences, and market strategy (Hutt and Speh 1998). While a common body of knowledge, principles, and theory applies to both consumer and business marketing, there are important points of departure that require special attention. Often, these differences cannot be adequately examined within the broad landscape of a marketing management or marketing strategy class. The business marketing course fills this gap in the undergraduate marketing curriculum.

Second, a day in the life of a marketing manager at an industrial firm differs from that of a counterpart at a consumer products company. Planning in the industrial setting requires more working relationships across functions and a tighter link to corporate strategy than planning in the consumer goods sector (Webster 1978). Cross-functional working relationships are vital because "changes in marketing strategy are more likely to involve capital commitments for new equipment, shifts in development activities, or departures from traditional engineering and manufacturing approaches, any one of which would have company-wide implications" (Ames 1976, pp. 95-96). Given the interfunctional nature of the content, students gain an understanding of how the different functional pieces of an organization fit together. Also, an opportunity is provided to link the course content to other core classes in the business curriculum, such as organizational behavior, finance, accounting, and strategic management.

Third, because of the concentrated nature of the business market and the reliance on direct channels, prominent attention is given in the business marketing course to customer-linking processes and account management. Close and enduring relationships in the business market require frequent communications, joint problem solving, and a high level of coordination between and among an array of personnel on both the buying and selling sides. Moreover, firms are increasingly using multifunctional teams to achieve the high level of information sharing and coordination that collaborative relationships require (Day 1994). The business marketing course can provide students with a solid grounding in account management strategies and expose them to the stream of supply chain activities that must be coordinated to achieve mutually profitable collaboration. For example, to customize a product and delivery schedule for an important customer requires close coordination among product, logistics, and sales personnel. Moreover, some customer accounts might require special field-engineering, installation, or equipment support, thereby increasing the required coordination between sales and service units.

Fourth, services are assuming a vital role in the economy and the business marketing course can isolate the special management challenges and marketing opportunities that this sector presents. Many original equipment manufacturers are now using effective service support as a strategy for creating sales growth; in addition, a vast array of "pure service" firms exist to supply organizations with everything from payroll processing or software applications to the complete management of their information technology or logistics functions. Firms such as Hewlett-Packard, IBM, and General Electric are deriving an increasing share of their sales and profit from services. To illustrate, General Electric (GE) is placing increased emphasis on service marketing strategies in each of its business units. Given his stunning record of profitable growth as Chairman and CEO at GE, some believe that Jack Welch's aggressive services strategy provides a blueprint for refashioning an industrial company in a postindustrial economy (Smart 1996). While downsizing in other areas, firms such as GE, IBM, and a host of others are adding to their ranks in the services area, thereby creating opportunities for marketing graduates who have specialized knowledge and skills in this area.

DIRECTIONS IN BUSINESS MARKETING PRACTICE

The business marketing course provides an ideal vehicle for exploring prominent themes in business practice that are transforming buyer-seller relationships, organizational processes, and marketing strategy patterns. Changes in practice call for corresponding adjustments in the content and focus of the business marketing course. To this end, five important trends in business marketing are highlighted.

First, the search for improved quality and superior performance has spawned a significant shift in the purchasing practices and priorities of organizations. Second, business marketing firms are seeking a "collaborative advantage" (Kanter 1994) by demonstrating special skills in managing relationships with key customers or by jointly developing inventive strategies with alliance partners. Third, rising attention is being given to how traditional marketing practices can be adapted for turbulent high-technology markets. Such markets represent a rapidly growing sector of the world economy and an intensely competitive battleground. Fourth, firms continue the search for better ways to manage business processes and integrate business functions, and ongoing changes here place special demands on the relationship management skills of marketing managers. Finally, "time to market" is a performance metric that is closely scrutinized by managers, and recent research provides some useful insights for accelerating the new product development process.

Strategic Trends in Purchasing

A variety of forces are reshaping the purchasing function and how organizations buy industrial goods and services (see Table 15). Purchasing managers are embracing the practice of supply chain management—a technique for linking a manufacturer's operations with those of all of its suppliers and its key intermediaries and customers. A buyer following a supply chain management strategy will reach several tiers back in the supply chain to assist second-, third-, and fourth-tier suppliers in meeting quality, just-in-time delivery, or other performance targets. The supply chain approach seeks to improve the speed, quality, and efficiency of manufacturing and delivery through strong vendor relationships (Mullin 1996). These goals are achieved through information sharing, joint planning, shared technology, joint problem solving, and shared benefits.

Firms that implement a supply chain management system often streamline the supplier base. Major industrial customers such as Ford, Xerox, Motorola, and others have cut the number of suppliers

TABLE 15. Trends Reshaping the Procurement Process

Trend	Description
Emphasis on Supply Chain Management	Synchronizing the activities and operations of multiple tiers of suppliers to increase speed, quality, and performance
Reduction in the Supplier Base	Longer-term and closer relationships with few suppliers (for example, over the past decade, the number of suppliers used by Chrysler and Motorola has been reduced by 60 percent or more)
Strategic Priorities in Purchasing	Forging relationships with those suppliers who can give the firm a competitive advantage in quality, cost, technology development, speed or response, or other performance areas
Closer Buyer-Seller Relationships	Frequent interactions and close working relationships among multiple functions—manufacturing, engineering, and logistics as well as sales and purchasing on both the buying and selling sides
A Focus on "Value in Use"	Moving beyond price to consider the total cost of ownership of a supplier's product: acquisition, possession, and usage costs

they use and demanded new supply chain arrangements for those that remain. From Table 15, observe that purchasing managers are also forging close relationships with those suppliers which can give their firms a competitive advantage. In many firms, purchasing strategy is becoming more closely tied to corporate strategy (Dyer 1996).

The trends in procurement place a premium on the supply chain capabilities of the business marketer. Organizational buyers emphasize the total value of the products and services a supplier provides. For example, Chrysler spends 90 percent of its purchasing dollars with 150 suppliers. Thomas Stallkamp, Chrysler's vice president of procurement supply, notes that once we decide on a supplier for a component or material, "the supplier will have the business forever, providing the supplier continues to meet quality, cost, technology and delivery requirements" (Chrysler 1995, p. 126). Of particular importance to Chrysler is the quality of technical support, innovative technology, and fresh ideas that it receives from suppliers.

The business marketer wishing to participate in leading-edge supply chains must possess the ability to deliver defect-free components exactly when they are required. Moreover, manufacturing flexibility and responsiveness to changing customer requirements are critical elements in forging a long-term relationship (Davis 1993). Information will play a central role: supplier data on costs and pricing, supplier input to product design, and the electronic linkage of all suppliers and the ultimate customer are all features of the buyer-seller relationship that are becoming more crucial. Importantly, a core component of marketing strategy now turns on how effectively a business marketing firm can manage its own supply network in a way that elevates the performance of its customer's supply chain. For those firms which can meet this requirement, the reward is significant: a sole-source position in a long-term relationship in which the supplier is viewed as an extension of the customer's company.

Course Coverage and Suggestions. In response to the trends that are changing the purchasing function, the business marketing course should provide increased coverage of (1) supply chain management issues, (2) the tools that organizational buyers employ in measuring "value in use," and (3) the strategic priorities that now occupy the attention of purchasing managers. Class discussion can be stimulated by considering the supply chain for a personal computer or an automobile. The goal here is to extend the traditional treatment of organizational buying behavior to reflect the changing nature of buyer-seller relationships. Rather than evaluating the product or service offerings of competing suppliers, organizational buyers examine the capabilities of these firms and the value of the product-service-information mix that they offer.

Purchasing provides a wealth of information on the buying patterns of Fortune 500 firms and each year provides a comprehensive profile of the structure and orientation of an award-winning purchasing department. To provide direct contact, students can be asked to interview a purchasing manager, explore the composition of the buying center for a specific product, and isolate the criteria that each member applied to a purchasing decision. As guest speakers, purchasing executives are well equipped to discuss the changing nature of buyer-seller relationships or the characteristics of effective sales-persons or successful relationship marketing programs.

Relationship Marketing

Responding to fundamental shifts on the procurement side, relationship marketing is a timely theme in practice, an area of long-standing interest among researchers (Wilson 1995; Dwyer, Schurr, and Oh 1987), and a topic of central importance in the business marketing course. Relationship marketing covers a broad domain and includes all marketing activities directed toward establishing, developing, and maintaining successful exchanges with customers, alliance partners, and other constituents (Morgan and Hunt 1994).

To effectively initiate and sustain a profitable relationship with a customer, the business marketer must carefully manage the multiple linkages that define the relationship. Several market forces, however, pose a challenge to the business marketer in implementing relationship strategies. Customers are demanding more customized services, emphasizing supply chain techniques to lower total "cost in use," and demanding more product variety. In turn, as firms have increased the speed of new product development cycles, little attention has been paid to the impact that the increased flow of new offerings has on downstream marketing activities (Cespedes 1995). Often, sales and service units do not have sufficient time to learn the new technology and to develop coordinated plans for strategy implementation.

Given these new marketing requirements, Cespedes (1995) emphasizes the importance of "concurrent marketing" among the groups that are most central to customer contact efforts: product, sales, and service units. In his view, these recent market developments place more emphasis on a firm's ability to

- generate timely market knowledge by market segment and by individual account,
- customize product service packages for diverse customer groups, and
- capitalize on local field knowledge from sales and service units to inform product strategy in real time.

Strategic alliances are also assuming an increasingly prominent role in the strategy of leading business marketing firms and pose a separate set of relationship management challenges worthy of consideration in the business marketing course. First, alliance agreements are broadly negotiated by senior executives who turn over the final details and day-to-day management of the alliance to middle managers. The implementation of alliance strategy can be hampered as managers flesh out the details with their counterparts in the partner firm (Ring and Van de Ven 1994). Second, many firms are involved in multiple alliances and this can provide an added source of tension to a relationship. Indeed, the partner firm may be a rival or be involved in other alliances with your competitors (Yoshino and Rangan 1995). Third, the basic idea behind an alliance is to create added value by effectively linking the core competencies of one firm with those of another firm. Often, however, the partner firms have incompatible systems and decision structures that delay decision making, create inefficiencies, and frustrate alliance personnel (Kanter 1994).

As in buyer-seller relationships, alliances involve a dense web of interpersonal connections. Research suggests that firms which are effective in managing strategic alliances use a flexible approach, letting their alliances evolve in form as conditions change over time; they invest adequate resources and management attention in these relationships; and they integrate the organizations so that the appropriate points of contact and communication are managed (Kanter 1994).

Course Coverage and Suggestions. Relationship management issues should constitute the heart of the business marketing course. Special attention can be given to account management issues such as (1) selecting key accounts, (2) developing a product-service offering, (3) coordinating and implementing the strategy, and (4) evaluating relationship outcomes.

Several excellent cases are available that explore the coordination issues that surround account management and strategic alliances. For example, Frank V. Cespedes (1996) gives special attention to relationship management issues in the cases that he authored for his excellent volume *Managing Marketing Linkages: Text, Cases, and Readings.* These and other relevant cases are available in the Harvard case series.

Assignments can also be created that ask students to develop a profile of the role that the service element assumes in the strategy of a firm such as Hewlett-Packard, PeopleSoft, Baxter International, or a local business marketing firm. An alternative exercise might ask students to interview a salesperson and explore the history of an important relationship.

High-Technology Markets

The business marketing course can also squarely address the complex question of how strategists can make informed decisions in rapidly changing high-technology industries. During the past quarter century, discontinuous innovations have been common in the computer and electronics industry, creating massive new influxes of spending, fierce competition, and a whole host of firms that are redrawing the boundaries of the high-technology marketplace.

A popular tool with strategists at high-technology firms is the technology adoption life cycle—a framework developed by Geoffrey A. Moore (1995) and detailed in his influential book *Inside the Tornado*. Fundamental to his framework are five classes of customers who constitute the potential market for a discontinuous innovation. Business marketers can benefit by putting innovative products in the hands of *technology enthusiasts*. They serve as a gatekeeper to the rest of the technology life cycle and their endorsement is needed for an innovation to get a fair hearing in the organization, but they do not have ready access to the resources needed to move an organization toward a large-scale commitment to the new technology. By contrast, *visionaries* have resource control and can often assume an influential role in publicizing the benefits of an innovation and giving it a boost during the early stages of market development. However, visionaries are difficult for a marketer to serve because each demands special and unique product modifications. Their demands can quickly tax the R&D resources of the technology firm and stall the market penetration of the innovation.

Truly innovative products often enjoy a warm welcome in an early market comprised of technology enthusiasts and visionaries, but then sales falter and often even plummet. Frequently, a chasm develops between visionaries who are intuitive and support revolution and the *pragmatists* who are analytical, support evolution, and provide the pathway to the mainstream market. If the business marketer can successfully guide a product across the chasm, an opportunity is created to gain acceptance with the mainstream market comprised of pragmatists and *conservatives*. Pragmatists make the bulk of technology purchases in organizations while conservatives include a sizable group of customers who are hesitant to buy high-tech products but do so to avoid being left behind. Meanwhile, *skeptics* are the ever-present critics of high-technology products.

The fundamental strategy for crossing the chasm and moving from the early market to the mainstream market is to provide pragmatists with a 100 percent solution to their problems. Many high-technology firms err by attempting to provide something for everyone and by never meeting the complete requirements of any particular market segment. Geoffrey A. Moore (1995, p. 22) notes that

> the key to a winning strategy is to identify a simple beachhead of pragmatist customers in a mainstream market segment and to accelerate the formation of 100 percent of their whole product. The goal is to win a niche foothold in the mainstream as quickly as possible—that is what is meant by *crossing the chasm.*

In technology markets, each market segment is like a bowling pin and the momentum achieved from hitting one segment successfully carries over into surrounding segments.

While economic buyers who seek particular solutions are the key to success in building momentum in the market, technical buyers in organizations can spawn a burst of demand—a tornado. Information technology (IT) professionals interact freely across company and industry boundaries and discuss the ramifications of the latest technology. IT managers watch each other closely—they do not want to be too early or too late. Often, they move together and create a tornado. Because a massive number of new customers are entering the market at the same time and because they all want the same product, demand dramatically outstrips supply and a large backlog of customers can appear overnight. Moore (1995) describes how such market forces have surrounded Hewlett-Packard's laser and inkjet printers, Microsoft's Windows products, and Intel's Pentium microprocessors.

In high-technology industries, Burgelman and Grove (1996; see also, Grove 1996) argue that the strategist must be alert to changes in competitive or customer behavior that might signal a strategic inflection point. A strategic inflection point describes "the giving way of one type of industry dynamics to another, the change of one winning strategy into another, the replacement of an existing technological regime by a new one" (Burgelman and Grove 1996, p. 10).

Course Coverage and Suggestions. High-technology markets pose special challenges and rewards for marketers, yet are given rather limited exposure in the marketing curriculum. The business marketing course can fill this gap by exploring concepts that are central to the management of high-technology products, such as the technology adoption life cycle and first-mover advantages; the nature of the organizational buying process for technology purchases; and the unique pricing, promotion, and services issues that the marketing strategist must consider. To this end, assignments can be built around identifying product winners and losers in the technology area or comparing and contrasting the strategies of firms such as Gateway versus Dell in the personal computer market or Hewlett-Packard versus Canon in the printer market. As guest speakers, management information systems directors or information technology officers from a local bank or manufacturing firm can explore trends and changing product-service requirements in their industry.

Cross-Functional Connections

As firms attempt to speed decision making, streamline their business processes, and become more market driven, a number of managerial prescriptions have been offered. Most center on this theme: emphasize the processes that clearly provide value to the customer and remove the barriers that divide functional areas (Hutt, Walker, and Frankwick 1995). Although many of these initiatives have improved performance by cutting cycle time, lowering costs, or increasing customer satisfaction, Majchrzak and Wang (1996) argue that many others have had disappointing results. After enduring the trauma of reengineering, some firms discovered that their performance is no better—and in selected cases, actually worse—than before.

Why? Managers and reengineering teams often underestimate the difficulty of transforming the way that employees behave and work with one another. "They assume that simply changing their organizational structures from functional units into process-complete departments will cause people to shed their functional mind-sets and will forge them instantly into a team intent on achieving common goals" (Majchrzak and Wang 1996, p. 93).

The business marketing course provides an ideal platform for exploring the critical cross-functional connections required in the design, development, and implementation of strategy. The strong inter-dependencies that exist between marketing and other functional units, such as R&D and logistics, are emphasized in conceptualizations of the unique dimensions of business-to-business marketing (for example, Webster 1978). Assuming a boundary position between the firm and its customers and an integrative role across functions (Day 1992), a central challenge for the business marketing manager is to minimize interdepartmental conflict while fostering shared appreciation of the interdependencies (Hutt and Speh 1984). This challenging interdisciplinary role raises important implications for the design of the business marketing course.

Course Coverage and Suggestions. Effective business marketing managers understand the critical role that each function assumes in the design and execution of strategy and, in turn, what each functional area requires from marketing. This suggests that special emphasis should be given in the course to the interrelationships between marketing and other business functions such as R&D, manufacturing, logistics, and procurement. (See Griffin and Hauser 1996 for a comprehensive review of the marketing-R&D interface.) All business marketing decisions are affected, directly or indirectly, by other functional areas. In turn, business decisions in R&D and in manufacturing and procurement, as well as adjustments in overall corporate strategy, are influenced by marketing considerations.

The work of a business marketing manager involves considerable interaction with customers and with superiors, subordinates, and peers from other functional units. To serve customers and to receive required support at various levels of the hierarchy and across functions, the marketing manager must initiate, develop, nurture, and sustain a network of relationships with a number of constituencies within the firm (Webster 1992; Hutt 1995). Special relationship skills are required in managing this cross-functional network. To this end, the business marketing course can explore common obstacles that divide functional areas—such as turf barriers, interpretive barriers, and communication barriers (Frankwick et al. 1994; Dougherty 1992). Moreover, treatment of relationship management can be extended beyond the buyer-seller context to include relationships with important cross-functional constituents. Marketing managers are involved in a diverse set of internal working relationships that are in various stages of development and take many forms. As in relationships with customers, cross-unit relationships involve a set of mutual expectations concerning performance, roles, trust, and influence (Gabarro 1987).

Some instructors of business marketing classes use speakers from other functional areas such as manufacturing or R&D to explore key cross-functional issues and to demonstrate the diverse perspectives that other functional areas hold. At many universities, opportunities exist for joint projects that involve marketing and engineering students. Annually, many engineering programs have undergraduate student teams involved in national product design competition and marketing expertise is welcomed. Moreover, the National Science Foundation is most receptive to educational initiatives that bring business and engineering programs together.

To secure insights into the working relationships of marketing managers, some instructors use an assignment that asks students to interview a marketing manager and develop a profile of the cross-unit communication patterns of that manager. In completing the profile, the manager is asked to describe the characteristics of effective and ineffective working relationships.

Fast-Paced Product Development

Product development is a favorite topic of business marketing students. Recent research in the new product development area provides timely content for the course. With shortening product life cycles, speed is the new weapon in the innovation battle (Deschamps and Nayak 1995). Rapid product development offers a number of competitive advantages. Speed allows a firm to respond to rapidly changing markets and technologies. Moreover, fast product development is usually more efficient because lengthy development processes tend to waste resources on peripheral activities and changes (Cooper and Kleinschmidt 1995). Of course, while an overemphasis on speed may create other pitfalls, it is becoming an important strategic weapon, particularly in high-technology markets.

How can a firm accelerate product development? A major study of the global computer industry by Eisenhardt and Tabrizi (1995) provides some important benchmarks. The research examined seventy-two product development projects of leading U.S., European, and Asian computer firms. The findings suggest that there are multiple approaches for gaining speed in product development. Speed comes from properly matching the approach to the technological and market conditions that surround the product development task.

For well-known markets and technologies, a *compression strategy* appears to speed development. This strategy views product development as a predictable series of steps that can be compressed. Speed comes from carefully planning these steps and shortening the time it takes to complete each step. This research indicates that the compression strategy increased the speed of product development for products that had predictable designs and that were targeted for stable and mature markets. Mainframe computers fit into this category—they rely on proprietary hardware, have more predictable designs from project to project, and compete in a mature market.

For uncertain markets and technologies, an *experiential strategy* accelerates product development. The underlying assumption of this strategy is that "product development is a highly uncertain path through foggy and shifting markets and technologies. The key to fast product development is, then, rapidly building intuition and flexible options in order to learn quickly about and shift with uncertain environments" (Eisenhardt and Tabrizi 1995, p. 91).

Under these conditions, speed comes from multiple design iterations, extensive testing, frequent milestones, and a powerful leader who can keep the product team focused. Here real-time interactions, experimentation, and flexibility are essential. The research found that the experiential strategy increased the speed of product development for unpredictable projects such as personal computers. The personal computer market is characterized by rapidly evolving technology and unpredictable patterns of competition. Rather than forcing all projects through a highly structured process, Eisenhardt and Tabrizi (1995) suggest that speed comes from adapting the process to the new product development task at hand.

Course Coverage and Suggestions. Built on a foundation that emphasizes marketing's interdisciplinary role in the firm, the business marketing course can explore the new product development process in greater detail than in the traditional marketing management class. Special attention can be given to alternative approaches for organizing the new product development process, the determinants of new product success, the special challenges involved in new service development, and alternative mechanisms for bringing R&D and marketing together. Moreover, since the prominent themes in practice center on the development of high-technology products and services, students secure additional grounding in high-technology marketing and how planning differs in that domain.

CENTRAL THEMES AND KNOWLEDGE AREAS

The business marketing course provides a valuable forum for developing a student's knowledge of the competitive realities of the business market, supply chain management, and other areas that occupy the attention of practitioners. Table 16 highlights the central themes and knowledge areas that comprise the undergraduate business marketing course.

Business Market Characteristics

To lay the groundwork for the business marketing course, the integrating questions are as follows: What are the similarities and differences between consumer goods marketing and business marketing? What customers comprise the business market? What forces influence the behavior of business market demand? Special attention is given to the unique characteristics of each of the three business market sectors—commercial firms, institutions, and government—and the nature of the procurement process in each sector. Emphasis is likewise given to supply chain concepts and the relationship management strategies that purchasing managers employ.

Organizational Buying Behavior

Since the market segments served are comprised of organizations rather than households, organizational buying behavior occupies a central position in the course. As purchasing assumes a more strategic role in the firm, the business marketer must understand the competitive realities of the customer's business and develop a value proposition that advances the performance goals of the customer organization. The specific objectives that frame this component of the course center on advancing the student's understanding of

- the decision processes that organizational buyers apply as they confront different buying situations and the resulting strategy implications for the business marketer;
- the formal evaluation systems and analytical approaches that organizational buyers employ when measuring value and evaluating supplier performance;
- the individual, group, organizational, and environmental variables that influence organizational buying decisions; and
- how a knowledge of organizational buying characteristics is of significant operational value to the business marketer when designing marketing strategy.

Evaluating Market Opportunity

Government at all levels, trade associations, trade publications, and private research companies publish a significant amount of economic data on a national, state, and county basis. Most of the data is collected by standard industrial classification (SIC) code—renamed the North American Industrial Classification System (NAICS)— allowing for an industry-by-industry analysis. These data sources are useful for defining target segments in the business market, estimating market potential, forecasting sales, evaluating competitors, and projecting market trends. Drawing on these information sources, students can explore specific techniques that can be applied in measuring market potential, segmenting the market, and forecasting sales.

Relationship Marketing

Some buyer-seller relationships in the business market fit the characteristics of transactional exchange while others are more collaborative in nature (Webster 1992). Knowledge of the different forms that relationships take in the business market provides the foundation for developing specific relationship marketing strategies for a particular customer. The central tasks of relationship marketing include identifying target segments, choosing individual accounts within these segments, developing product-service offerings for these customers, and evaluating relationship outcomes. Since strategic alliances are assuming an increasingly important role in business marketing strategy, attention can likewise be directed to the special challenges and opportunities that these relationships present.

TABLE 16. The Ingredients of the Business Marketing Course: Themes and Knowledge Areas

Theme	Desired Knowledge
Business Market Characteristics and the Nature of the Procurement Process	The distinguishing features of the business market, the major types of organizational customers, the structure and orientation of the procurement process
Organizational Buying Behavior	Themes of organizational buying behavior and the individual, group, organizational, and environmental forces that shape the decision-making process
Evaluating Market Opportunity	The concepts, methodologies, and information sources for evaluating and measuring market opportunities, analyzing the bases of competition in an industry, and selecting market segments
Relationship Marketing	Theories, concepts, and strategies for managing relationships with customers, organizations in the channel of distribution, and strategic alliance partners
Marketing's Cross-Functional Relationships	Concepts, organizing frameworks, and special requirements for managing relationships with other functional areas during new product development and during the design, development, and implementation of marketing strategy
Managing and Integrating Business Marketing Strategy Variables	Selected theories and concepts for managing each strategy variable, strategic options for combining them into an integrated marketing strategy program on a domestic or global scale, and procedures for monitoring and controlling business marketing programs

Marketing's Cross-Functional Relationships

By exploring the relationship between marketing and other business functions such as R&D, manufacturing, and logistics, students gain a more integrated and realistic view of strategy design, development, and implementation. Strategic plans emerge out of a bargaining process among functional areas and special relationship skills are required to work effectively across functions. Various functional units operate under unique reward systems, time horizons, and orientations. By understanding the common barriers that divide functions and by recognizing the contribution that each makes to strategy, the cross-functional knowledge of the student is advanced.

The marketing-R&D interface merits special coverage in the course. A shared appreciation of each function's distinctive skills contributes to creating competitive advantage. When harmony prevails, R&D can articulate the technological possibilities, while marketing thoughtfully assesses the possibilities in light of market opportunities and competitive realities. Collaboration creates new, sharper conceptualizations of how technology can profitably serve customers and strengthen competitive advantage.

Managing and Integrating Strategy Variables

Business marketing programs increasingly involve a combination of tangible products, service support, and ongoing information services both before and after the sale (Cespedes 1995). When organizational buyers select a product, they are buying a given level of product quality, technical service, and delivery reliability. Other elements may be of importance—the reputation of the supplier, friendship, and other personal benefits flowing from the buyer-seller relationship. Consistent with a relationship marketing perspective, this suggests that special attention should be given to the service elements that support product strategy and define the total customer offering. Other distinctive marketing strategy topics that can be covered in the business marketing course include high-technology product management, national account management, industrial channel strategy, value-based pricing, logistical support, and new service development processes.

A valuable organizing framework for exploring the integration and control of marketing programs is the *balanced scorecard* approach developed by Kaplan and Norton (1996). By complementing financial measures of past performance with specific measures of the drivers of future performance, the approach seeks to translate a firm's strategy into a comprehensive set of performance measures that guides strategic control and action. Organizational performance is examined across four perspectives: financial, customers, internal business processes, and learning and growth. Well suited to business marketing applications, the scorecard examines financial results as well as the underlying factors that drive long-term financial performance and competitive advantage.

COURSE DESIGN

To achieve desired learning outcomes, lectures can be augmented with a variety of learning tools in the undergraduate business marketing course (Lichtenthal and Butaney 1991). Included here are cases, industry analysis projects, demand analysis exercises, and small-group class discussion assignments. The particular blend chosen varies based on the preferences of the instructor and the background and needs of the students. As a rule, lectures assume an important role in providing students with a business market perspective and an appreciation of the special challenges that marketers confront in serving organizational customers. Once a foundation is developed in particular areas, cases and other learning aids can be used to add variety to the course, to integrate key concepts, and to enhance the students' skill set.

Skill Development

From Table 17, observe the important role that cases and course projects can assume in developing the skill set of business marketing students. For example, cases and industry analysis projects provide a vehicle for improving the analytical, critical, and communication skills of the students. For the undergraduate course, a mix of cases is appropriate. Shorter cases can be used to isolate particular areas, such as organizational buying behavior, while longer, more comprehensive cases can be employed to integrate important content areas and to bring closure to the course.

Industry analysis projects provide an alternative vehicle that can be used in the course. The goal here is to improve the students' analytical and research skills by providing them with hands-on experience at using a wide variety of sources of industry and company in formation that supports decision making in business marketing (Bunn 1995). Such projects can be built around an assessment of a particular

TABLE 17. Skill Development in the Business Marketing Course: An Illustrative Profile

Skills	Description	Learning Vehicle
Analytical Skills	Ability to identify and analyze market data presented in secondary sources or cases, evaluate this data using appropriate concepts and theories, and apply the resulting information in reaching sound conclusions to new and recurring marketing problems	Cases Industry Analysis Projects Market Analysis Exercises
Critical Skills	Ability to analyze and evaluate proposed solutions to marketing problems by exploring the adequacy of supporting evidence, the theoretical or practical relevance of the choice options, and the unique characteristics of the environmental context	Cases
Research Skills	Ability to use secondary sources of information in exploring the nature of competition in a market, industry trends, the composition of markets, market potential, and a firm's financial position	Industry Analysis Projects Market Analysis Exercises
Communication Skills	Ability to organize, write, and effectively present a marketing plan that appropriately details and persuasively supports a proposed marketing strategy	Cases

firm's product, its competitive standing in the industry, and its current strategic course. Shorter market analysis exercises that center on market opportunity assessment can also be used.

A Two-Course Sequence

To strengthen the skill set of its business marketing students, Miami University offers an innovative two-course sequence. Here students who perform well in the first course and meet certain grade point average benchmarks in the undergraduate business program are given the opportunity to register for the advanced workshop in business marketing.

The workshop is organized around a series of "live cases" that business marketing executives present. In advance of the presentation, the executive provides some background on the company and a particular marketing problem. Likewise, the students do library research to secure additional background on the industry and the company's performance history. The executive then visits the campus, presents the situation, and addresses questions. After deliberations, a preliminary set of recommendations is offered by the students and the visiting executive provides feedback. Following the visit, a student team develops a comprehensive final report for the client firm. The advanced seminar is embraced by students and has received long-standing support from business marketing practitioners.

CONCLUSIONS

The undergraduate business marketing course provides value to the important constituents of a marketing department. First, the content and focus of the business marketing course are closely aligned with important themes in business practice. This strikes a responsive chord with practitioners and recruiters. Clearly, recruiters who seek marketing graduates place a premium on those students who understand business-to-business markets, organizational buying processes, and relationship management. Indeed, at most universities, the roster of companies that recruit on campus is dominated by business marketing firms. Most entry-level positions in marketing are in sales and a large portion of these are concentrated in industrial sales. Candidates who demonstrate a grasp of business marketing fundamentals are easier to train and, compared to their peers, offer the potential to make a more immediate contribution to the firm's operations.

Such evidence strongly suggests an expanded role for business marketing in the undergraduate curriculum through a more frequent offering of the class and through multiple sections as resources permit. By increasing the proportion of students who are exposed to business marketing, a marketing department is providing added value to its students and business constituents alike. Some marketing departments may further strengthen their relationships with the business community by building an area of specialization in the business marketing area. This could be achieved by augmenting the business marketing course with personal selling and sales management electives. Such a concentration provides students with the knowledge fundamentals and practice skills that are sought by the majority of campus recruiters.

Opportunities also exist for strengthening the coverage of organizational markets in other courses in the marketing curriculum, such as in the required consumer behavior course. By infusing a systematic treatment of organizational buying behavior into the course, students develop a sharper grasp of how buyers behave and how markets operate. The traditional consumer behavior course provides a conceptual foundation for moving from individual decision making to group decision making and from the household to the organization. Selected readings can be used to aid the transition.

Second, the business marketing course occupies a unique niche in the undergraduate business curriculum and provides a contribution to other departments in the college. As major accreditation organizations, such as the American Assembly of Collegiate Schools of Business (AACSB), are placing increased pressure on business schools to integrate the curriculum, cross-functional themes provide the heart of the business marketing course. Emphasizing an interdisciplinary orientation, the course ties together core business concepts from different business disciplines and demonstrates the managerial relevance of these concepts.

Third, and most important, the business marketing course serves the needs of students. By extending their knowledge of markets beyond the consumer goods domain, by deepening their understanding of how organizations make buying decisions, by strengthening their grasp of relationship marketing theories, by exposing them to the competitive realities of high-technology markets, and by providing them with decision-making skills in this important area of marketing, the business marketing course provides special value to students.

REFERENCES

Ames, B. C. (1976). "Trappings vs. Substance in Industrial Marketing." *Harvard Business Review* 48(July-August), 95-96.

Bunn, M. D. (1995). *Industry Analysis Workbook.* Fort Worth, TX: The Dryden Press.

Burgelman, R. A. and A. S. Grove (1996). "Strategic Dissonance." *California Management Review* 38(Winter), 8-28.

Cespedes, F. V. (1995). *Concurrent Marketing: Integrating Product, Sales, and Service.* Boston, MA: Harvard Business School Press.

———(1996). *Managing Marketing Linkages: Text, Cases, and Readings.* Englewood Cliffs, NJ: Prentice-Hall.

"Chrysler Pushes Quality Down the Supplier Chain" (1995). *Purchasing* 118(13), 126.

Cooper, R. G. and E. J. Kleinschmidt (1995). "Performance Typologies of New Product Projects." *Industrial Marketing Management* 24(October), 439-456.

Davis, T. (1993). "Effective Supply Chain Management." *Sloan Management Review* 34(Summer), 35-46.

Day, G. S. (1992). "Marketing's Contribution to Strategic Dialogue." *Journal of the Academy of Marketing Science* 20(Fall), 323-329.

———(1994). "The Capabilities of Market-Driven Organizations." *Journal of Marketing*, 58(October), 37-52.

Deschamps, J. P. and P. R. Nayak (1995). *Product Juggernauts: How Companies Mobilize to Generate a Stream of Market Winners.* Boston: Harvard Business School Press.

Dougherty, D. (1992). "Interpretive Barriers to Successful Product Innovation in Large Firms." *Organization Science* 3(May), 179-202.

Dwyer, F. R., P. H. Schurr, and S. Oh (1987). "Developing Buyer-Seller Relationships." *Journal of Marketing* 51(April), 11-27.

Dyer, J. H. (1996). "How Chrysler Created an American Keiretsu." *Harvard Business Review* 74(July-August), 42-56.

Eisenhardt, K. M. and B. N. Tabrizi (1995). "Accelerating Adaptive Processes: Product Innovation in the Global Computer Industry." *Administrative Science Quarterly* 40(March), 84-110.

Frankwick, G. L., J. C. Ward, M. D. Hutt, and P. H. Reingen (1994). "Evolving Patterns of Organizational Beliefs in the Formation of Strategy." *Journal of Marketing* 58(April), 96-110.

Gabarro, J. J. (1987). "The Development of Working Relationships." In *Handbook of Organizational Behavior*, ed. J. W. Lorsch. Englewood Cliffs, NJ: Prentice-Hall, 172-189.

Griffin, A. and J. R. Hauser (1996). "Integrating R&D and Marketing: A Review and Analysis of the Literature." *Journal of Product Innovation Management* 13(May), 191-215.

Grove, A. S. (1996). *Only the Paranoid Survive.* New York: Currency-Doubleday.

Hutt, M. D. (1995). "Cross-Functional Working Relationships in Marketing." *Journal of the Academy of Marketing Science* 23(Fall), 351-357.

———, and T. W. Speh (1984). "The Marketing Strategy Center: Diagnosing the Industrial Marketer's Interdisciplinary Role." *Journal of Marketing* 48(Fall), 53-56.

_____and_____ (1998). *Business Marketing Management: A Strategic View of Industrial and Organizational Markets,* Sixth Edition. Fort Worth, TX: The Dryden Press.

_____, B. A. Walker, and G. L. Frankwick (1995). "Hurdle the Cross-Functional Barriers to Strategic Change." *Sloan Management Review* 36(Spring), 22-30.

Kanter, R. M. (1994). "Collaborative Advantage: The Art of Alliances." *Harvard Business Review* 72(July-August), 96-108.

Lichtenthal, J. D. and G. Butaney (1991). "Undergraduate Industrial Marketing: Content and Methods." *Industrial Marketing Management* 20(August), 231-239.

Majchrzak, A. and Q. Wang (1996). "Breaking the Functional Mind-Set in Process Organizations." *Harvard Business Review* 74(September-October), 93-99.

Moore, G. A. (1995). *Inside the Tornado: Marketing Strategies from Silicon Valley's Cutting Edge.* New York: HarperCollins.

Morgan, R. M. and S. D. Hunt (1994). "The Commitment-Trust Theory of Relationship Marketing." *Journal of Marketing* 58(July), 20-38.

Mullins, R. (1996). "Managing the Outsourced Enterprise." *Journal of Business Strategy* 17(July/August), 32.

Ring, P. S. and A. H. Van de Ven (1994). "Developmental Processes of Cooperative Interorganizational Relationships." *Academy of Management Review* 19(January), 90-118.

Smart, T. (1996). "Jack Welch's Encore: How G.E.'s Chairman Is Remaking His Company—Again." *Business Week* (October 28), 155-160.

Webster, F. E. Jr. (1978). "Management Science in Industrial Marketing." *Journal of Marketing* 42(January), 21-27.

_____ (1992). "The Changing Role of Marketing in the Corporation." *Journal of Marketing* 56(October), 1-17.

Wilson, D. T. (1995). "An Integrated Model of Buyer-Seller Relationships." *Journal of the Academy of Marketing Science* 23(Fall), 336-346.

Yoshino, M. Y. and U. S. Rangan (1995). *Strategic Alliances: An Entrepreneurial Approach to Globalization.* Boston, MA: Harvard Business School Press.

Business Marketing Education's Distinctive Role in the Undergraduate Curriculum: A Commentary

Gul Butaney

New marketing philosophies and core technologies have emerged. Relational marketing orientation, increasing global opportunities and competition, forging closer working relationships with value chain partners, increasing use of information technologies in the marketing processes, and organizing for creating time-based competitive values—all have revolutionized the way marketers create and nurture exchange relationships and transact business in the marketplace. These trends have important ramifications for what and how we teach the business-to-business marketing course (BMC). Students need to be prepared to operate in the complex and dynamic world of the future.

Seen from this perspective, Hutt and Speh's paper makes an important and timely contribution in the field of business marketing education. Because a large portion of business school graduates enter firms that have direct involvement in the business market, the business marketing course fills an important gap in the curriculum. Their paper suggests how current *specific topical directions* in the business marketing field affect the BMC. In this paper, however, this issue is looked at through a broader perspective on these directions. Specifically, strategic trends in purchasing and supplier relations management; relationship marketing; high-technology product marketing; faster, better, and friendlier product development; and cross-functional integration are reviewed. Specific aspects of these practices that need to be covered in the BMC are identified, with suggestions on pedagogical tools where necessary. The goal of this commentary is to enhance

Hutt and Speh's contribution in providing stronger supporting material for the instructors teaching BMC.

STRATEGIC TRENDS IN PURCHASING AND SUPPLIER RELATIONS MANAGEMENT

As prospective business (industrial) marketers, students need to understand the strategic trends shaping the purchasing and supply management functions. An understanding of the organizational buying process and strategies is fundamental to the development of sound marketing strategies for targeting as well as managing working relationships with business customers. Some students are likely to end up on the purchasing and supply management side of the business organization. As prospective managers, the students need to understand the impact of purchasing and supply chain management practices on the competitive success and profitability of the modern organization. The students also must understand the nature of interactions and issues between purchasing and other major intraorganizational functional activities, such as product design, manufacturing planning and control, quality management, information system design, customer service standards, and requirements of the company's customers. This understanding plays a key role in their responsibilities as the supplier relations managers. Hutt and Speh emphasize that the business marketing course should provide increased coverage of supply chain management issues and strategic priorities that now occupy purchasing managers. The coverage should be sufficiently expanded as noted in the following.

Supply Chain Management. A basic motivation of buyers for cultivating closer working relationships with suppliers is to improve the buying organization's performance on total quality, cost, delivery, and responsiveness to its external customers. Strategic supply management involves developing the strategies, approaches, and methods for realizing a competitive advantage and for improving the sourcing process, through direct involvement and interactions with suppliers. Selecting the right suppliers is important to satisfy the quality, cost, delivery, and technology requirements of the purchaser. It also creates the foundation for working closely with suppliers for continuing performance improvement arrangements. Global sourcing, which is becoming an important part of strategic supply management as firms search worldwide for the best source of supply, increases the level of challenge and complexity for the purchasing and supply management requirements, and for conducting business between two firms. A BMC, therefore, would clearly benefit from full-fledged discussion of the reasons, motivations, and specific values that customer organizations seek in entering closer working relationships with their vendors.

The topics of vender selection and value analysis for selecting suppliers for closer relationships should play a major role. How should the traditional vendor selection criteria be modified, the focus of value chain analysis, if at all, be expanded to include the relationship dimensions to the traditional product cost, quality, and performance factors? The value-in-use analysis should also take into account the cost of acquiring and maintaining the long-term relationship.

The role of information technology in achieving superior values in the supply chain relationships needs to expand substantially. The collection, creation, management, and communication of information are critical to the efficiency and effectiveness of operations and relationships in closer buyer-seller relationships. The BMC, therefore, should examine how information technology is used and how specific benefits are realized. For example, in-class demonstration of electronic data interchange (EDI) use in facilitating purchasing activities, order processing, automatic replenishment of inventory on a timely basis, in addition to providing structure for creating intranet and extranet as communication channels, would go a long way to illustrate how and why purchasing functions have been involved in forming closer buyer-seller working relationships. This will allow the student to understand some of the aspects of the total cost analysis of ownership of a supplier's product—acquisition, possession, and usage costs—much more clearly. Once the purchasers focus on the values rather than the cost, they must evaluate values within the buyer-seller relationship.

Pedagogically, how should the domain of issues related to the strategic trends in purchasing be tapped in the BMC course? Guest speakers from different buying and selling organizations illustrating their experiences and observations on operational aspects of the buying-selling relationships would provide firsthand information as well as an opportunity for students to ask specific questions and interact with the guest speaker. A case study describing a "before-after" scenario of how buying-selling operations were done before and after the formation of the closer relationship with the vendor (or customer) would be an effective vehicle to evaluate favorable impact of the relationship on inventory management costs, production costs, speed of communication, and other efficiencies and effectiveness achieved in organizational performance. In-class demonstration of EDI and efficient customer response (ECR) technologies also is seen as a value-adding pedagogical tool.

RELATIONSHIP MARKETING

Relationship marketing generally involves creating unique values and business arrangements for the customer for forging long-lasting business relationships. Developing and timely updating the customer-related unique offerings of product, services, and other undertakings by the supplier builds up the customer switching costs. If the customer is satisfied with the unique values and customized arrangements received from the supplier, the customer is less motivated to switch or develop other supply sources because of the cost and effort involved in educating the vendor of the customer operations, requirements, and processes as well as the customer's own learning of the supplier's processes, offerings, and other transaction costs. Sheth and Sharma (1997) feel that with increasing turbulence in the marketplace, it is clear that firms would have to move away from transaction-oriented marketing strategies and toward relationship-oriented strategies for enhancing marketing performance. Several marketing, economic, competitive, and organizational performance-related factors would support this viewpoint.

The increasing importance and practice of relational marketing strategies and tactics are likely to affect several areas of business marketing decisions. First, identification and development of superior competitive values unique to each major customer account or group of business customers/organizations will be necessary for targeting the customer uniquely, to build lasting relationships. Because these efforts will involve strategic resources, new marketing strategies, and changes in marketing processes, the coverage of business marketing strategy formulation (target market selection, strategic planning, and marketing strategy development) needs to be expanded in the BMC. Effective implementation of the relational marketing philosophy orientation, establishing closer working relationships, and what it would mean for the customer and the supplier in terms of their organizational structures and processes should be discussed. How relational philosophy affects design of product, customer services offerings, and account management strategies should be included. After-marketing (Vavra 1992) programs and tactics to maintain and enhance customer patronage should be emphasized. This will affect the industrial marketing promotion topic.

Baxter International, Inc., the world's largest manufacturer and distributor of hospital and institutional medical supplies and specialty products, best illustrates the nature of relationship philosophy, strategies, and some of the areas of their impact. The company manufactures and/or distributes more than 200,000 products to hospitals, clinics, and medical research laboratories worldwide. Its relationship marketing strategy focuses on such decision areas as customer service, inventory management, marketing research and information systems, and product pricing and promotion strategies. For example, Baxter uses just-in-time inventory management with its key customers through its value link program and uses four other unique inventory programs for different customer groups. The company has invested resources in technology investment and established common data communication standards (e.g., through EDI) for both its suppliers and customers, resulting in lower transaction costs, faster transmission of data and communication, and better product and order status information. In Baxter's value link inventory management program, Baxter does not limit itself to delivering materials to a hospital loading dock but distributes products to point of use (such as a nursing station on a specific floor of a hospital) and delivers products in exact quantities as needed on a daily basis (Berman 1996).

The goal of relationship marketing is customer retention. Relationships are built on familiarity and knowledge of customers, their experiences with the products, information on their business problems, as well as preferences for and importance of various benefits and incentives that the vendor might offer. The relationship marketing, therefore, necessitates two things. First, the marketer needs to develop a relationship marketing strategy with a well-designed customer information file (CIF) and system where the customer-related information is accessible to all relevant parties for timely decisions and activities. Second, a customer satisfaction and feedback measurement structure should be in place. Therefore, a separate session is warranted for designing and developing effective customer services strategies as well as customer satisfaction measurement systems, the essential requirements for cultivating long-lasting relationships.

Strategic alliances between organizations are also becoming an increasingly important marketing strategy choice in business marketing. The alliances are strategic in nature, allowing organizations to enter into favorable arrangements; gather marketing resources, strategic sourcing, technology, and strength; and gain power and control that otherwise would be difficult to achieve by an individual firm without partnering with other organizations. More than 20,000 new alliances were formed between 1987 and 1992, compared with 5,100 between 1980 and 1987, and only 750 during the 1970s (Harbinson and Pekar 1993). The scope of BMC should, therefore, be expanded to reflect the incidence and impact of strategic alliances, specifically, in the areas of business strategy development, issues related to terms and conditions of business contracts, selection of appropriate partners, management and evaluating performance of partner relationships, adaptation of interorganizational culture, and conflict management techniques (Barnes and Stafford 1993). Training of boundary-spanning personnel (e.g., middle managers and sales reps) becomes important, as Hutt and Speh suggest that alliances are broadly negotiated by senior executives who turn over the details of day-to-day management of the alliance itself to middle managers and sales reps. Their attitudes, orientations, and account management skills are crucial for furthering the performance of the alliance.

HIGH-TECHNOLOGY PRODUCT MARKETING

Technology is advancing at a tremendous pace. New developments in artificial intelligence and information technology are reported almost every day (Bearden, Ingram, and LaForge 1998). The emergence of EDI systems, videoconferencing technology, computer-to-computer linkages between organizations, transmission and receipt of data on real-time bases, software technology facilitating marketing operations and decision making, and, more recently, the World Wide Web—all these technological breakthroughs challenge marketers to embrace a technology perspective. There are opportunities for translating emerging technologies into successful new products and services, and for using technology to improve marketing operations and practices.

In today's fast-paced business climate and with rapid diffusion of emerging information technologies, it is especially important for students of business marketing, the technology practitioners and leaders of the future, to understand the issues and uses of marketing technologies. High-ticket and complex product technologies such as CASE tools, videoconferencing, and voice recognition are likely to have a longer acceptance and diffusion period (Butaney, Chand, and Chand 1994). Hutt and Speh's chapter promotes the understanding of the technology adoption life cycle very well. This knowledge is essential for designing effective strategies and tactics to penetrate the organizational buying process for technology purchases as well as for managing the unique pricing, promotion, and services issues that the technology marketing strategist must consider. Management of marketing opportunities for developing new technological products should play an important role in the session on new industrial product development and marketing strategies.

Students, however, need to be exposed to one other aspect of high-tech marketing, that of Internet-based marketing and opportunities.

Electronic commerce (EC) eliminates a number of national and global market entry barriers, such as distribution and marketing costs. Thomas Register, which provides manufacturers' directories for purchasing agents, now offers this service online also. Their revenues in 1996 from the Web site alone were $16 million (Bearden, Ingram, and LaForge 1998). A recent study by Honeycutt, Flaherty, and Benassi (1998) suggests that Web technology improved public relations and communication among suppliers, customers, and employees in three specific business marketing firms marketing welding, flooring, and metal products. The Web site also attracted new customer segments, feedback from customers on companies' products and customer services, as well as information on factors influencing their buying over the Internet. The authors also offer several guidelines to industrial marketers wishing to venture into cyberspace. Specific company examples should be brought in to expand the discussion of practices and issues of marketing business products and services online.

FASTER, BETTER, AND FRIENDLIER
PRODUCT DEVELOPMENT

Flexibility, integration, and velocity are the three words that, according to Weimer et al. (1992) sum up current business philosophy when it comes to manufacturing success and outmaneuvering competitors while reaping a profit as well. Nayak (1992) from Arthur D. Little also suggests that unless U.S. companies can accelerate their cycle of new product design development, Japanese and European companies will continue to come out with new technologies and improved products. The biggest obstacle to product introduction, according to Nayak (1992), is usually poor management, including bureaucratic cycles, pursuing sequential development processes, and trying to hit home runs with bigger and costlier innovations. For faster product development, Nayak suggests companies

1. aggressively pursue opportunities or incremental innovation,
2. support continuous improvement strategy structure,
3. plan thoroughly and keep the planning team lean,
4. pursue simultaneous engineering, and
5. make it a team effort reporting to a single senior executive.

Hutt and Speh's paper appropriately emphasizes the importance of fast-paced product development in business marketing, and the compression and experiential strategies for accelerating product development. The product development philosophy, however, needs to be broadened to include faster, better, and friendlier products. The instructor needs to discuss disadvantages of compressing developmental cycle time (e.g., cost overruns, product deficiencies, poor market information or testing, people stress), and how they can be avoided to bring out faster and better products, as well as how to eliminate bottlenecks and streamline processes for designing, developing, manufacturing, and marketing. Finally, firms need to implement ecological orientation in designing products, including the product packaging decisions. In the United States, there have been several enactments controlling the environmental safety standards as well as marketing practices (e.g., product design, packaging, disposal of chemicals, product labeling) that have harmful effects on the environment (Ottaman 1992). Marketers have been criticized for their products' effects on the environment. The design of some products, such as automobiles and trucks, clearly contributes to air pollution. Manufacturers of plastics and certain packaging materials that have an adverse effect on the environment have also been targeted by environmental groups.

Basically, those in the business-to-business sector are under pressure from their own customers and from pending legislation. They are overhauling their operations and asking for support to satisfy end users (Ottaman 1992). IBM corporation, for example, is now demanding alternatives to CFC-based cleaning agents. Sears, Roebuck & Company asked its 2,300 suppliers to cut packaging use by 25 percent through such tactics as lightweighting and recycled content. Home Depot hired the Scientific Certification System testing organization to review all manufacturers' environmental claims. The BMC, therefore, needs to incorporate ecological orientation, as several marketing decision areas are impacted. Product and packaging decisions seem affected the most, followed by physical distribution and industrial marketing promotion tools and strategies.

CROSS-FUNCTIONAL INTEGRATION

Webster (1984) stated that marketing in industrial (business) organizations is a responsibility of general management. By the very nature of the industrial customer's product and service requirements, all business functional areas must be involved in implementing the marketing concept philosophy. Building cross-functional relationships and marketing personnel partnering with other functional areas in the organization, therefore, continue to be key in integrating structural arrangement (Bondra and Davis 1996) to produce superior values. A separate session might be devoted to this subject matter in the BMC, including the mechanisms that are available to establish cross-functional connections (e.g., multifunctional teams), issues of composition, performance measurement, motivation of team members, and how to integrate the multifunctional teams in the marketing process, as well as how to resolve interdepartmental and within-team marketing conflicts. A practitioner's point of view should be brought in on these issues. Because of the increasing incidence and involvement of multifunction teams in selecting vendors (or customers) and maintaining closer working relationships, implementing a company's strategic alliance and/or outsourcing strategy with external business partners, and managing customer services strategy locally, nationally, globally, and on the Internet, the team needs training in two areas. First, since within-organization and interorganizational conflicts among team members are inevitable, expertise in selecting or avoiding specific methods and mechanisms of conflict management is essential. Thomas's (1976) conflict management orientations—avoidance, competition, domination, accommodation, and collaboration—would provide useful insights for team members. Second, the team members need to be empowered to make timely decisions as necessary to maintain efficiency and effectiveness in the working relationships with customers, vendors, and strategic alliance partners. Real-life examples of conflicts and empowerment scenarios depicting a variety of marketing disagreements can be brought in, either through case method or by inviting guest speakers in the class.

CONCLUDING SUMMARY

The past several years have witnessed several strategic trends and philosophies that have redefined business-to-business marketing strategies. Many of the business marketers have yet to realign their thinking to address opportunities and threats in the changing marketing environments. Complementing Hutt and Speh's contributions on the trends in business marketing practice, and their impact on business marketing education, this paper further examined these trends and slightly broadened their labels. These business trends are reviewed to convey the dynamic nature of changing values in the business-to-business marketing field. Their relevance is linked to business marketing decisions as well as education, including recommendations of what and how these trends might be covered in the business marketing course, when appropriate.

REFERENCES

Barnes, John W. and Edwin R. Stafford (1993). "Strategic Alliance Partner Selection: When Organizational Cultures Clash." *American Marketing Association* (Summer), 424-432.

Bearden, William O., Thomas N. Ingram, and Raymond W. LaForge (1998). *Marketing: Principles and Perspectives.* Massachusetts: Irwin McGraw-Hill, Inc.

Berman, Barry (1996). *Marketing Channels*. New York: John Wiley and Sons, Inc.

Bondra, James C. and Tim R. V. Davis (1996). "Marketing's Role in Cross-Functional Information Management." *Industrial Marketing Management Systems* 25, 181-195.

Bowersoy, Donald J. (1996). "The Strategic Benefits of Logistics Alliances." *Harvard Business Review* (July-August), 36-45.

Butaney, Gul T., Donald Chand, and Renuka Chand (1994). "Examining the Role of Innovation Attributes in Positive Opinion Leadership." *Journal of Management Systems* (6), 87-103.

Harbinson, John R. and Peter Pekar Jr. (1993). *A Practical Guide to Alliances: Leapfrogging the Learning Curve*. Los Angeles, CA: Booz-Allen and Hamilton, Inc.

Honeycutt, Earl D. Jr., Teresa B. Flaherty, and Ken Benassi (1998). "Marketing Industrial Products on the Internet." *Industrial Marketing Management*, 27, 63-72.

Nayak, P. Ranganathan (1992). *Boardroom Reports* (April), 87.

Ottaman, Jacquelyn A. (1992). "Industry's Response to Green Consumerism." *Journal of Business Strategy* (July-August), 3-7.

Sheth, Jagdish N. and Arun Sharma (1997). *Industrial Marketing Management*, 26, 91-100.

Thomas, Kenneth W. (1976). In *Conflict and Conflict Management Handbook of Industrial and Organizational Psychology*, Marwin D. Dunnette, ed. Chicago: Rand-McNally, 889-935.

Vavra, Terry G. (1992). *Aftermarketing—How to Keep Customers for Life Through Relationship Marketing*. New York: Irwin Publishers.

Webster, Frederick E. Jr. (1984). *Industrial Marketing Strategy*. New York: John Wiley and Sons, Inc.

Weimer, George, Bernie Kill, James Manji, and Beverly Beckert (1992). *Integrated Manufacturing*, IM 2-IM 16.

Linking Content to Practice in the Business Marketing Course: A Reply to Commentary

Michael D. Hutt
Thomas W. Speh

Gul Butaney provides thoughtful and constructive commentary on our paper that affirms our core position that the business marketing course provides an ideal platform for exposing students to fundamental changes that are occurring in business practice. Moreover, the commentary lends support to the particular trends in practice that we chose as most deserving of special coverage in the business marketing course. To this end, Butaney explores these trends in business practice by using more broadly defined labels: strategic trends in purchasing and supplier relations management; relationship marketing; high-technology product marketing; faster, better, and friendlier product development; and cross-functional integration. The commentary complements our paper and contributes to the business marketing education literature by providing additional course content and design recommendations that respond to each of these trends.

STRATEGIC TRENDS IN PURCHASING

In many firms, purchasing strategy is becoming more closely tied to corporate strategy (Spekman, Stewart, and Johnston 1995). Organizations are focusing on core competencies and relying on key suppliers as a source for product and process technology to continuously improve performance. For the purchasing function, this reflects a shift away from a tactical perspective (for example, cost savings) to a more strategic orientation (for example, forging relationships with those suppliers which can enhance the value of the firm's offerings)

(Moncka and Trent 1995). As purchasing adopts a more strategic orientation, we endorse Butaney's position that the business marketing course should give careful attention to the reasons, motivations, and specific values that customer organizations seek in entering close working relationships with suppliers. To achieve this goal, the business marketing course should isolate the role of purchasing in the firm, explore the tools of analysis that purchasing managers employ (for example, value analysis and vendor analysis), examine the rich information environment that supports vendor evaluation, and assess the complex influence patterns that encircle organizational buying decisions. The commentary provides several valuable suggestions for bringing purchasing tools—such as electronic data interchange (EDI) systems—to life in the classroom.

RELATIONSHIP MARKETING

By demonstrating superior skills in managing relationships with key customers as well as with alliance partners, business marketers can create a competitive advantage. Butaney argues that a relationship marketing perspective provides the foundation for the business marketing course because relational issues surround nearly every element of strategy. We agree. To develop responsive and profitable relationship marketing strategies, special attention must be given to

1. segmenting the market,
2. selecting specific customers to target in each segment,
3. developing account-specific offerings,
4. implementing relationship strategies, and
5. evaluating relationship outcomes.

Consistent with Cespedes (1995), Butaney argues that successful relationship strategies place more emphasis on the firm's ability to generate timely market knowledge by individual customer account. Some valuable suggestions are offered for a dedicated class session on the design of customer service strategies and customer satisfaction measurement systems. We believe that these topics fit nicely into a course module that can be organized around the balanced scorecard (Kaplan and Norton 1996; Hutt and Speh 1998).

HIGH-TECHNOLOGY PRODUCT MARKETING

The business marketing course can fill a gap in the marketing curriculum by examining the unique challenges and opportunities that high-technology products and markets present. Butaney outlines several areas where the Internet is assuming a more prominent role in business marketing programs. We would add a wealth of other content areas where Internet-based applications and strategies might be incorporated into the course. These applications include the use of the Internet for competitive analysis, market research, postsale communications with customers, self-service technical support and customer training, as well as marketing communications and public relations (Moore, Johnson, and Kippola 1998). Quelch and Klein (1996, p. 74) argue that a "company must assess who its diverse Web audiences are, what specific customer needs the medium will satisfy, and how its Internet presence will respond to a changing customer base, evolving customer needs, competitor actions, and technological developments."

FASTER, BETTER, AND FRIENDLIER PRODUCT DEVELOPMENT

Rather than providing a comprehensive inventory of topics that might be covered in the business marketing course, we chose instead to isolate important themes from practice—such as fast-cycle product development—and to explore the resulting implications for course design. As Butaney suggests, the new product development area also provides a vehicle for exploring the barriers to new product success as well as the complex ecological issues that emerge in the new product development process.

CROSS-FUNCTIONAL INTEGRATION

Managing conflict, promoting cooperation, and developing coordinated strategies are all fundamental to the business marketer's interdisciplinary role. By understanding the concerns and orientations of personnel from other functional areas, the business marketing manager is better equipped to forge effective cross-unit relationships and fulfill the needs of customers (Hutt and Speh 1998). Butaney suggests that the business marketing course should devote special attention to composition, performance measurement, and the forces that motivate and divide multifunctional teams. Such an approach has merit in illuminating the challenging interdisciplinary role that a marketing manager performs. In line with Butaney, we believe that managing relationships with other functions, with alliance partners, with channel members, and with customers constitutes a major component of the managerial work of a business marketing manager.

A CONCLUDING NOTE

A review of our paper and the related commentary reveals that fundamental topics such as supply chain management, organizational buying behavior, relationship marketing, cross-functional integration, and related strategy areas constitute the common ground of the business marketing course. A diverse portfolio of approaches can be employed by the instructor to bring these concepts to life and to expand the knowledge and skills of students. Butaney highlights the unique place that the business marketing course occupies within the business school curriculum and offers a rich set of suggestions for designing the undergraduate course.

REFERENCES

Cespedes, Frank V. (1995). *Concurrent Marketing: Integrating Product, Sales, and Service.* Boston: Harvard Business School Press, 14-18.

Hutt, Michael D. and Thomas W. Speh (1998). *Business Marketing Management: A Strategic View of Industrial and Organizational Markets,* Six Edition. Fort Worth, TX: The Dryden Press.

Kaplan, Robert S. and David P. Norton (1996). *The Balanced Scorecard: Translating Strategy into Action.* Boston: Harvard Business School Press.

Moncka, Robert M. and Robert J. Trent (1995). *Purchasing and Sourcing Strategy: Trends and Implications.* Tempe, AZ: Center for Advanced Purchasing Studies, 69-71.

Moore, Geoffrey A., Paul Johnson, and Tom Kippola (1998). *The Gorilla Game: The Investor's Guide to Picking Winners in High Technology.* New York: HarperCollins.

Quelch, John A. and Lisa R. Klein (1996). "The Internet and International Marketing." *Sloan Management Review* 37(Spring), 60-75.

Spekman, Robert E., David W. Stewart, and Wesley J. Johnston (1995). "An Empirical Investigation of the Organizational Buyer's Strategic and Tactical Roles." *Journal of Business-to-Business Marketing* 2(4), 37-63.

PART V:
ALTERNATIVE TECHNOLOGIES

Technology in the Classroom: Teaching Business Marketing in the Twenty-First Century

Richard P. Vlosky
David T. Wilson

INTRODUCTION

Since the invention of writing there has been a continued passing parade of new technologies, each of which it is claimed has the potential to "revolutionize learning." These technologies are released in a flurry of excitement but often end in disappointment when evaluation studies fail to reveal the much-anticipated improvement in learning (Alexander 1995). During the past decade and a half, American higher education has invested about $70 billion in information technology goods and services, as much as $20 billion of which has gone to the support of teaching and learning (Geoghegan 1994). But despite the size of this investment in instructional technology, numerous examples of innovative and successful instructional applications, and a growing comfort level with technology among both faculty and students, instructional technology has not been widely adopted by faculty, nor has it become deeply integrated into curricula. By some estimates, no more than 5 percent of faculty utilize information technology in their teaching as anything more than a "high-tech" substitute for blackboard and chalk, overhead projectors, and photocopied handouts (Geoghegan 1994). Alexander (1995) cites a review of a number of studies by Clark (1983) that questioned the methods of instruction used in the computer-based instruction (CBI) "experiments" and suggested that CBI authors have simply computerized methods of programmed instruction rather than capitalizing on the possible "added value" of using computers. It seems surprisingly obvious that there is no reason to expect the quality of learning to improve if we simply transfer a learning experience from one medium to another (Alexander 1995).

In spite of past disappointments, the ramifications of adopting technology into instructional settings can be significant and far-reaching. As a direct result of technology implementation, methods of information delivery by instructors and reception by students in the future will be very different from traditional methods employed today. From a practical standpoint from the educator's perspective, Green and Gilbert (1995) suggest that technology in the classroom will allow the same number of faculty to teach more students at the current level of learning or allow campuses to serve the same number of students with fewer faculty.

The purpose of this paper is to review current technology-driven instructional methods and prognosticate how teaching marketing will be redefined at the university level in the future. The essay addresses issues and comments relative to marketing instruction in general. Educators can apply these technologies to the teaching of both consumer and business-to-business marketing.

WHY USE TECHNOLOGY IN THE CLASSROOM?

It is no secret that computer-based instructional technology is evolving at a rapid pace, with new applications being developed and adapted almost daily. In discussing learning using different media, Kozma (1989) states that computers help students connect the real worlds to the symbols that are used to represent them in the classroom. Computers can be used to create microworlds, or as simulations of real-world events, that facilitate learning nonconcrete ideas or building complex mental models of knowledge domains.

Ellis (1996) cites Schmidt (1996) who found that since the early 1980s educators have been pressured to provide students with skills, knowledge, and attitudes needed to be successful in a technological workplace and globally competitive marketplace. In the Secretary of Labor's Commission on Achieving Necessary Skills (SCANS) Report, the commission identified "using technology" as one of the critical competencies required to be competitive in a global economy. Examples of such emerging technologies are multimedia "virtual classrooms," the use of sophisticated presentation software, use of the World Wide Web for research and data collection, and Internet-facilitated distance learning. This world of computer learning is relatively uncharted to date.

According to Robert Robicheaux (1996), marketing students need to develop a differential advantage in order to compete after graduation. He believes that technology is going to be this differentiator creating a new type of student that is prepared to function effectively. A study of technology use by marketing students (Miller and Mangold 1996) suggests that students consider these technology-based sources to be important to business professionals but attach a relatively low rating to their skills at acquiring information through these sources. In an unpublished study of use of technology by marketing students at the Pennsylvania State University and Louisiana State University (Wilson and Vlosky, no date), it was found that 43 percent of the students did not use computers in their marketing courses, and 57 percent of respondents said that technology was used in the classroom for less than one-quarter of the marketing courses they had taken. In many instances, the only technology used was the replacement of acetate overheads with PowerPoint slides.

The possibilities of what can be taught through the aid of computers and multimedia approaches are seemingly endless and very rapidly developing (Vickery 1996). However, whether or not technology in the classroom results in improved learning and test scores remains to be seen. For example, Miller and Mangold cite Reisman (1993) who reported that the use of multimedia approaches in a computer applications course resulted in higher test scores than more traditional approaches, while Coye and Stonebraker (1994) reported no such improvement in an operations management course.

One good reason to use technology in the classroom is because students are demanding it. In the study by Wilson and Vlosky (no date), nearly three-fourths of marketing students surveyed felt that it was important to use technology in the teaching of marketing. However, on the downside, 31 percent felt that the use of technologies was ineffective in their learning of marketing. The study identified a potential gap, at least at the two universities, between student demand and education supply of technology in the marketing classroom.

ADVANCED TECHNOLOGY CLASSROOMS

Many universities have made a commitment and investment for the hardware, software, and support necessary to offer interactive multimedia educational instruction to marketing students. As the name implies, interactive multimedia programs allow students to become more involved in the learning process by fostering interaction with other students and the instructor (Tippins and Su 1996). Instead of passively listening to a lecture or reading a textbook, students using interactive multimedia are given some control in deciding the speed and direction of the learning process (Davies 1995).

One example of a multimedia learning application is at the School of Business at Indiana University in Bloomington. A variety of technology has been installed in several classrooms so that faculty can use the latest software, incorporate electronic presentations into their teaching, present video, and/or connect to the Internet. Technology in their high-tech classrooms includes computers, video equipment, CD-ROMs, VCRs, laser disc players, document cameras, and audiotape players. Capabilities in these rooms include networking, digital/video projection, and enhanced lighting. Technology services, with support from electronics, maintains these classrooms and provides training about how to use the technology. Each of these classrooms is networked to the School of Business Classrooms local area network (LAN) with a complete array of software available. Instructional support services also can help faculty get ideas about how to effectively incorporate the technology available in these classrooms into their instruction (Anonymous 1996a).

An integral component of the multimedia learning environment is the use of interactive CD-ROM. CD-ROM discs can store over 600 megabytes of information (one megabyte = one million characters). In addition to storing text, the CD-ROM is also capable of storing audio and visual graphics. Because of its speed and storage capacity, CD-ROM has become an ideal storage medium for interactive multimedia programs (Tippins and Su 1996). In describing benefits of interactive CD-ROM, Tippins and Su (1996) state that while textbooks or class lectures are usually rigidly structured, CD-ROM-based learning tools possess very few limiting restrictions. Students are able to branch off in various directions, learning as they venture through each program. By being able to move through different topics at a comfortable pace, students get the added benefit of not having to move on to new material until they are comfortable with the current task at hand. In addition, they believe that CD-ROM allows for more student interaction. Whether in small groups or as a class, CD-ROM lessons encourage students to participate and discuss among themselves how best to proceed through the lesson. Students find that, in a team setting, they are able to work through problems and make decisions more efficiently.

A number of integrated marketing courses that use both textbooks and CD-ROM have been developed. At Louisiana State University, some sections of the introductory marketing course are being offered using this format. A study is under way to evaluate the relative effectiveness of using CD-ROM only, textbooks only, and a combination of CD-ROM and textbooks in the teaching of marketing.

Van Winkle (1996) cautions that a number of practical hurdles have to be overcome before multimedia courses can be successfully implemented and presented in the classroom. Considerations of infrastructure, equipment, personnel, and pedagogy need to be taken into account early in the planning stages of any single or coordinated multimedia teaching effort.

INTEGRATED SOFTWARE

Integrated software packages, such as Microsoft Office or Lotus SmartSuite typically include a word processor, spreadsheet program, database, and communications in one low-cost package. With an integrated software package, teachers have a "one-stop" solution to a majority of their computing needs, such as writing lesson plans, tests, electronic grade books, student databases, and remote computer dial-up. Presentation software packages, such as Microsoft PowerPoint or Lotus Freelance Plus, allow teachers and students to create dazzling overhead slide shows, electronic screen shows, and 35 mm slide packages. Integrating visually exciting visual aids into platform instruction helps get and keep students' attention. Desktop publishing software, such as Microsoft Publisher, gives teachers the ability to create brochures, newsletters, custom textbooks, and other educational products that are of professional quality.

THE INTERNET AND MARKETING EDUCATION

The Internet offers marketing instructors and students the opportunity to communicate and exchange information nationally and internationally. Although only a handful of online courses are currently available over the Internet, the number is expected to increase rapidly in the next few years (Service 1994). Indeed, educators and publishers have started to worry about a time when the Internet might become like public-access cable television, clogged with programs and courses that are mediocre or, even worse, filled with inaccuracies. "Quality control is really important, especially in science," says James Lichtenberg, vice president of the Association of American Publishers. Because publishers have traditionally played that role, Lichtenberg predicts that they will move into online course distribution as the field grows (Service 1994).

Internet communication can facilitate many learning opportunities for marketing students. In one example, a Purdue University pilot study instituted in the spring of 1996 had students in a marketing principles course augment textbook instruction with the Internet and e-mail (Seibert 1996). The Internet was used to access course-specific information (syllabus, announcements, handouts, and assignments) and general information to complete assignments. E-mail was used for communication with the instructor and for course announcement distribution. Students in this pilot program found that the Internet and e-mail could be used to gather marketing intelligence from around the world and seek out information that may not be published. In the two short years since that pilot study, the use of e-mail and other Internet functions in marketing instruction has become commonplace. Most marketing curricula include some element of Internet interaction, including data acquisition, market research, and collaborative research projects. Table 18 conveys a small sample of the many opportunities that exist for Internet-supported marketing instruction.

Distance learning deserves particular mention, as this dimension of education can significantly expand the reach and level of learning opportunity to a wide population of potential students. The following are ten advantages of using distance education and Internet courses in curricula (Anonymous 1996b):

1. You can serve students anywhere—remote or rural areas where students do not have a community college or university nearby.
2. You can teach courses that normally could not be taught at a specific institution because of the lack of a qualified instructor.
3. The student becomes an "active" learner rather than a "passive" learner.
4. This technology will empower learners to be lifelong masters of their learning.
5. The Internet enables the teacher's role to shift from that of a "knowledge dispenser" to a "learning facilitator."
6. The Internet will liberate students and instructors to explore previously untapped worlds of information both inside and outside traditional classroom walls.
7. Learning will become more interactive; therefore it will become more relevant and stimulating.
8. With the use of the Internet, technology will become a vehicle for widespread educational reform.
9. Parents, community members, businesspeople, and other educational institutions will be more closely connected with learners, teachers, and the entire educational process.
10. Because this is self-directed learning, students can work at their own pace and their own schedule.

THE WORLD WIDE WEB

If the Internet global network is akin to a sanctum of information and commerce, the World Wide Web is the means to enter this domain. The World Wide Web, also known as WWW or just the Web, is a network of servers, "talking across the Internet," that know how to display text and graphic information (Vlosky and Gazo 1996). Much of the Internet's growth can be attributed to the proliferation of Internet access programs called browsers, such as Netscape Communicator and Microsoft Internet Explorer. Capable of displaying formatted text, graphics, and links to other WWW sites, a Web home page provides the most visual presence possible on the Internet. The

TABLE 18. Internet-Supported Marketing Instructional Activities

Type of Instruction	Description
Links to Corporate Sponsors and Partners	Would interact with students in an electronic mentoring role (cyber mentors)
	Answer general questions in the context of classroom activities
	Technologies: e-mail, WWW, two-way video/audio links
Distance Learning	Wide-band access to students' homes
	Interact with professors at host institution and at other institutions
	Take tests interactively
	Submit papers electronically
Student/Faculty Special Marketing Interest Groups	Set up mailing lists
	Encourage dialogue with others in the field of interest
	Exchange of ideas
Cross-Regional/National Class-room Project Teams	Collaborate with professors so students can collaborate across universities
	Electronic presentations
	Linked via WWW, e-mail

WWW, which has only been in existence since 1992, offers the benefits of the "information superhighway" with its protocols and client-server technology and takes advantage of the global telecommunications infrastructure that is already in place (Abate 1993). The WWW presents the first tangible example of the world of the future, with information just a click away and low barriers to entry for information providers. World Wide Web home pages on the Internet can generate substantial customer interest for companies and general interest for researchers.

The challenge for educational developers is to use this knowledge of learning, together with an understanding of the features of the WWW, to design learning experiences that promote a deep approach to learning so that "what" students learn is a deep understanding of the subject content, the ability to analyze and synthesize data and information, and the development of creative thinking and good communication skills (Alexander 1995). With this proviso in mind, the WWW offers a number of learning opportunities for marketing students. Areas that will be dramatically changed with WWW technology include the conveyance of information about individuals, classroom environments, and research efforts.

CHALLENGES AND SUCCESS

Although the need to adopt technology into the classroom environment is exceedingly clear for some educators, others are not embracing these approaches for a number of reasons. The problem is that only a very small proportion of faculty are actively developing or using such applications, and that once developed, they rarely find their way beyond the individuals or teams whose innovative efforts brought them into existence in the first place. The vast majority never reaches more than a tiny handful of "mainstream" teaching faculty (Geoghegan 1994). For many, the application of technology in the classroom constitutes a dramatic departure from teaching platforms that have been used forever. The transition to technology is often too overwhelming for faculty. In a conversation with the author, a professor said that he could not wait to retire so he did not have to learn to use computers to help him teach.

In a study commissioned by the Learning and Technology Committee of the Further Education Funding Council, United Kingdom, it was found that successful integration of educational technology into the curriculum in order to maximize learning gains needs careful planning, supported by teachers who are confident in the potential that such facilities offer (Smith 1994). The study indicated that, at present, there is a lack of strategic planning which takes account of the use of technology to support teaching and the delivery of curricula. Existing computing facilities were not found to be utilized to their maximum potential, as teachers lack experience in using technology to deliver the curricula and there are few teaching and learning models to draw on.

One possible solution to this problem is to departmentally develop and support a structured, and perhaps required, technology training and development program for faculty. This program would involve hands-on training and ongoing technical support administered by trained technology-based educational facilitators.

To expand on comments made by Hoskinson (no date), we offer some guidance for instructors who wish to employ technology in the classroom. First, the instructor needs to be technically proficient in the system used in teaching. This can be as simple as knowing how to "point and click" icons or as complicated as audio/video real-time linkages. Regardless of application, only current technology should be used. In addition, an analysis should be conducted to identify appropriate applications of technology and gaps in student needs relative to capabilities. Maximize available time by teaching students only those tasks which are critical to being a functional, "computer-literate" user and those which support course objectives. Teach computer usage as a tool to accomplish a specific task.

Boettcher (1996) points out that life cycle funding is another critical success factor for effective technology-based instruction. Implementing technology requires funding for start-up as well as maintenance. Funding also needs to include support personnel, an often overlooked part of long-term maintenance. Constant interruptions in service are not workable, as faculty generally do not have the expertise or time to maintain equipment.

SUMMARY

Ellis (1996) cites the Business Education Forum Policy Statement Number 53 (McDowell 1993) that states "business educators must review their instructional goals and strategies in light of advances in technology to ensure that identified student outcomes encompass that technological skills need today and in the future."

To quote Judith Boettcher (1996):

> Providing technology classrooms on our campuses today means thinking substantively about the intersection of teaching and learning processes with the capabilities of information technologies. When you consider the infrastructure and organizational issues surrounding this intersection of teaching and technology, you find that implementing technology classrooms is not for the faint of heart; indeed, it takes deep courage.

REFERENCES

Abate, Tom (1993). "Apple Plans New On-Line Service." *The San Francisco Examiner,* December 16.

Alexander, Shirley (1995). "Teaching and Learning on the World Wide Web." Institute for Interactive Learning, University of Technology, Sydney, Australia. <http://www.scu.edu.au/ausweb95/naDers/education2/alexander/>.

Anonymous (1996a). "Advanced Technology Classrooms." Indiana University, Bloomington, Indiana. <http://www.bus.indiana.edu/isweb/classtec/clastech.htm>.

Anonymous (1996b). "Conference Registration Materials. Emerging Technologies for Educators. Office Systems Technology." Pitt Community College, Greenville, North Carolina. November 1, 1996. <http://nemesis.pitt.co.nc.us/pb/Advant. htm>.

Boettcher, Judith V. (1996). "Technology Classrooms, Teaching, and Tigers." For Faculty. V.1.9:10-12.

Clark, R. E. (1983). "Reconsidering Research on Learning from Media." *Review of Educational Research* 4, 445-459.

Coye, Ray W. and Peter W. Stonebraker (1994). "The Effectiveness of Personal Computers in Operations Management Education." *International Journal of Operations and Production Management,* 35-46.

Ellis, Richard S. (1996). "Internet Applications in Marketing Education and Business Education." Department of Vocational and Adult Education, Auburn University. <http://www.duc.auburn.edu/~ellisrs>.

Geoghegan, William H. (1994). *What Ever Happened to Instructional Technology? IBM Academic Consulting.* Paper presented at the 22nd Annual Conference of the International Business Schools Computing Association, Baltimore, MD, July 17-20. <http://w3.scale.uiuc.edu/scale/library/geoghegan/wpi.htm>.

Green, Kenneth C. and Steven W. Gilbert (1995). "Great Expectations: Content, Communications, Productivity, and the Role of Information Technology in Higher Education." *Change* (March/April), 8-18.

Hoskinson, Ronald A. (no date). "Technology: Teaching It and Using It As a Teaching Tool." <http://users.aol.com/andyhask/techprep.html>.

Kozma, R. B. (1989). "Learning with Media." *Review of Educational Research* 61, 179-211.

McDowell, R. G. (1993). "Statement Number 53: This We Believe About the Role of Business Education in Technology." *Business Education Forum* (October), p. 12.

Miller, Fred and W. Glynn Mangold (1996). "Developing Information Technology Skills in the Marketing Curriculum." *Marketing Education Review* 6(1), 29-39.

Reisman, Sorel (1993). "A Comparative Study of Multimedia Personal Computing and Traditional Instruction in a Business School Curriculum." *Information Resources Management Journal* (Fall), 15-21.

Robicheaux, Robert (1996). Southern Marketing Association Presentation.

Schmidt, B. J. (1996). "Student Experiences in Business, Vocational, and Nonvocational Classes: The Instructional Environment." *Business Education Forum* (February), 14.

Seibert, Larry J. (1996). "Using the Net, E-Mail in Marketing Education." *Marketing Education* (August), 10-11.

Service, Robert F. (1994). "Assault on the Lesson Plan; Includes Related Article on Using the Internet for Curriculum Reform; Campus Innovations: Curricula," American Association for the Advancement of Science. *Science* 266 (5186), 856.

Smith, I. (1994). "Technology and Learning in Further Education." National Council for Educational Technology, Coventry, England. <http://ncet.csv.warwick.ac.ukWWW/projects/tech-learn/summary.html>.

Tippins, Michael J. and Wanru Su (1996). "Preparing Students for the Marketplace: An Investigation of the Potential Uses of Multimedia CD-ROM." *Proceedings of the American Marketing Association Summer Educators Conference.*

Van Winkle, Barrik (1996). "Video for Classroom Multimedia Instruction." Syllabus, 10-11.

Vickery: <http://www.largnet.uwo.ca/news/OR_apr95/BenefitsofMM.html>.

Vlosky, R. P. and Rado Gazo (1996). "The Internet and the Forest Products Community: The Role of the Forest Products Society." *Forest Products Journal* 46, 19-26.

Wilson, David T. and Richard P. Vlosky (no date). "Technology Applications in the Marketing Classroom: A Study of Two Universities." Unpublished study.

Technology in the Business Marketing Classroom: A Commentary

Carlos M. Rodriguez

The authors of the previous paper bring to marketing educators the opportunity to analyze and evaluate the positive impact of technology in education and learning. The central statement is that instructional technology has not been widely adopted and integrated into the marketing curriculum. The purpose of their work is to review current technology-driven instructional methods and project the role of technology in teaching marketing in the future. The paper discusses the alternative educational technologies available as advanced technology classroom (ATC) developed initially by IBM, integrated software, the Internet (WWW), and distance learning to enhance the learning experience. However, it falls short in connecting how these technologies may be used to enhance the learning experience as a process.

Instructional technologies may be used as delivery systems or as enhancing learning mediators. Ronchetto et al. (1992) suggest that multimedia technology may be used as delivery systems to accomplish a learning objective. Once learning outcomes are defined, the learning process is a function of the learning environment, teaching method, and student learning style (Frontezak 1990). Student learning and study styles, methods of instruction, and educational objectives are components of the learning process (Rumelhart and Norman 1981). Thus, there are several dimensions that define the learning experience and the design and adoption of technology in the classroom should be observed within a holistic view of learning as a process. These dimensions are student learning style, content area to deliver, learning outcomes, nature of skills to develop, and degree of intrinsic motivation to learn.

The identification of student learning styles is critical for the design and success of technology educational strategies. According to

Wynd and Bozman (1996) student learning style can be related to identifiable demographic traits. There are four types of learners: *accomodators,* who learn by concrete experience; *assimilators,* who use deductive reasoning to conceptualize; *convergers,* who focus on problems and apply ideas through active experimentation; and *divergers,* who develop ideas from concrete experience through reflective observation.

There is no agreement about what style characterizes marketing students. Biberman and Buchanana (1982) suggest that students in marketing tend to be divergers, compared to students in finance and economics who are accommodators, and students in accounting characterized by being convergers. Wynd and Bozman (1996) distinguish learning styles of traditional students from adult learners. Overall traditional students, being assimilators, learn better when exposed to experiences that involve reflective observation and abstract conceptualization. On the other hand, nontraditional students, being convergers, respond better when dealing with activities that include abstract conceptualization through active experimentation.

Marketing requires that students develop critical thinking capabilities. It emphasizes knowing and comprehension of concepts (as in a typical introductory marketing class), application skills (as in marketing research), and analysis, organization, synthesis, and evaluation (as in marketing strategy). This suggests that instructional technology should be seen as enhancing learning mediators and not simply as delivery systems (Ronchetto et al. 1992). Benefits derived from multimedia technologies are multisensory delivery (assimilation of information through multiple sensory channels: audio, visual, and kinesthetic), critical thinking (promotion of higher-level thinking skills), active learning (stimulation and involvement), motivation (make learning exciting and relevant), and individualization (self-paced learning) (Barron and Orwing 1995). Then, the question is, How can technology assist marketing instructors in adding value to the learning process?

The design of instructional methods must be based on sound learning principles (Rockman 1992; Clark 1989). Technology should be organized around the level of thinking, questioning, and learning. It is useful to develop application, analysis, and synthesis skills (Bloom's taxonomy). Students will enhance their application skills through using previously learned material to solve problems (software business application); analysis through identification of reasons, causes, and motives used to reach a conclusion; and inference or generalization. Synthesis is attained through skills to combine ideas, make predictions, and solve problems using different sources. Different media delivery systems, such as audiovisual aids, interactive computer simulations, and multimedia are more appropriate for certain learning styles (Ronchetto, Buckles, and Barath 1992).

Instructional technology strategies for the classroom should blend with a process that starts from a concrete experience which induces reflective observation. Later, students develop comprehension and analytical skills following the development of abstract conceptualization generally through processes that foster synthesis. Finally, students get involved in active experimentation in which models learned are continuously evaluated.

Educational systems should enhance the value creation and build on traditional instructional activities used in the classroom. For example, reflective observation is achieved through group discussions and participative question-answer sessions, while active experimentation can be attained through case analysis, fieldwork, and simulations. For instance, distance-learning environments and technology are adequate to develop problem-solving and critical-thinking skills and foster a multicultural education. Each learner must be able by himself or herself to analyze the problem, prepare a diagnostic, and implement a solution (Levenburg and Major 1998).

Ultimately, we as marketing instructors have to be educated in the new developments in educational technology and its benefits to enhance the learning process. Moreover, be alert not to overemphasize the use of multimedia instruction in the classroom. Still, there is tremendous need for one-to-one interpersonal encounters to build knowledge and skills in the marketing students of the twenty-first century. The challenge is to balance "high tech" with "high touch" (Barron and Orwig 1995).

REFERENCES

Barron, Ann E. and Gary W. Orwig (1995). *Teaching with New Technology in New Technologies for Education,* Second Edition. Colorado, pp. 1-10.

Clark, R. E. (1989). "Current Progress and Future Directions for Research in Instructional Technology." *Educational Technology Research and Development* 37(1), 57-66.

Frontezak, Nancy T. (1990). "The Role of Learning Styles in Marketing Education." In *1990 Western Marketing Educator's Association Conference Proceedings,* Jeffrey T. Doutt and Gary F. McKinnon, eds. Provo, UT: Brigham Young University Press, 57-62.

Levenburg, Nancy M. and Howard T. Major (1998). "Distance Education: Good for What?" *Marketing Educator* (Winter), 4-5.

Rockman, S. (1992). "Learning from Technologies: A Perspective on the Research Literature." U.S. Office of Technology Assessment, ERIC Document Reproduction Service, No. ED361499.

Ronchetto, John R., Tom A. Buckles, Robert M. Barath, and James Perry (1992). "Multimedia Delivery Systems: A Bridge Between Teaching Methods and Learning Styles." *Journal of Marketing Education* (Spring), 12-21.

Rumelhart, D.E. and D.A. Norman (1981). "Analogical Processes in Learning." In *Cognitive Skills and Their Acquisition,* J.R. Anderson, ed. Hillsdale, NJ: Lawrence Erlbaum.

Wynd, William R. and Carl S. Bozman (1996). "Student Learning Style: A Segmentation Strategy for Higher Education." *Journal of Education for Business* (March/April), 232-235.

Technology and Learning in the Classroom: A Reply to Commentary

Richard P. Vlosky
David T. Wilson

Professor Rodriguez makes an excellent point in reminding us of the importance of the "identification of student learning styles" in designing successful educational strategies. Educators are concerned about how students learn and we need to be flexible in accommodating different learning styles. Novak and Gowin (1984), in their book *Learning How to Learn,* state, "We are concerned with helping people learn to educate themselves. We want to help people get better control over the meanings that shape their lives. Educating is powerfully liberating: failures in educating are powerfully oppressive." As academics we all share their concern about helping our students to educate themselves and it is likely that we are quite competent in using traditional teaching methods to help our students educate themselves. The new technologies discussed in the paper present an opportunity to liberate the student learning process. However, we may have to adjust our role in the educating process if the learning is to be liberating for the student. The educational experience has four distinct elements: teacher, learner, curriculum, and climate (Schwab 1973, in Novak and Gowin 1984). Teachers set the educational agenda and decide what knowledge is present and how it will be presented. Learners may participate in agenda planning as in mastery learning where learners set their own goals in terms of knowledge acquisition (Bloom 1968, 1976). "Learners must choose to learn; learning is a responsibility that cannot be shared" (Novak and Gowin 1984). Teachers cannot force students to learn; we can only punish them for not learning what we teach. The knowledge, skills, and values that comprise the educational experience define the curriculum.

175

The educational climate defines how students and teachers define meaning in the curriculum. Forces such as enrollment policies that set class size, AACSB requirements, attitudes toward the importance of teaching, and college and department policies are examples of climate factors.

While we are probably comfortable with these elements in a traditional educational environment, we must adjust to the new demands and freedom created by the new technologies. We have an opportunity to increase meaningful learning over rote learning. David Ausubel (1968; Ausubel, Novak, and Hanesian 1978) defines meaningful learning as

> individuals must choose to relate new knowledge to relevant concepts and propositions they already know. In rote learning, on the other hand, new knowledge may be acquired simply by verbatim memorization and arbitrarily incorporated into a person's knowledge structure without interacting with what is already there.

Table 18 shows that learning can vary from being very meaningful to rote learning, and from reception learning, where information is provided directly to the learner to individual discovery learning, where the learner manages his or her own learning process by choosing the information to be learned.

Technology has arrived, but are we prepared to take advantage of the opportunity to redefine the educational process? Based upon a limited sample, the answer is no. Many faculties teach undergraduate and MBA courses using a combination of lectures and case material. Sometimes in a capstone course a simulation such as Markstrat is used. These technologies place us in the middle range on the meaningful-to-rote-learning dimension of Table 18 and in the reception-learning mode. On a good day we may hit the meaningful-learning level as we integrate the concepts for the students. Simulations likely fall into the midrange of discovery learning. Unfortunately, too many of our colleagues, present readers excepted, spend most of their time in the reception area somewhere in the middle between rote and meaningful learning. Our challenge is to help students move from rote learning to autonomous discovery learning and be accommodating to their preferred learning styles.

Examining how educational technology impacts the four elements helps define the changes required to fully utilize these technologies. Teachers set the agenda and selected the knowledge and its order of presentation because it was assumed that they had greater competence than the learner did. This assumption holds for the substantive aspects of the course but in courses using Internet and Web technology it is likely that many of the students have equal or better knowledge than the teacher about Internet and Web operation. The learner who is able to reach out on the Internet and Web is no longer dependent upon the teacher for all of the knowledge provided in the course. We teachers may have to share more of the agenda setting with the learner as the Web opens access to information equally for both the learner and the teacher.

New twenty-first century curricula may be products of interaction between learners and teachers. They may be less well defined in content, as one does not always know what the Web will yield over the semester. The process of how the course will proceed may place a heavier burden upon the learner to engage in more autonomous discovery learning. The climate is a major influence in the rate of integration of technology into curricula. The cost of providing computers, networks, and access determines the rate of adoption of technology. Even with a positive supportive environment, constrained resources make it very difficult to integrate technology into the learning process.

REFERENCES

Ausubel, David P. (1968). *Educational Psychology: A Cognitive View.* New York: Holt, Rinehart and Winston.

Ausubel, David P., Joseph D. Novak, and Helen Hanesian (1978). *Educational Psychology: A Cognitive View,* Second Edition. New York: Holt, Rinehart and Winston.

Bloom, Benjamin S. (1968). "Learning for Mastery." *UCLA Evaluation Comment* 1(2), 1.

Bloom, Benjamin S. (1976). *Human Characteristics and School Learning.* New York: McGraw-Hill.

Novak, Joseph D. and D. Bob Gowin (1984). *Learning How to Learn.* New York: University of Cambridge.

Schwab, J. (1973). "The Practical 3: Translation into Curriculum." *School Review* 81(4), 501-22.

PART VI:
BUSINESS MARKETING TEXTBOOKS

Business-to-Business Marketing Textbooks: A Comparative Review

Klaus Backhaus
Katrin Muehlfeld
Diana Okoye

INTRODUCTION

More than half the graduates of American business schools will work in firms that are active in business-to-business markets. Yet, some years ago, it was estimated that less than 6 percent of these graduates would take a course in business-to-business marketing[1] (Hlavacek 1980). With the recognition of industrial marketing as an important area of research and instruction in its own right, this situation has improved considerably since the early 1980s (see the impressive account of research activity on business marketing from 1978 to 1997 in the Reid and Plank 2000a review). Yet, a considerable proportion of graduates will still start working without having taken a course in business-to-business or industrial marketing. In acquiring the necessary knowledge finally on the job, they are then likely to fall back upon business-to-business textbooks at that point. For those who have taken part in a business-to-business marketing course, it is likely that a textbook will have shaped their understanding of business-to-business marketing: Even in this high-tech age, many teachers still heavily rely on a textbook to structure their course (Rich, Powers, and Powell 1988; Rugimbana and Patel 1996). One in two instructors uses a textbook as the basis for their business-to-business marketing courses (Narus and Anderson 1998), so textbooks remain

The authors thank Dr. David Lichtenthal and three anonymous *JBBM* reviewers for their helpful comments on an earlier version of this manuscript. This English version was translated and edited by Brian Bloch. The authors are also grateful to Dr. Bloch for his comments and suggestions relating to the clarity and precision of the text.

a prime component of instruction (Becker and Watts 1996; Tootelian, Bush, and Stern 1992)—and one that may influence student satisfaction with the course considerably and thus also course evaluations (Rich, Powers, and Powell 1988). Against this background, selecting the appropriate textbook on business-to-business marketing is a crucial issue for both practitioners and academics involved in teaching business-to-business marketing. In this paper, we focus on the academic side of the problem, although some practitioners may also find the assessment helpful. What follows relates to a comparative analysis of the leading business-to-business marketing texts in an attempt to answer the earlier question. This issue has not yet been addressed sufficiently in the literature, let alone to a comprehensive extent. For example, while representing a remarkable exception in this field, Rugimbana and Patel's work (1996), covers only three books (all on general marketing) and focuses on a single criterion (understandability).

THE SELECTION OF TEXTBOOKS FOR COMPARISON

A selection of seven textbooks forms the basis for the comparative analysis (see Table 19). The selection is orientated around the textbooks recommended in the business-to-business marketing section of the *Marketing Education Review* (1999), the *Industrial Marketing Practitioner* (1999), and a study of Narus and Anderson (1998).

An allocation of textbooks to *undergraduate* or *graduate* levels is not a priori considered in this investigation, because, first, no criteria for unambiguously placing the books in one or the other group could be established.[2] For instance, in the listing from the *Marketing Education Review,* the textbook of Hutt and Speh[3] is regarded as an undergraduate text, whereas in the study by Narus and Anderson (1998) it is considered the most-used book at the master's level, that is, in the graduate arena. Second, rejecting such an a priori distinction allows for arriving deductively at a clear differentiation of the books' different structures. However, we have made an a priori allocation to the literature for two other aspects: first, textbooks exclusively targeted for master's-level executive programs and, second, for doctoral programs are explicitly excluded, because of the significant differences between the various stated programs (Danneels and Lilien 1998; Narayandas, Rangan, and Zaltman 1998).

TABLE 19. Selection of Business-to-Business Marketing Textbooks for Comparison

Textbooks
Anderson, James C. and Narus, James A. (1999). *Business Market Management: Understanding, Creating, and Delivering Value.* Upper Saddle River, NJ: Prentice-Hall.
Bingham, Frank G. (1998). *Business Marketing Management,* Second Edition. Homewood, IL: NTC Business Books.
Brierty, Edward G., Eckles, Robert W., and Reeder, Robert R. (1998). *Business Marketing,* Third Edition. Upper Saddle River, NJ: Prentice-Hall.
Eckles, Robert W. (1990). *Business Marketing Management.* Upper Saddle River, NJ: Prentice-Hall.
Haas, Robert W. (1995). *Business Marketing: A Managerial Approach,* Sixth Edition. Cincinnati, OH: South-Western College Pub.
Hutt, Michael D. and Speh, Thomas W. (1998). *Business Marketing Management,* Sixth edition. Fort Worth: Dryden Press.
Webster, Frederick E. (1995). *Industrial Marketing Strategy,* Third Edition. New York: Wiley.

CRITERIA AND METHODOLOGY

The objectives of textbooks on business-to-business marketing, as formulated in the literature, form the basis for this study.

First, the fundamental objective of any textbook is to convey knowledge (Berry 1993; Wills 1982). Thus, the challenge is to cover a large range of the discipline at a state-of-the-art level (Jaffe 1997), and this applies to business-to-business marketing books as well. Lichtenthal and Butaney (1991) comment further on the importance of integrating the latest research findings and their application in business-to-business books. Second, above and beyond the pure transfer of knowledge, a business-to-business marketing textbook should promote the development of cognitive capabilities. These capabilities refer to the understanding and application of business-to-business marketing concepts and to creative and effective problem solving (Lichtenthal and Butaney 1991). Third, if used in a course, a textbook is arguably the core teaching instrument, sometimes complemented by additional materials as, e.g., case studies. Thus, it is necessary that a business-to-business marketing book provides the basic structure of a course as well as the basis for achieving the learning objectives (Lichtenthal and Butaney 1991; Narus and Anderson 1998). It should be designed in such a way as to allow students to learn as much as possible about the subject matter from the course (Rich, Powers, and Powell 1988). In the context of a course on business-to-business marketing, a textbook should thus contribute toward the development of a variety of capabilities: analysis, research, evaluation and critique, communication, synthesis and organization (Hutt and Speh 1998a; Lichtenthal and Butaney 1991; Rodriguez 1998).

However, this specific derivation of business-to-business marketing objectives requires augmentation through the use of more generally accepted principles for evaluating textbooks that could also be useful for business-to-business books. We therefore used a general evaluation approach: Bloom's (1956) taxonomy of educational objectives for the cognitive domain.[4] This taxonomy provides a classification scheme that is characterized by a hierarchical construction and theoretical grounding. The taxonomy of educational objectives for the cognitive domain was developed by thirty academics in order to eradicate vagueness in discussions relating to learning objectives and to create a theoretical framework for communication among experts. Its practical relevance has been documented in empirical evaluation and in the application of this taxonomy concept in management theory (e.g., Hampton, Krentler, and Martin 1993). The concept has been criticized in various aspects (for examples, see Furst 1981; Moore 1982; Paul 1985), but, with about 2,000 citations in the ERIC (Educational Resources Information Center) database alone, a vast amount of literature referring to or based on the taxonomy and recent studies still using it, the concept remains the prime framework for defining educational objectives (see, as examples, Anderson 1999; Clabaugh Jr., Forbes, and Clabaugh 1995; Guthrie 2000; Marzano 2001; Stearns and Crespy 1995; Sultana and Klecker 1999; Wentland 2000; Zabudsky 2000). The taxonomy has been used as the basis for empirical research undertaken, for instance, in the United States, Australia, or Turkey and has been applied in different educational settings, ranging from microbiology to professional selling, physics or fine arts. With respect to its impact on theoretical research, there have been numerous modifications, refinements, and general discussions (see Imrie 1995; King, Wood, and Mines 1990; Solman and Rosen 1986; Stuart and Burns 1984).

In terms of its meaning, it is important to stress that the taxonomy for the cognitive domain actually defines teaching intentions associated with the development of knowledge and intellect. The actual attainment of these capabilities, and hence the degree to which they are realized, may differ and lies largely in the responsibility of the student. This has implications for the operationalization of the taxonomy. For instance, in his work on stating behavioral objectives, Gronlund focuses on the actual outcome of the teaching/learning process, that is, in terms of actual student behavior (Gronlund 1970). By doing so, he provides statements for defining objectives in behavioral terms (e.g., "Describes the characteristics of a given historical period"; Gronlund 1970). Each statement for a specific learning outcome starts with a verb, by this indicating observable behavior. Our approach differs from Gronlund, as we do not focus on actual student behavior. Instead, we attempt to assess the degree to which the books in the analysis are appropriate material in relation to a given objective (from the taxonomy) that a teacher might have in mind. So what objectives might a teacher following Bloom's taxonomy have in mind?

Bloom's taxonomy identifies the following six fundamental cognitive abilities, which combine in hierarchical order all conceivable capabilities.

Basic Capabilities

1. *Knowledge* (level 1): rote memory of previously learned material
2. *Understanding* (level 2): involves translation of one level of abstraction to another; requires understanding of facts and principles to restate problems in own words or give examples

Skills

3. *Application* (level 3): use of learned material/principles on new problems
4. *Analysis* (level 4): recognition of unstated assumptions and logical fallacies in reasoning; distinction between facts and opinions
5. *Synthesis* (level 5): ability to form a hypothesis or theory of his or her own (new problem solution) from different aspects (often requires creativity and/or material from other disciplines)

6. *Evaluation* (level 6): ability to assess value of material at disposal for a given purpose; use of internal (consistency) and external (relevant standards) criteria to discuss the quality of the material

These capabilities include all those which were derived without a theoretical grounding, in the context of the learning objectives of business-to-business marketing textbooks. The previously formulated textbook goals need to be further operationalized so as to enable their implementation in practice. By so doing, not only all dimensions that define a textbook can be analyzed and compared but also the appropriate learning objectives for a text. Rugimbana and Patel (1996) point out that very few publications compare textbooks. Furthermore, in these publications, textbooks are compared only in terms of one criterion and without a methodologically sound derivation, but in a purely applied manner (as examples, see Cline 1972; Doane 1994; Spinks and Wells 1993). A comprehensive comparison of several textbooks on the basis of various criteria is not available in the literature. Therefore, criteria and methodology for this analysis need to be derived from the cognitive skills of Bloom's taxonomy. Despite the considerable impact this concept has exerted on the theory and practice of education during the past three decades, no conclusive and general operationalization of Bloom's six fundamental cognitive abilities as educational objectives has yet been undertaken (Clabaugh Jr., Forbes, and Clabaugh 1995; for examples, see Karns, Burton, and Martin 1983; Gronlund's work [1970] constitutes an exception but is not appropriate in our context, as explained earlier). An operationalization of the elements of Bloom's taxonomy is thus achieved in this paper by referring to various sources in the literature on marketing, marketing education, and education (e.g., from a study by Rich, Powers, and Powell 1988, resulting in guidelines for textbook satisfaction from a student perspective). In subsequently assessing the textbooks according to these criteria, it is important to note that a strong subjective element will inevitably remain—of this all readers should be aware as the authors are themselves.

Knowledge

The knowledge conveyed in a textbook can be compared on several dimensions. To start with, the *formal structure* of any text constitutes a purely quantitative, first-sight indicator in terms of amount of material covered and of the systematic order of discussed topics. In our case, it hence provides information on the extent to which the actual design of the books varies. Therefore, the net page area (i.e., total page area without case studies and references) with characters per page as a standard indicator (measure) for varying page formats (average number of characters of the first five normally formatted lines of each textbook, multiplied by the number of lines in the first full-text page of the book), the depth of subdivisions, and the use of various structuring modules are comparative bases.

The more content-oriented criterion of *approach* focuses on the selection and sequencing of the various themes. In the literature, mainly two approaches relevant to business-to-business marketing can be distinguished: First, the instrumentally oriented approach and, second, the marketing management approach (Backhaus 1997; Blotnicky 1991; Engelhardt and Witte 1990; Lamont and Friedman 1997; Smith and Robbins 1991). The conventional instrumental approach is characterized by the perspective that business-to-business marketing problems can be resolved through the instruments of product, price, distribution/placement, and communication/promotion ("four P's"). This approach has been extended to the marketing management approach that considers, in addition to the four instruments, the managerial functions of analysis, planning (strategic and operative), implementation, and control (Haas 1995; for a documentation of the relatedness between the two approaches, see, e.g., Smith and Robbins 1991). In order to facilitate identification of the marketing management approach in the comparison, the phases of the approach must be covered appropriately thematically. An allocation of the content of individual themes to the phases of the approach could not be found with respect to business-to-business marketing books. Consequently, specifying the nature of the content is based on Kotler's *Marketing Management* textbook (1997). The comparison of textbooks proceeds through an understanding of the structure of contents, based on the characteristics of the stated approaches.

A textbook, especially an introductory or general one, should cover a large percentage of all themes that are generally regarded as relevant for a particular teaching discipline (Kuhn 1970). Ray, Stallard, and Hunt (1994) suggest that, particularly in the case of undergraduates, a broad knowledge is appreciated by employers. Therefore, the *breadth of coverage* in the various books is compared. In order to make judgments, the themes that are considered in the literature as relevant for business-to-business marketing are compared with the lists generated from the textbooks. The studies of Narus and Anderson (1998) and Plank (1982) and recently a very thorough study by Reid and Plank (2000a) provide the academic perspective (Narus and Anderson; Reid and Plank) and practical perspective (Plank), and thus the foundation for this comparison. In detail, the topics depicted in Table 20 are considered.

In this manner, statements can be made as to which themes are handled in the textbooks, the spread in terms of thematic breadth, and the extent to which the themes are relevant to business-to-business marketing.

In addition to the themes that can generally be assumed to be regarded as relevant, Hutt and Speh (1998a) emphasize the need to consider *current themes* in a business-to-business marketing course, while Rich, Powers, and Powell (1988) state this in general terms for any marketing course. As the basis of a course, a textbook reflects the themes that can be covered in the course using the books' conceptual framework. The integration of current topics and up-to-date material therefore seems an important characteristic for the relevance of a textbook (Rich, Powers, and Powell 1988). This is important in terms of providing a conclusive, coherent, and at the same time up-to-date framework of the subject. Also, it allows students to relate more easily to their own daily business background (business news in the media, etc.), which also fosters the ability to learn from the course (see Henke et al. 1988 on increasing students' motivation to learn by bringing real-life marketing to the classroom). In order to assess the books, a (nonexclusive) list of topics considered as current in the literature was collected (see Table 21) and compared with those topics handled in the textbooks.[5] The list itself is derived partly from general literature (books or articles), which considers this issue, and partly from several commentaries on the Reid and Plank (2000a) study. The study itself being of a more retrospective character, the commentaries are clearly also concerned with current and future challenges of business marketing.

TABLE 20. General Themes in Business-to-Business Marketing

General Themes	Source
Differences between Business-to-Business and Consumer Marketing	Narus and Anderson (1998)
Organizational Buying and Purchase	Reid and Plank (2000a) (overall)
Purchasing and Materials Management	Narus and Anderson (1998); Plank (1982)
Buying Center and Related Models	Reid and Plank (2000a)
Value Assessment	Narus and Anderson (1998)
Relationship Marketing	Narus and Anderson (1998)
Strategic Alliances	Narus and Anderson (1998)
Business Marketing Intelligence System	Narus and Anderson (1998); Reid and Plank (2000a)
Analysis of Demand	Narus and Anderson (1998); Plank (1982)
Market Segmentation	Narus and Anderson (1998); Plank (1982)
Marketing Instruments (Product, Price, Placement, Promotion)	Narus and Anderson (1998); Plank (1982); Reid and Plank (2000a)
Implementation and Control	Narus and Anderson (1998)
Trends	
International Business-to-Business Marketing	Narus and Anderson (1998); Reid and Plank (2000a)
Business Service Marketing	Narus and Anderson (1998); Plank (1982)
Marketing Ethics	Reid and Plank (2000a)

Although not stated explicitly in the literature, there is an additional criterion that is pertinent to the comparison of textbooks. The fact that a topic is handled in a textbook gives no indication as to the extent and weighting accorded to this theme. Consequently, the criterion of *depth of treatment (of themes)* supplements our criteria catalog. The depth of the themes handled is compared by means of the marketing-mix instrument of price as an example, because this instrument is accorded the highest significance in both the Narus and Anderson and the Plank studies. In this respect, particular attention is paid to the models and concepts that are introduced, in order to draw conclusions as to the level of detail that is conveyed in the books.

Understanding

If a textbook is to be understood by students, it needs to fulfill the conditions for a successful transfer of knowledge. In the literature, *readability* is given as a basic and necessary, although not sufficient, criterion (Adelberg and Razek 1984; Cline 1972; Rugimbana and Patel 1996). Readability is regarded as a significant selection criterion and thus represents an appropriate basis for a first-sight comparison on understanding (Spinks and Wells 1993). A procedure for measurement discussed in the literature is a "readability index" based on average word and sentence length. The LIX, developed by Björnsson (1968) as "Läsbarhetsindex," is one such index and is regarded as superior to the others (Adelberg and Razek 1992). Applications can be found to English as well as French, German, or Greek texts (Anderson 1983). The formula is

$$LIX = S + W$$

TABLE 21. Current Themes in Business-to-Business Marketing

Current Themes	Source
Business Networks	Achrol (1997); Best (1990); Moore (1996); Spekman (2000)
Cross-Functional Relationships	O'Reilly (1994); Reid and Plank (2000a); Wright, Bitner, and Zeithaml (1994)
International Dimensions of Business-to-Business Marketing	Bea (1997); Gaugler (1994); Johnston and Borders (1998); Koch (1997); Narus and Anderson (1998)
High-Tech Marketing	Lamont and Friedman (1997); O'Reilly (1994)
Relationship Marketing	Lamont and Friedman (1997); Palmer (1994); Reid and Plank (2000b)
Value Assessment	Reid and Plank (2000b); Spekman (2000)

where S = average number of words; W = percentage of words with seven or more letters.

Both the LIX and other indices of this kind are heuristic procedures that are constructed through the addition of absolute numbers and percentages. Nonetheless, empirical investigations have shown that the LIX represents comprehensibility quite adequately (Adelberg and Razek 1992). Indices such as the LIX for measuring readability have been somewhat criticized for basing the assessment on formal characteristics of the text itself alone. Other aspects such as the reader's knowledge or the difficulty of the subject cannot be captured. Against this background, other procedures have been suggested in the literature to integrate a content dimension, such as the cloze procedure (see Rugimbana and Patel 1996; Taylor 1953). Certain words are eliminated from a text, thereby creating a completion text that has to be filled in by the respondents. The better they manage, the higher the text's score in terms of *understandability* (as opposed to readability) for this particular group. However, there is a major drawback to this index, leading to our preference of the LIX for this study: The method originates from the learning theory of communication that, among others, deals with redundancy in language. Low redundancy is interpreted essentially as low understandability by the cloze procedure (see Taylor 1954). Efficient and precise use of language, that, in the original text, may even enhance comprehensibility, is likely to produce a low score for readability in the cloze procedure. Moreover, a measurement of real understanding as suggested by the method is not possible since consistency of arguments as a crucial element in determining understanding cannot be included. Hence, explicitly restricting ourselves to measuring only readability seemed a more objective approach, although it certainly captures only a very basic prerequisite of deep understanding of a text.

The design of our study is oriented around that of Spinks and Wells (1993). Using ten sample passages from each book, we obtained a higher number per book than in the Spinks and Wells study. Furthermore, the LIX measures the number of letters, rather than the word length, based on the number of syllables, as for the index used by Spinks and Wells.

In a review of the first edition of *Industrial Marketing Management* by Hutt and Speh (1982), LaPlaca indicates that the comprehensibility of the textbook is well supported by clear graphics. The literature also concurs that *visualization* contributes to an understanding of the material (Moore 1993; Peeck 1993; Evans, Watson, and Willows 1987) and as a result to higher student satisfaction with the book and the course (Rich, Powers, and Powell 1988). Interrelated networks of knowledge can be portrayed more effectively through appropriate visualization than through verbal explanation (Eysenck and Keane 1990; Hunter, Crismore, and Person 1987; Winn 1987). The reason is that complex informational linkages can be absorbed simultaneously, whereas verbal explanations can be portrayed and absorbed only linearly. A very basic proposition associated with visualization in general is, however, that the degree of abstraction should match the complexity of the underlying ideas. The more difficult the latter, the simpler the visual object should be in terms of structure as well as coloring (unless colors are integral and a necessary part of the object) to allow for a stronger focus. Evidence suggests that colors may enhance realism of pictures, may direct attraction to some particular information, or may allow for clearer distinction of elements (Chute 1979). However, it is suggested in the literature that there is a limit to which the use of colors is helpful: some authors even suggest a maximum number of colors for symbolic objects (Stary 1997). In any case, studies suggest that in order to realize the full potential of spatial aids, students should receive training on how to use these aids most effectively (Moore 1993; Scevak and Moore 1990).

In order to evaluate the figures or graphics in textbooks, the investigative design of Evans, Watson, and Willows (1987) was used. Accordingly, on the quantitative level, the frequency of illustrations is determined and, qualitatively, the type and complexity of figures are considered. As types of figures, the following categories were used: tables, maps, inserted text (boxes), diagrams/graphs, and pictures (Evans, Watson, and Willows 1987). Tables are defined as general presentations of verbal or numerical data in lines and columns (Hunter, Crismore, and Pearson 1987). Inserted texts are passages containing verbal presentations (text), distinctively set apart from the floating text. Diagrams are visual depictions of pairs of values, symmetrically related, usually presented in a coordinate system (Kosslyn 1987). Maps are schematic geographic presentations using symbols (Kosslyn 1987). Given the fact that complex interrelationships, in particular, are most effectively and understandably explained by means of illustrations, figures that visualize structures are differentiated according to whether they depict linear or complex interrelationships. It is assumed that the latter, in particular, support understanding, since complex interrelationships are more difficult to depict by verbal presentation than are linear ones.

Applications

In terms of their subsequent careers in industry, it is decisively important that students be able to apply appropriately the theories they have learned (Lichtenthal and Butaney 1991). This means in the first place that they acquire a solid theoretical foundation that will allow them to move to higher levels in the cognitive hierarchy (Clabaugh Jr., Forbes, and Clabaugh 1995; Lamont and Friedman 1997). In a second step, however, the crucial objective is to convey theory in such a manner that students have at their disposal instruments capable of solving practical problems (Ames and Hlavacek 1984). Theory must be formulated accordingly, and, consequently, the *theory-practice connection* emerges as additional criteria in the investigation (Blotnicky 1991).

No explicit procedures for evaluating this criterion in textbooks are evident in the literature, although it is generally suggested that case studies can "bridge the gap between classroom training and real-world experiences" (Clabaugh Jr., Forbes, and Clabaugh 1995) (see also Lamb Jr. and Baker 1993). In this study, we regarded a textbook as theoretically oriented to the extent that various models and concepts are presented. The practical emphasis can be introduced through examples, demonstrations of applications, or more actively in case studies (Rich, Powers, and Powell 1988). The subject of "market segmentation" is particularly well suited to comparisons in this context. Its significance within the marketing curriculum is emphasized by Stearns and Crespy (1995). A study by Wind and Cardozo (1973) shows that market segmentation proceeds intuitively in practice, rather than on the basis of prevailing theoretical approaches. Furthermore, it has been established that the literature contains few practical demonstrations of segmentation processes (Webster 1995; Haas 1995), so that inclusion in a textbook would seem very helpful.

Analysis, Synthesis, and Evaluation

The development of *more complex capabilities* (especially analysis, synthesis, and evaluation) can be supported in a textbook by *appropriately formulated* case studies and test questions (Clabaugh Jr., Forbes, and Clabaugh 1995; Kelley and Gaedeke 1990; Krishnan and Porter 1998). The studies of Hampton, Krentler, and Martin (1993) and Karns, Burton, and Martin (1983) indicate that test questions in textbooks can contribute to the development of complex cognitive capabilities, but that the degree to which this applies is less than optimal in terms of generally accepted normative rules and the subjective perceptions of the instructor. Consequently, based on the named studies, test questions were investigated with the aid of the taxonomy (of educational objectives), in terms of their contribution toward the development of complex capabilities. The same procedure was applied to the case studies.

Table 22 provides an overview of the formulated goals and the criteria used in the investigation.

RESULTS

The comparison of textbooks culminated in the identification of three groups, with the first group containing five of seven books. The books of Anderson and Narus and Webster differ significantly from the others with respect to the investigated criteria and thus each form their own "group." Consequently, the results will be presented in terms of the identified groups.

FORMAL STRUCTURE

Textbook Group 1

The first set comprises the books of Bingham; Brierty, Eckles, and Reeder; Eckles; Haas; and finally Hutt and Speh. With respect to page coverage, it is confirmed that this varies between the textbook of Eckles, with 401 net pages and 3,741 characters per page, and that of Haas, with 644 net pages and 3,698 characters per page. Three to four subdivision levels and eighteen to twenty-two chapters seem typical,

TABLE 22. Comparative Criteria Derived from the Objectives of Books on Business-to-Business Marketing

Objectives of a Textbook	Formulation of the Goals Based on the Taxonomy of Educational Objectives	Derived Criteria	
Conveying Knowledge	Knowledge	1.	Formal structure
		2.	Approach
		3.	Themes: breadth, current topics, depth of treatment
Development of Cognitive Skills	Understanding	4.	Comprehensibility of the ext
		5.	Visual comprehensibility
	Application	6.	Theory-practice link
	Analysis, synthesis, evaluation	7.	Development of complex skills

although the text of Bingham has only fifteen chapters. The extensive use of supplementary material, above and beyond the main text, is conspicuous in all textbooks in this group. All contain chapter summaries, text questions, literature citations (endnotes and bibliography), as well as case studies. Furthermore, some have chapter outlines (Bingham; Brierty, Eckles, and Reeder), learning objectives (Bingham; Hutt and Speh), key terms (Bingham; Haas), practice exercises (Eckles; Hutt and Speh), and embedded texts (Bingham; Hutt and Speh).

Textbook Groups 2 and 3

The textbooks of Anderson and Narus as well as Webster have a smaller page area and a lower number of capital and structure modules than the books in Group 1. With 349 net pages and 2,710 characters, Webster's book has the smallest page area of all the books under consideration. The Anderson and Narus text has 414 net pages and 3,834 characters per page, and is thus also at the lower end of the area continuum. Both books have three subdivision levels and ten (respectively eleven) chapters. Both books have chapter summaries and literature references, but none of the other supplementary material mentioned in the previous paragraph, by that possibly encouraging teachers to select their own supplementary materials (case studies, etc.). The Anderson and Narus book also includes chapter outlines, a characteristic much appreciated by students, according to a study by Rich, Powers, and Powell (1988).

It can thus be confirmed that the textbooks in the second group have a quantitatively smaller area and lower number of chapters, which suggests a more limited and/or focused content. Furthermore, they have considerably fewer structuring modules, although examination of the first group shows that structuring models can be regarded as a general characteristic of business-to-business marketing textbooks.

APPROACH

Textbook Group 1

The investigation of the first group reveals that in the structuring of content, these textbooks use the theory-building phases of the marketing management approach. For all the books in this group, the basis for the following text is an introductory background chapter on business-to-business marketing. Accordingly, in the first part, the differences between business-to-business and consumer marketing are discussed in general terms and do not correspond to any particular phase of the marketing management approach.

After the introductory part, the five books under consideration deal with procurement (purchasing), information collection in business-to-business markets (business marketing intelligence system), market segmentation, and demand analysis. This coincides with the first phase of the marketing management process, that of analysis (Kotler 1997).

For three textbooks, after the analysis component, there is a chapter devoted to the second phase—strategic marketing planning (Brierty, Eckles, and Reeder; Eckels; Hutt and Speh). In Bingham's book, this topic is not treated explicitly.

Subsequently, the books consider the individual marketing-mix instruments. This is the operative part of the second phase—operative marketing planning (Kotler 1997).

The third and fourth phases in the marketing management approach deal with implementation and control (Kotler 1997). These thematic areas are handled in all the books apart from that of Bingham.

However, *implementation* is considered explicitly in a separate chapter only in Hutt and Speh's book.

It is therefore evident, that, apart from Bingham's text, the business-to-business marketing books under consideration, are structured according to the marketing management approach. They present their content with small deviations in the sequencing of phases within this approach. In Bingham's book, the phases of strategic planning and of implementation and control cannot be identified and the text follows the marketing management approach to only a limited extent.

Textbook Group 2

As in the case of the books discussed earlier, the first chapter deals with the differences between business-to-business and consumer marketing. The second and third chapters are devoted to organizational purchasing. Webster devotes the fourth chapter to various market segmentation strategies. The thematic areas of the second to fourth chapters correspond with the first phase of the marketing management approach. Nonetheless, there is no focus on the areas of information collection (business marketing intelligence systems), including market research and demand analysis. The following six chapters handle the marketing instruments and can thus be allocated to the broader topic of operative planning. Strategic marketing planning is considered in only the last chapter. This isolated treatment of strategic marketing planning strongly suggests that the marketing management approach is not an integral component of the overall presentation of business-to-business marketing. The approach is far more that of an instrumentally oriented approach, with a concluding chapter integrating the marketing management perspective. In order to understand the entire process of strategy development and implementation, the discussions of strategy development should have preceded the section on operative planning. Furthermore, the sections on information collection and demand analysis (parts of the first phase) and implementation (third phase) and control (fourth phase) are not considered. If one includes the detailed handling of the instruments, the approach in Webster's book can be considered essentially as instrumentally oriented.

Textbook Group 3

Although the textbook of Anderson and Narus is titled *Business Market Management,* their definition of *business market management* does not correspond to the marketing management approach in the sense of analysis, planning (strategic and operative), implementation, and control. Anderson and Narus define business market management as the "process of understanding, creating and delivering value to targeted business markets and customers" (p. 4). The Anderson and Narus book thus seems to follow a quite recent approach, because, until now, the value process has not been discussed in the literature as a specific textbook approach, although it has been established that "value assessment" exerts an influence on the development of marketing strategies (Anderson, Jain, and Chintagunta 1993). Sheth, Gardner, and Garrett (1988) actually claim that "the main purpose of marketing is to create and distribute values."

It is worth considering the extent to which the phases of the value approach correspond with those of the marketing management approach. Through the discussion of market segmentation, competitive analysis, and customer satisfaction, the first phase of the value approach conforms partly to the first phase of the marketing management approach. However, in this section, the second phase of the marketing management approach, *strategic marketing planning,* is also considered in detail. Anderson and Narus argue that their depiction of marketing-mix instruments does *not* follow the instrumentally oriented approach and that they integrate from a value perspective into the overall depiction, components of the marketing mix that they consider relevant (p. I). Accordingly, the third phase of the marketing management approach can be identified only to some extent. However, once again, it is clear that the actual structuring of content does not correspond to the traditional marketing management approach. The last phase of the value approach deals with relationship-marketing themes, which does not correspond with any phase of the marketing management approach. It is, therefore, clear that the phases of the value approach do not correspond with those of the marketing management approach. Thus, the Anderson and Narus book can be regarded as characterized by its own distinct approach: the value approach. It thus differs considerably from "traditional" business-to-business textbooks.

In addition, we analyzed the extent to which other approaches were used in all the textbooks considered. With the exception of Webster and Anderson and Narus, the authors indicate in the introduction, the need not only to develop different kinds of marketing strategies for different kinds of products, but also to demonstrate, with the aid of examples, what these strategies might look like. However, in the course of the books, the authors do not follow through on these thoughts, and they do not in fact develop specific marketing strategies. This confirms the statement made by Backhaus (1998) that no English-language textbook really uses a transaction-types approach for structuring (for a detailed example of this approach, see Backhaus 1999).

BREADTH OF THEMATIC PORTRAYAL AND INCLUSION OF CURRENT THEMES

Textbook Group 1

The textbooks in the first group cover 73 to 85 percent of all topics covered in the given business-to-business marketing textbooks (for detailed results of all criteria, see <http://www.uni-muenster/wiwi/ias>). The depiction and weighting of topics can thus be regarded as essentially comparable. Furthermore, for the most part, they cover the themes hinted at as relevant in the Narus and Anderson (1998) and in the Plank (1982) studies as well as in the Reid and Plank review (2000a). Bingham's book is an exception, because, as discussed earlier when considering his approach, some fully relevant thematic areas are neglected. The treatment of current themes reveals differences in depiction for the books of the first group.

Table 23 shows the variance among the books with respect to the handling of current topics. Hutt and Speh's book emerges as positive with regard to giving an overview of the subject, because, apart from the subject of "business networks," all the topics considered as current (see Table 20) are handled. Some topics even emerge as integral components of the overall treatment, because they recur at various points in the text, rather than being dealt with in one section only.

TABLE 23. Treatment of Current Themes in the Books of the First Group

Current Topic	Textbook	Location and Nature of Handling
International Dimensions of Business-to-Business Marketing	Bingham (1998)	Isolated treatment: 516+* onward Integrated in overall treatment: 19+, 301+, 336+, 465+, 503+
	Brierty, Eckles, and Reeder (1998)	Isolated treatment: 552+
	Eckles (1990)	Isolated treatment: 379+
	Haas (1995)	Isolated treatment: 64+
	Hutt and Speh (1998b)	Integrated in overall treatment: 60+, 284+, 338, 404+
High-Tech Marketing	Hutt and Speh (1998b)	Integrated in overall treatment: 243+, 264, 307+, 455
Relationship Marketing	Bingham (1998)	Isolated treatment: 45
	Hutt and Speh (1998b)	Isolated treatment: 505
Cross-Functional Relations	Hutt and Speh (1998b)	Isolated treatment: 249+
Business Networks	Haas (1998)	Isolated treatment: 199
Value Assessment	Bingham (1998)	Isolated treatment: 84+
	Eckles (1990)	Isolated treatment: 65+
	Hutt and Speh (1998b)	Isolated treatment: 6

*The numbers refer to pages and the + sign indicates that the subject is treated in a varying number of ensuing pages.

Textbook Group 2

With a value of 50 percent, Webster's textbook has a far more limited thematic coverage than the books in the first group. Investigation of the criterion "approach" already suggests that entire thematic areas considered relevant for a textbook on business-to-business marketing are missing.

In Webster's book, current themes play a relatively minor role. Value assessment and relationship marketing are emphasized. Although Webster regards the international dimension as a trend in business-to-business marketing, he devotes only three pages to this perspective (pp. 79, 130, 195).

Textbook Group 3

With a thematic coverage of 43 percent, Anderson and Narus's book has the most limited range of all the books under consideration. The reason lies in the approach selected, because only those themes which relate directly to the value concept are considered. The book's target clearly is the introduction of a new perspective.

The introductory section considers general issues on the subject of "value" with respect to business-to-business marketing. Furthermore, Anderson and Narus discuss the international dimension, working relations, and business networks. However, they do not deal with the differences between business-to-business and consumer marketing. Yet, this topic is of decisive importance, precisely because it is these differences that constitute the need for a specialized textbook on this subdiscipline of marketing.

Furthermore, only those components of the marketing mix which are regarded as relevant to value creation are discussed. Consequently, the instrument "price" is considered, with the focus on value-based pricing, and channel management as a component of the instrument "distribution." All other aspects of the marketing mix are consequently ignored. A similar situation prevails with respect to the depiction of organizational purchasing behavior. The section Adding Value to the Purchasing Process Through Buying Teams (p. 107) emphasizes the focus on value creation.

The lack of analysis of the procurement of information (including market research), demand analysis, marketing-mix instruments, as well as implementation and control may constitute some problems if the book is used as a basic textbook on business marketing. The missing themes are of interest both theoretically and in practice for business-to-business marketing (see, e.g., Plank 1982; Reid and Plank 2000a), because information provides a necessary basis for developing a marketing concept.

However, one should keep in mind that the Anderson and Narus book integrates a new perspective in the depiction of business-to-business marketing—and that this is the key target. Furthermore, current developments in business-to-business marketing play a decisive role. The considerations of "value" in relationship marketing, cross-functional relations, the international dimension, and business networks are not treated in isolation (as in the other books, if included at all) but are an integral component of the overall treatment. Hence, the book seems more appropriate for readers who already possess a basic knowledge in the field and want to focus on a special perspective (value) more in-depth.

DEPTH OF THEMATIC TREATMENT

Textbook Groups 1 and 2

With respect to depth of treatment (for detailed results, see <http://www.wiwi.uni-muenster.de/ias>), it is apparent that most authors cover all major themes relating to "price." However, there is variation in the level of detail. No author considers all determinants of pricing decisions and Webster ignores this area completely. The treatment of pricing strategies also varies considerably among the books. All authors present their own particular selection of strategies and none provides a complete discussion.

It is conspicuous that for "common pricing practices," Hutt and Speh consider only one area, whereas all other authors deal with the topic exhaustively. Bingham's book is the only one that deals with *international* pricing policy.

Textbook Group 3

The Anderson and Narus text is quite distinct from the others in its handling of price. Apart from the consideration of individual pricing strategies, all other areas (significance of pricing policy, objectives, determinants, common pricing strategies) are excluded. The emphasis is on value-based pricing in particular and is supplemented through the consideration of only two further "traditional" pricing strategies. Penetration and skimming strategies are treated as an integral component of "value-based pricing." This confirms the hypothesis that Anderson and Narus's book concentrates on the value perspective at the expense of neglecting some traditional thematic areas.

COMPREHENSIBILITY OF THE TEXTS

Table 24 presents the results of the LIX for all the books. Column two shows, in increasing rank order, the empirical LIX values for the various books. In order to make statements about readability, the textbooks are grouped into the LIX value groups suggested in the literature (Fry 1977; Anderson 1983). These groups correspond with the readability levels in column four. It should be noted that a higher value for the magnitude "associated level of readability" in column four means a *lower* level of comprehensibility in LIX terms.

The LIX values range over three levels of readability. For college textbooks, the appropriate level runs from 13 to 17 (Anderson 1983; Fry 1977). The style of writing used by Bingham; Brierty, Eckles, and Reeder; and Eckles reveals greater comprehensibility in terms of LIX than that of Anderson and Narus, which has a value two levels higher. However, given that it falls in the middle of the college-level range, it can be regarded as quite sufficiently comprehensible.

VISUAL COMPREHENSIBILITY

Table 25 presents the quantitative analysis of the graphics and figures used in the books.

An examination of the frequency of figures shows that three of the books (Brierty, Eckles, and Reeder; Eckles; Haas) have one figure on average for every double page. In the books of Anderson and Narus; Bingham; and Hutt and Speh, there is a figure on almost every third

TABLE 24. Comparison of the Criterion "Text Readability"

Textbook	LIX for the Books	Continuum of LIX Values	Associated Level of Readability
Eckles	56.7		
Brierty, Eckles, and Reeder	58.4	56-59	13
Bingham	58.9		
Webster	61.2		
Haas	62.5	60-63	14
Hutt and Speh	62.9		
Anderson and Narus	64.8	64-67	15

TABLE 25. Results of the Quantitative Analysis of the Criterion "Visual Comprehensibility"

	Number of Figures	Net Number of Pages	Frequency of Figures	Frequency of Pages Per Figure
Brierty, Eckles, and Reeder	251	578	0.43	2.30
Bingham	146	533	0.27	3.65
Eckles	185	401	0.46	2.17
Haas	330	644	0.51	1.95
Hutt and Speh	191	555	0.34	2.91
Anderson and Narus	145	414	0.35	2.86
Webster	39	349	0.11	8.95

page. On the other hand, Webster's book is an exception, with a figure on only every ninth page.

It is not easy to evaluate these results, because there are no indications in the literature as to what frequency of figures *aids* comprehensibility and above what frequency breaking the flow of text actually *reduces* comprehensibility. Thus, only through questioning instructors was it possible to confirm that figures do not necessarily promote understanding but may also be disruptive and distracting (Evans, Watson, and Willows 1987). With respect to Webster, one may pose the question as to whether, given the low frequency of the figures, the potential of figures to aid understanding of the material presented is fully exploited by Webster.

For the remaining texts, it could be established that figures are manifest with a significantly higher frequency, which, as indicated earlier, could also reduce understanding through constantly interrupting the flow of the text. There is, therefore, something of a trade-off in terms of figure usage.

Nonetheless, various types of figures aid understanding to varying degrees, so that different forms will be considered. Figures can present the simultaneous dimension of complex interactions (relationships) better than verbal explanations. Consequently, the visualization of complex interactions is regarded as contributing to a higher level of comprehensibility. Inserted text, on the other hand, illustrates the surrounding themes in another, different context and thus contributes only indirectly to an understanding of the material. The remaining types of figure are those which contribute to understanding, but not in the same way as the visualization of complex interactions (see Table 26).

The visualization of complex interactions plays a significant role in all the books and accounts for between 20 percent and 28 percent of all figures. The books of Webster and Haas are exceptions, with 48.8 percent and 11.8 percent, respectively. While the visualization of complex interactions plays a decisive role for Webster, the converse applies to Haas.

The most frequently used form of figure is the table. Particularly in the books of Brierty, Eckles, and Reeder (57.8 percent); Bingham (42.5 percent); and Haas (45.5 percent), their extensive use is conspicuous. The Anderson and Narus text is characterized by a comparatively large number of inserted text passages (boxes). The results of an extensive "field research" comprise almost half of all figures.

Additional statements on the contribution of figures to textbook comprehensibility can be generated only if the application and quality of the individual figures can be evaluated meaningfully and validly. Compared to the research devoted to understandibility of texts, research into the quality of visualization in terms of its improvement on understanding has been rather poor (Weidenmann 1993). Some procedures have meanwhile been suggested in the literature for assessing the quality of individual spatial aids, but they relate to a comparison of a smaller number of figures and thus a high level of detail (Kosslyn 1989). Such an analysis cannot be undertaken in the context of this investigation (that is, seven textbooks and 1,287 figures).

LINK BETWEEN THEORY AND PRACTICE

Table 27 shows the complete results of the analysis of the criterion "link between theory and practice."

With the exception of Anderson and Narus, it is evident that all books present both macro and micro segmentation approaches. The Anderson and Narus book presents market segmentation criteria, but no particular approach. Hutt and Speh present only Wind and Cardozo's

TABLE 26. The Results of Qualitative Investigation of the Criterion "Visual Understanding"

	Visualization of Linear Relationships	Visualization of Complex Relationships	Tables	Maps	Inserted Text (Boxes)	Diagrams	Pictures
Brierty, Eckles, and Reeder	2.0	19.9	57.8	0.4	7.2	2.0	10.8
Bingham	5.5	25.3	42.5	0.0	17.8	0.0	8.9
Eckles	4.9	28.6	26.5	0.5	16.2	10.8	12.4
Haas	2.1	11.8	45.5	0.6	16.1	8.5	15.5
Hutt and Speh	6.3	25.1	26.7	0.5	26.7	11.0	3.7
Anderson and Narus	4.8	25.5	13.1	0.0	48.3	4.8	3.4
Webster	2.6	48.7	23.1	0.0	5.1	7.7	12.8

Note: All figures in percentages

TABLE 27. Results of the Analysis of the Criterion "Link Between Theory and Practice"

	Hutt and Speh	Webster	Haas	Eckles	Brierty, Eckles, and Reeder	Bingham	Anderson and Narus
Two-Stage Approach (Wind and Cardozo)							
Nested Approach (Bonoma and Shapiro)							
Market Segmentation and Positioning Approach (Doyle and Saunders)							
Corporate Culture Approach (Eisenhart)							
CUBE							
Thomas							
McKinsey Strategic Gameboard							
Market Segmentation and Positioning Approach (Kotler)							
Rangan, Moriarty, and Swartz							
Haas and Wotruba							
Demonstration: Applications Approaches	175+*; 181+	121	280+	130+		161	
Practical Examples	167; 168; 180	100; 101; 120	265	122+; 127; 129	203; 205; 206	159; 160	44; 45; 46
Case Studies	No. 2, 5, 14, 15, 16		No. 6, 8, 10, 22	No. 3	No. 8, 14, 19	No. 5, Case for Part 3	
Practice Exercises				132+			

*The numbers refer to pages and the + sign indicates that the subject is treated in a varying number of ensuing pages. The abbreviation No. refers to the case number specified in a book.

207

"two-stage approach," while Eckles introduces only the modified "nested approach." Webster; Haas; Brierty, Eckles, and Reeder; and Bingham present both approaches.

The depiction of other approaches to market segmentation varies considerably among the various textbooks. Apart from the approaches of Doyle and Saunders as well as that of Thomas, the others presented in Table 26 are introduced in only one of the books. Furthermore, the approaches are not so detailed as the macro or micro segmentations, being little more than cited and explained briefly. As was already established with respect to the observation of the criterion "depth of themes treated" for the marketing-mix instrument "price," the authors make no claims of an exhaustive depiction of *all* market segmentation approaches but illustrate, by way of example, that other approaches to market segmentation can be developed in research processes.

When discussing the criterion of the theory-practice link (see Criteria and Methodology), it was suggested in the literature that only a few examples demonstrating the application to segmentation can be found in the literature. However, the application is in fact presented in five books (Bingham; Eckles; Haas; Hutt and Speh; Webster).

All authors supplement the depiction of market segmentation with practical examples. They do so by means of examples that show how a particular aspect is applied to practical problems and often support this with the results of studies relating to this aspect.

Case studies offer the possibility of an active application of theories in practical situations. However, because the textbooks of Anderson and Narus and Webster have no cases, such an application is clearly not possible if no complementary material is used. All other books have at least one case study on market segmentation. In addition, Eckles's book provides two application exercises for market segmentation. The relationship of theory to practice thus plays an important role in all the books, although, as indicated, two do not offer cases.

DEVELOPING MORE COMPLEX CAPABILITIES

According to the taxonomy of educational objectives for the cognitive domain, the required skills for solving the test questions and case studies were examined. For the analysis of the test questions, the chapters on organizational purchasing behavior, demand analysis, strategic marketing planning, channel management, personal selling, and marketing controlling were chosen. This ensured that all components[6] of a textbook (analysis, strategic planning, operative planning, implementation, and control) were integrated.

The classification of test questions and case studies reveals a subjective character. However, comparable studies also indicate that the subjective character of such results cannot be excluded (as examples, see Hampton, Krentler, and Martin 1993; Karns, Burton, and Martin 1983).

The textbooks of Webster and Anderson and Narus contain no test questions or case studies.

In addition to test questions at the end, Bingham's book also offers "concept questions" within the chapters. However, because, according to the author himself (p. xxii), these questions test pure learning, they were excluded from consideration.

The classification of test questions reveals that the books of Hutt and Speh, Eckles, and Bingham aim predominantly at reproducing what has been learned. Thus, the questions merely ask what was presented in a particular chapter. Nonetheless, the books do contain some test questions that test evaluative skills and thus all other capabilities specified in the taxonomy. Yet, the emphasis falls clearly on mechanical learning. Conversely, the questions in the book of Brierty, Eckles, and Reeder and that of Haas, focus on evaluative skills. Therefore, these books promote the development of complex capabilities to a far greater extent.

An analysis of capabilities that can be developed through *case studies* reveals a uniform picture. All case studies of all textbooks under consideration require the application of evaluative skills. Through the hierarchical structure of the taxonomy of educational objectives, they also target the development of all skills specified in the taxonomy. The observation of case studies makes it quite clear that they are the most effective tool that textbooks have at their disposal for developing complex cognitive skills.

As indicated earlier, the books of Anderson and Narus and Webster do not offer either case studies or test questions. Therefore, it is doubtful that, on their own, they contribute much toward developing complex skills. For this reason, Webster stresses the importance of supplementing the use of textbooks with case studies, so as to ensure a focus on applying the themes presented (p. v). Supplementary material to support the development of complex capabilities is a crucial requirement in case either one of these two books is used as the basis for a course. In this respect they provide less support for the instructor who focuses on complex skills.

CONCLUSIONS

Our main findings are depicted in Table 28 at a fairly aggregated level. The results are described in more detail verbally in the following section on the two basic objectives of Bloom's taxonomy.

Table 29 contains some additional aspects that became conspicuous in our study. Although not directly related to the taxonomy scheme, and being of a rather subjective nature, they may still add value to the overall analysis.

Objective 1: Knowledge

The textbooks of the first group reveal the most extensive content and hence seem most suitable for undergraduate courses, although there are considerable differences within the group as well. The Anderson and Narus and the Webster books, on the other hand, both neglect some central themes in terms of a general overview of the subject. Both books rather seem targeted mainly at the undergraduate level. Particularly the Anderson and Narus book provides a focused view from a special perspective. The particular approach used in a book can be regarded as decisive in this respect, because it influences not only the structuring of content but also the selection of themes. The value approach presented by Anderson and Narus leads to a focused selection related directly to the "value" concept and also to a rather biased presentation of the themes in terms of their contribution to "value creation" that makes the book less suitable for obtaining an overview of business marketing. The advantage of the value approach is that business-to-business marketing is portrayed from a new perspective and, at the same time, discussions on the development of marketing strategies are grouped around a significant theme, making the book more appropriate for an advanced or specialized course or reader. The structuring through the marketing management approach, as found in most of the books, is more appropriate for a broader treat-

TABLE 28. Synopsis of Main Results

Contribution to Level According to Bloom Textbook	Knowledge	Understanding	Application (ex.: Market Segmentation)	Complex Capabilities
Anderson and Narus	focused (value)	text: appropriate visual: appropriate	significant role	supplementary material for case studies required
Bingham	limited	text: appropriate visual: appropriate	significant role	test questions: reproductive cases: evaluative
Brierty, Eckles, and Reeder	broad	text: appropriate visual: appropriate	significant role	test questions: evaluative cases: evaluative
Eckles	broad	text: appropriate visual: appropriate	significant role	test questions: reproductive cases: evaluative
Haas	broad	text: appropriate visual: appropriate	significant role	test questions: evaluative cases: evaluative
Hutt and Speh	broad	text: appropriate visual: appropriate	significant role	test questions: reproductive cases: evaluative
Webster	limited (instrumental)	text: appropriate visual: potentially low	significant role	supplementary material for case studies required

TABLE 29. Additional Aspects of Comparison

| Textbook | Additional Features | | |
	Content	Volume	Other
Anderson and Narus	new approach (value)		
Bingham	rather limited, but without particular focus		
Brierty, Eckles, and Reeder	strongly related to Eckles and Brierty/Reeder/Reeder (not in sample)		
Eckles			less vivid language
Haas		very detailed, but considerable redundancies	
Hutt and Speh	Broad range of themes (general overview, current topics); comprehensible case studies	very detailed	
Webster	limited		

ment of the overall spectrum of topics. Nevertheless, this concept also shows some inconsistency: although the authors frequently acknowledge that the various transactions in business-to-business markets are particularly heterogeneous, and that this requires differentiated marketing strategies, the actual approach followed in the books is *un*differentiated. A possible solution to this, in line with Reid and Plank (2000) who stress the significance of identification and definition of relationship types, could be found in structuring a textbook according to an explicit typology of transaction (or business relationships). Originating from the commodity school (for a focused overview of this concept, see Sheth, Gardner, and Garrett 1988), transaction-types approaches attempt to account for the extreme heterogeneity of marketing processes in business-to-business markets. While the commodity school concentrated on the objects of the transaction for classification, recent transaction-types approaches focus on the transaction itself: according to certain criteria (e.g., physical characteristics of the goods or specificity of necessary investment) that are assumed to shape the way a transaction takes place, different types are identified (e.g., Cannon and Perreault 1999; Miracle 1965) and type-specific marketing requirements are derived (for examples, see Plinke 1992 and 1997; Kleinaltenkamp 1994). A textbook could then start with a general derivation of transaction types. After that, the structuring of the book on the uppermost level could be done according to these types, while the structure within each type could follow a marketing management approach or whatever the author might regard as useful. An advantage of this system would be that the transaction lying at the heart of marketing (Kotler 1972; Sheth, Gardner, and Garrett 1988) is placed at the center of the structuring. At the same time it would be able to capture explicitly the significance and characteristics of relationship marketing, the importance of which has increasingly been emphasized in the recent literature (Hutt and Speh 1998a; Reid and Plank 2000b; Sheth and Sharma 1997; on its significance for the marketing curriculum, see Koch 1997). Moreover, transaction-types approaches may provide a link to new microeconomic theory (Cannon and Perreault 1994; for the economic perspective, see, in general, e.g., Williamson 1985; a recent typology is provided by Wathne and Heide 2000) and by that allow for a stronger cross-subject perspective. The advantage of these approaches lies therefore not only in the differentiated development of general type-specific marketing strategies but also in their ability to integrate a broad spectrum of topics. While the textbooks of the first group come closest to depicting the entire range of business-to-business marketing knowledge, all books reveal some weaknesses in their structuring of content, which could possibly be at least partly overcome through using a transaction-types approach.

Objective 2: Contribution to the Development of Cognitive Capabilities

All groups reveal an appropriate level of linguistic comprehensibility. Furthermore, this is supplemented through visualization, although to a greater (e.g., Hutt and Speh) or lesser degree (e.g., Webster).

The practical and related application orientation is achieved through practical examples, and especially case studies, in the books of the first group. These factors contribute substantially toward the development of complex cognitive capabilities. However, the presentation of appropriate and sufficient theoretical instruments for problem solving remains a basic condition for practical application. All observed books have deficiencies in this respect in certain areas, because the depiction of theory proceeds very selectively, offering only a cross section of the instruments actually available for practical problem solving. Furthermore, the undifferentiated presentation of content based on the marketing management approach in most sample books requires substantial adaptation for practical application in a specific situational context. A transaction-types approach might possibly facilitate practical application and situation-specific adaptation more effectively, through its differentiated marketing strategies. Thus, despite the creation of a practical linkage through examples and cases, the way in which theory is presented in the books under examination renders a true applications orientation more difficult.

LIMITATIONS AND DIRECTIONS FOR FUTURE RESEARCH

All in all, in this study we have attempted to demonstrate a way of generating useful results from Bloom's taxonomy of educational objectives for the cognitive domain when comparing different textbooks on business marketing. The concrete investigation itself has shown that, despite the variety of available textbooks on business-to-business marketing, none fulfills all of the identified educational criteria exhaustively. It seems likely that this may not, in completion, be possible at all, even if this is due only to the related volume. However, the study suggests that there is a certain "gap" in the English-language textbook market for business-to-business marketing for work beyond the marketing management approach (see also Smith and Robins 1991). A textbook structured according to transaction types may provide a further fruitful perspective, allowing for a broad inclusion of themes and at the same time for a focused, business-marketing-specific perspective. For the time being, our results may however help teachers or interested practitioners in selecting a textbook on business marketing that might best conform to their particular purpose. The study does not, though, provide a general ranking of the books' overall quality.

Despite these findings there certainly are considerable limitations to our study that might at least partly be overcome by further research. First, despite the use of a well-recognized theoretical underpinning, there is a strong subjective element to our study in the actual assessment of the books. In some of our operationalizations greater objectivity in measurement is achieved, but at the expense of requiring more subjective interpretation in the subsequent evaluation. Therefore, further research into operationalization of Bloom's taxonomy would be very helpful. Second, in our study we considered only English-language textbooks. Similar studies on textbooks in other languages not only might provide helpful evaluations of these books themselves, but could also reveal interesting aspects in terms of a cross-language comparison. For instance, it could be interesting to see whether there is a general difference in focus on a certain level of the taxonomy for books in a specific language. Targeted at general business-to-business marketing textbooks, a similar comparison of books explicitly addressing MBA or PhD courses might reveal helpful aspects for teachers in these areas. Last but not least, books may more or less significantly be changed with every new edition. This would not only impact individual criteria (e.g., current themes) but also could influence the entire focus of the book. New textbooks may be published and some may not see new editions, so a new sample may have to be analyzed at some point in time.

NOTES

1. The terms *business-to-business marketing, industrial marketing,* and *business marketing* will, despite the debate about the distinction between the fields, be used synonymously in this chapter, because the textbooks in comparison do not share a uniform understanding of these terms.

2. The authors are aware of the shortcomings of this lack of an a priori distinction. In an undergraduate course, greater emphasis has to be placed on laying a theoretical foundation, while in a graduate course, specific topics can be accorded a more in-depth treatment. However, for the sake of providing a more comprehensive deductive analysis, we decided to avoid this a priori classification.

3. In 2001 the seventh edition of the book was published. However, as all of the other books dated from the 1990s, we have chosen not to integrate the latest edition of Hutt and Speh. This contemporary analysis was completed in early spring 2001. Coupled to the double-blind review process, textbooks dated 2001 or later could not appear.

4. Bloom advances two further areas associated with the learning process, the affective domain and the domain of motor capabilities. These are, however, excluded from our analysis as they are not that relevant for an analysis of textbooks on business marketing, nor have they been as well explored as the cognitive domain.

5. The role of the Internet is a topic that has emerged as a major factor in marketing literature in general and also in business marketing literature (Reid and Plank 2000a; Spekman 2000; Wilson 2000). It has not been included due to the different publishing dates of the textbooks. The comparison might have been considerably distorted by its inclusion.

6. Components were decided according to the most frequently used approach in our sample, namely, the marketing management approach.

REFERENCES

Achrol, Ravi S. (1997). "Changes in the Theory of Interorganizational Relations in Marketing: Toward a Network Paradigm." *Journal of the Academy of Marketing Science* 25(1), 56-71.

Adelberg, Arthur H. and Razek, Joseph R. (1984). "The Cloze Procedure: A Methodology for Determining the Understandability of Accounting Textbooks." *The Accounting Review* 59(1), 109-122.

Ames, B.C. and Hlavacek, J.D. (1984). *Managerial Marketing for Industrial Firms.* New York: Random House.

Anderson, James C., Jain, Dipak C., and Chintaunta, Pradeep K. (1993). "Customer Value Assessment in Business Markets: A State-of-Practice Study." *Journal of Business-to-Business Marketing* 1(1), 3-29.

Anderson, James C. and Narus, James A. (1999). *Business Market Management: Understanding, Creating, and Delivering Value.* Upper Saddle River, NJ: Prentice-Hall.

Anderson, Jonathan (1983). "LIX and RIX: Variations on a Little-Known Readability Index." *Journal of Reading* (March), 490-496.

Anderson, Lorin W. (1999). "Rethinking Bloom's Taxonomy: Implications for Testing and Assessment." ERIC No. ED435630.

Backhaus, Klaus (1997). "Entwicklungspfade im Investitionsgütermarketing [Development paths in industrial goods marketing]." Backhaus, Klaus (ed.), *Marktleistung und Wettbewerb: strategische und operative Perspektiven der marktorientierten Leistungsgestaltung* [Market performance and competition: Strategic and operational perspectives of market-oriented performance design]. Wiesbaden: Gabler, 33-62.

Backhaus, Klaus (1998). "Industrial Marketing: A German View." *Thexis* 15(4), 2-6.

Backhaus, Klaus (1999). *Industriegütermarketing* [Industrial goods marketing], Sixth Edition. München: Vahlen.

Bea, Franz Xaver (1997). "Globalisierung" [Globalization]. *WiSt* 26(8), 419-421.

Becker, William E. and Watts, Michael (1996). "Teaching Undergraduate Economics." *AEA Papers and Proceedings* 86(2), 448-453.

Berry, Leonard L. (1993). "Our Roles As Educators: Present and Future." *Journal of Marketing Education* 15(3), 3-8.

Best, Michael (1990). *The New Competition.* Cambridge, MA: Harvard University Press.

Bingham, Frank G. (1998). *Business Marketing Management,* Second Edition. Homewood, IL: NTC Business Books.

Björnsson, Carl H. (1968). *Läsbarhet* [Readability]. Stockholm, Sweden: Bokförlaget Liber.

Bloom, Benjamin S. et al. (1956). *Taxonomy of Educational Objectives, Handbook 1: Cognitive Domain.* New York: Longmans.

Blotnicky, Karen A. (1991). "The Marketing Concept As the Foundation of Marketing in the Classroom: An Educational Dilemma." *Journal of Marketing Education* 13(2), 11-17.

Bonoma, Thomas V. and Shapiro, Benson P. (1983). *Segmenting the Industrial Market.* Lexington, MA: Lexington Books.

Brierty, Edward G., Eckles, Robert W., and Reeder, Robert R. (1998). *Business Marketing,* Third Edition. Upper Saddle River, NJ: Prentice-Hall.

Cannon, Joseph P. and Perreault, William D. (1999). "The Nature of Buyer-Seller Relationships in Business Markets." *Journal of Marketing Research,* 36(4) (November), 439-460.

Chute, Alan G. (1979). "Analysis of the instructional functions of color and monochrome cueing in media presentations." *Educational Communication and Technology Journal* 27(4), 151-163.

Clabaugh Jr., Maurice G., Forbes, Jessie L., and Clabaugh, Jason P. (1995). "Bloom's Cognitive Domain Theory: A Basis for Developing Higher Levels of Critical Thinking Skills in Reconstructing a Professional Selling Course." *Journal of Marketing Education* 17(3), 25-34.

Cline, Terry A. (1972). "Readability of Community College Textbooks." *Journal of Reading* 17(October 1972), 33-37.

Danneels, Erwin and Lilien, Gary L. (1998). "Doctoral Programs in Business-to-Business Marketing: Status and Prospects." *Journal of Business-to-Business Marketing* 5(1/2), 7-33.

Doane, David P. (1994). "Assessing Textbook Coverage of Quality Topics in Business Education." *Journal of Education for Business* 69(5), 299-302.

Eckles, Robert W. (1990). *Business Marketing Management.* Upper Saddle River, NJ: Prentice-Hall.

Engelhardt, Werner Hans and Witte, Petra (1990). "Konzeptionen des Investitionsgüter Marketing—eine kritische Bestandsaufnahme ausgewählter Ansätze" [Conceptions of industrial goods marketing—A critical taking stock of selected approaches]. In Kliche, Mario (ed.), *Investitionsgütermarketing: Positionsbestimmung und Perspektiven* [Industrial goods marketing: Position and perspectives]. Wiesbaden: Gabler, 3-17.

Evans, Mary Ann, Watson, Cathrine, and Willows, Dale M. (1987). "A Naturalistic Inquiry into Illustrations in Instructional Textbooks." Houghton, Harvey A. and Willows, Dale M. (Eds.), *The Psychology of Illustration.* Volume 2, New York: Springer-Verlag, 86-115.

Eysenck, Michael W. and Keane, Mark T. (1990). *Cognitive Psychology-A Student's Handbook.* Hove: Erlbaum.

Fry, Edward (1977). "Fry's Readability Graph: Clarifications, Validity, and Extension to Level 17." *Journal of Reading* December 1977, 242-252.

Furst, Edward J. (1981), Bloom's Taxonomy of Educational Objectives for the Cognitive Domain: Philosophical and Educational Issues, in: *Review of Educational Research,* Vol 51, No. 4, 441-453.

Gaugler, Eduard (1994). Der Wandel der betriebswirtschaftlichen Universitätsausbildung im Zuge der Internationalisierung der Wirtschaft [Changes in Business Education due to Internationalization], in: *ZfB* (special edition) (February) 3-13.

Gronlund, Norman E. (1970). *Stating Behavioral Objectives for Classroom Instruction.* New York: Macmillan.

Guthrie, Barbara (2000). "Thinking about Student's Thinking." Practitioner Research Briefs, 1999-2000 Report Series. Full text from <http://www.vcu.edu/aelweb/Barbara_Guthrie.pdf>.

Haas, Robert W. (1995). *Business Marketing: A Managerial Approach,* Sixth Edition. Cincinnati, OH: South-Western College Pub.

Hampton, David R., Krentler, Kathleen A., and Martin, Aleza B. (1993). "The Use of Management and Marketing Textbook Multiple-Choice Questions: A Case Study." *Journal of Education for Business* 69(1), 40-43.

Henke Jr., John W., Locander, William B., Mentzer, John T., and Nastas, George III (1988). "Teaching Techniques for the New Marketing Instructor: Bringing the Business World into the Classroom." *Journal of Marketing Education* 10(1), 1-10.

Hlavacek, James. D. (1980). "Business Schools Need Industrial Marketing." *Marketing News* Vol. 13 (April 4), 1, 23.

Hunter, Barbara, Crismore, Avon, and Pearson, P. David (1987). "Visual Displays in Basal Readers and Social Studies Textbooks." Houghton, Harvey A. and Willows, Dale M. (Eds.), *The Psychology of Illustration.* Volume 2, New York: Springer-Verlag, 116-135.

Hutt, Michael D. and Speh, Thomas W. (1982), *Industrial Marketing Management: A Strategic View of Business Markets,* Chicago: Dryden Press.

Hutt, Michael D. and Speh, Thomas W. (1998a). "Business Marketing Education: A Distinctive Role in the Undergraduate Curriculum." *Journal of Business-to-Business Marketing* 5(1/2), 103-126.

Hutt, Michael D. and Speh, Thomas W. (1998b). *Business Marketing Management,* Sixth Edition, Fort Worth: Dryden Press.

Imrie, Bradford W. (1995). "Assessment for Learning: Quality and Taxonomies." *Assessment and Evaluation in Higher Education* 20(2), 175-189.

Industrial Marketing Practitioner (1999). Industrial Marketing Library. <http://www.practitioner.com/library1.htm>. Retrieved: September 13.

Jaffe, Eugene D. (1996). "International Marketing Textbooks—A Citiation Analysis As an Indicator of the Discipline's Boundaries." *International Marketing Review* 14(1), 9-19.

Johnston, Wesley J. and Borders, Leila X. (1998). "The Industrial Marketing Strategist in the New Millennium." *Thexis* 15(4), 12-14.

Karns, James M.L., Burton, Gene E., and Martin, Gerald D. (1983). "Learning Objectives and Testing: An Analysis of Six Principles of Economic Textbooks, Using Bloom's Taxonomy." *The Journal of Economic Education* Volume 16 (Summer) 1983, 16-20.

Kelley, Craig A. and Gaedeke, Ralph M. (1990). "Student and Employer Evaluation of Hiring Criteria for Entry-Level Marketing Positions." *Journal of Marketing Education* 12(3), 64-71.

King, Patricia, Wood, Philip, and Mines, Robert (1990). "Critical Thinking Among College and Graduate Students." *The Review of Higher Education* 13(2), 167-186.

Koch, Adam J. (1997). "Marketing Curriculum: Designing Its New Logic and Structure." *Journal of Marketing Education* 19(3), 2-16.

Kosslyn, Stephen M. (1989). "Understanding Charts and Graphs." *Applied Cognitive Psychology* 3(3), 185-226.

Kotler, Philip (1972). "A Generic Concept of Marketing." *Journal of Marketing* 36(April) 46-54.

Kotler, Philip (1997). *Marketing Management: Analysis, Planning, Implementation, and Control.* Ninth Edition. Upper Saddle River, NJ: Prentice-Hall.

Krishnan, H. Shanker and Porter, Thomas W. (1998). "A Process Approach for Developing Skills in a Consumer Behavior Course." *Journal of Marketing Education* 20(1), 24-34.

Kuhn, Thomas S. (1970). *The Structure of Scientific Revolutions,* Second Edition, Chicago: University of Chicago Press.

Lamb, Charles W. Jr. and Baker, Julie (1993). "The Case Method of Instruction: Student-Led Presentations to Videotaping." *Marketing Education Review,* Volume 3, (Spring), 44-52.

Lamont, Lawrence M. and Friedman, Ken (1997). "Meeting the Challenges to Undergraduate Marketing Education." *Journal of Marketing Education* 19(3), 17-30.

LaPlaca, Peter J. (1982). *Industrial Marketing Management,* Volume 11, 165-166.

Lichtenthal, J. David and Butaney, Gul (1991). "Undergraduate Industrial Marketing: Content and Methods." *Industrial Marketing Management,* Volume 20, 231-239.

Marketing Education Review (1999). "Business Marketing Textbooks, Case Books, Readers, Trade Books, and Simulation Games." <http://cbpa.louisville.edu/ mer/business_textbooks.htm>. Retrieved: September 13.

Marzano, Robert J. (2001). *Designing a New Taxonomy of Educational Objectives: Experts in Assessment,* Thousand Oaks, CA: Corwin Press.

Miracle, Gordon E. (1965). "Product Characteristics and Marketing Strategy." *Journal of Marketing,* Volume 29, January, 18-24.

Moore, David S. (1982). "Reconsidering Bloom's Taxonomy of Educational Objectives, Cognitive Domain." *Educational Theory* 32(1), 29-34.

Moore, James F. (1996). *The Death of Competition,* New York: Harper Business.

Moore, Phillip J. (1993). "Metacognitive Processing of Diagrams, Maps and Graphs." *Learning and Instruction,* Volume 3, 215-226.

Narayandas, Narakesari, Rangan, V. Kasturi, and Zaltman, Gerald (1998). "The Pedagogy of Executive Education in Business Markets." *Journal of Business-to-Business Marketing* 5(1/2), 41-63.

Narus, James A. and Anderson, James C. (1998). "Master's Level Education in Business Marketing: *Quo Vadis?*" *Journal of Business-to-Business Marketing* 5(1/2), 75-91.

O'Reilly, Brian (1994). "Reengineering the MBA." *Fortune* 129(January 24), 38-47.

Palmer, Adrian (1994). "Relationship Marketing: Time to Enrich the Marketing Curriculum?" *Journal of Marketing Education* 16(2), 34-41.

Peek, Joan (1993). "Increasing Picture Effects in Learning from Illustrated Text." *Applied Cognitive Psychology,* Volume 3, 227-238.

Paul, Richard W. (1985). "Bloom's Taxonomy and Critical Thinking Instruction." *Educational Leadership* May, 36-39.

Plank, Richard E. (1982). "Industrial Marketing Education: A Practitioner's View." *Industrial Marketing Management,* Volume 11, 311-315.

Plinke, Wulf (1992). "Ausprägungen der Marktorientierung im Investitionsgütermarketing [Different Forms of Market-orientation in Industrial Goods Marketing]." *Schmalenbachs Zeitschrift für betriebswirtschaftliche Forschung* 44(9), 830-846.

Plinke, Wulf (1997). "Grundlagen des Geschäftsbeziehungsmanagements [Principles of business relationship management]." Plinke, Wulf and Kleinaltenkamp, Michael (eds.), *Geschäftsbeziehungsmanagement* [Business relationship management], Berlin, 113-159.

Ray, Charles M., Stallard, John J., and Hunt, C. Steven (1994). "Criteria for Business Graduates' Employment: Human Resource Managers' Perceptions." *Journal of Education for Business* 69(3), 140-144.

Reid, David A. and Plank, Richard E. (2000a). "Business Marketing Comes of Age: A Comprehensive Review of the Literature." *Journal of Business-to-Business Marketing* 7(2/3), 9-185.

Reid, David A. and Plank, Richard E. (2000b). "A Reply to the Commentaries on Business Marketing: A Twenty Year Review." *Journal of Business-to-Business Marketing* 7(4), 55-67.

Rich, D. Layne, Powers, Thomas L. and Powell, Judith D. (1988). "Textbook Satisfaction: A Preliminary Examination of the Student Perspective." *Journal of Marketing Education* 10(2), 29-33.

Rugimbana, Robert and Patel, Chris (1996). "The Application of the Marketing Concept in Textbook Selection: Using the Cloze Procedure." *Journal of Marketing Education* 18(Spring), 14-20.

Scevak, Jill J. and Moore, Phillip J. (1990). "Effective processing of visual information." *Reading* 24(1), 28-36.

Sheth, Jagdish N., Gardner, David M., and Garrett, Dennis E. (1988). *Marketing Theory: Evolution and Evaluation,* New York: Wiley.

Sheth, Jagdish N. and Sharma, Arun (1997). "Supplier Relationships—Emerging Issues and Challenges." *Industrial Marketing Management* 26(1), 91-100.

Smith, Michael F. and Robbins, John E. (1991). "Marketing Education and Marketing Management: Some Thoughts on Compatibility and Integration." *Journal of Marketing Education* 13(3), 33-39.

Solman, Robert and Rosen, Gaye (1986). "Bloom's Six Cognitive Levels Represent Two Levels of Performance." *Educational Psychology* 6(3), 243-263.

Spekman, Robert E. (2000). "A Commentary on Business Marketing: A Twenty Year Review and an Invitation for Continued Dialogue." *Journal of Business-to-Business Marketing* 7(4), 11-32.

Spinks, Nelda and Wells, Barron (1993). "Readability: A Textbook Selection Criterion." *Journal of Education for Business* 69(2), 83-88.

Stary, Joachim (1997). *Visualisieren: ein Studien-und Praxisbuch* [Visualization: A book for study and practice], Berlin: Cornelsen Scriptor.

Stearns, James M. and Crespy, Charles T. (1995). "Learning Hierarchies and the Marketing Curriculum: A Proposal for a Second Course in Marketing." *Journal of Marketing Education* 17(2), 20-32.

Stuart, John and Burns, Richard (1984). "The Thinking Process: A Proposed Instructional Objectives Classification Scheme." *Educational Technology,* July, 21-26.

Sultana, Qaisar and Klecker, Beverly M. (1999). *Evaluation of First-Year-Teacher's Lesson Objectives by Bloom's Taxonomy.* Paper delivered at the Annual Meeting of the Mid-South Educational Research Association, Point Clear, Alabama, November 17-19.

Taylor, Wilson L. (1953). 'Cloze Procedure': A New Tool for Measuring Readability. *Journalism Quarterly,* 30(Fall), 415-433.

Taylor, Wilson L. (1954). Application of 'Cloze' and Entropy Measures to the Study of Contextual Constraint in Samples of Continuous Prose, n.p.

Tootelian, Dennis H., Bush, Ronald F., and Stern, Bruce L. (1992). "Business Educators' Use of Conferences, Journals, and Textbooks." *Journal of Education for Business* 67(6), 366-370.

Wathne, Kenneth H. and Heide, Jan B. (2000). "Opportunism in Interfirm Relationships: Forms, Outcomes and Solutions." *Journal of Marketing,* Volume 64, October, 36-51.

Webster, Frederick E. (1995). *Industrial Marketing Strategy,* Third Edition, New York: Wiley.

Weidenmann, Bernd (1993). Informierende Bilder [Informational pictures]. *Wissenserwerb mit Bildern: instruktionale Bilder in Printmedien, Film/Video und Computerprogrammen* [Gaining knowledge through pictures: Instructional pictures in print media, film/video and computer software], Weidenmann, Bernd (Ed.), Bern: Hans Huber Verlag.

Wentland, Daniel (2000). "A Framework for Organizing Economic Education Teaching Methodologies." ERIC ED 442702.

Williamson, Oliver E. (1985). *The Economic Institutions of Capitalism,* New York: The Free Press.

Wills, Gordon (1982). "Marketing a School to Industry." *Industrial Marketing Management,* Volume 11, 303-310.

Wilson, David T. (2000). "Commentary: Thoughts on the Future of Business Marketing." *Journal of Business-to-Business Marketing* 7(4), 33-43.

Wind, Yoram and Cardozo, Richard N. (1974). "Industrial Market Segmentation." *Industrial Marketing Management* 3(2) (April), 153-166.

Winn, Bill (1987). "Charts, Graphs, and Diagrams in Educational Materials." Hoghton, Harvey A. and Willows, Dale M. (eds.), *The Psychology of Illustration,* Volume 1, New York: Springer-Verlag, 152-198.

Wright, Lauren K., Bitner, Mary Jo, and Zeithaml, Valerie A. (1994). "Paradigm Shifts in Business Education: Using Active Learning to Deliver Services Marketing Content." *Journal of Marketing Education* (Special Issue on Services), (Fall), 5-19.

Zabudsky, Jeff (2000). "The Digital Curriculum Database: Meeting the Needs of Industry and the Challenge of Enhanced Student Learning." *TEND 2000, Proceedings of the Technological Education and National Development Conference,* "Crossroads of the New Millennium," Abu Dhabi, United Arab Emirates, April 8-10.

Comparative Review of Business-to-Business Marketing Textbooks: A Commentary

Gul Butaney

The previous paper by Bacchus, Muehlfield, and Okaye makes an important contribution to business marketing education. At the very outset, I would like to commend the authors for their painstaking effort to systematically derive the criteria and evaluate the leading textbooks on business-to-business marketing. Benjamin Bloom's (1956) taxonomy of educational objectives serves as an appropriate framework for the criteria. Business-to-business marketing faculty members and the authors of the textbooks stand to gain from the comparative review, which is done quite objectively and impartially. The faculty member gains insight on the textbook selection decision variables as well as the issues surrounding the determination of business-to-business marketing content, approaches, pedagogical direction, and the overall course mission. Clearly, selecting a textbook for the business-to-business marketing course at the undergraduate or graduate level is an important decision and deserves careful consideration for effective execution of the course strategy. Many of us view the textbook as a prime component of instruction and do rely on it heavily to structure and organize the course, and the issue has not been addressed sufficiently in the literature.

Almost three-quarters of today's graduates become employed in firms that manufacture and market products and services for non-consumer markets. My informal conversations with several students, who enroll in a business-to-business marketing course at Bentley College as a part of their preparation to pursue a career in the business-to-business marketing arena, do hold on to their textbook long after they have graduated. Perhaps they feel equipped and assured of their resources and skills, having that book on their shelves. It is not unusual for students to buy an updated edition of the book if they perceive its value in terms of gaining the latest insights on business-to-business research findings and industry practices. Thus, these students could account for a continuously expanding revenue stream for textbook publishers. Textbook authors, therefore, should find the review useful in terms of determining what major or minor revisions, if any, are warranted to update their textbooks to effectively serve two of their prime constituencies: marketing students and faculty. Bloom's (1956) taxonomy and its operationalization should become a catalyst for streamlining and revitalizing the educational objectives as they relate to each major business-to-business marketing topic and, hence, the pedagogy of the text for treating the material. The purposes of this commentary, therefore, are to reinforce the appropriateness of the taxonomy, and to recommend an enhancement to its operationalization and assessment through the inclusion of a qualitative review and judgment method. Specifically, we raise an issue of student information overload and the challenges that textbook authors must face to address it.

ABOUT THE TAXONOMY

Bloom's (1956) taxonomy seems to be an appropriate framework for evaluating business-to-business textbooks. The practical significance of this taxonomy has been well acknowledged and documented in the educational literature across several disciplines (e.g., Anderson 1999; Bower 1981; and Chacon 1992). Even industry practitioners have recommended and expect the business-to-business marketing course to provide students not only the fundamentals of business-to-business marketing concepts, practices, and techniques (the knowledge-based educational objectives) but to impart to students higher-level skill sets emphasizing application, analytical, managerial, critical thinking, and research capabilities (e.g., Clabaugh et al. 1995). The taxonomy thus remains a prime framework for defining the educational objectives of the textbooks as well as influencing the faculty members' instructional goals and strategies. The taxonomy is robust enough to encompass the fundamental cognitive abilities and application skills that we all desire in our students. By applying this taxonomy as the evaluative criteria, all dimensions that define the textbooks are analyzed and compared.

ENHANCEMENT OF THE CRITERIA
AND THEIR APPLICATION

The assessment criteria and its application could be enhanced to better serve the faculty members' textbook selection decision and adaptation. First, the operationalization of the knowledge criteria needs to be broadened to examine the issue of conceptual complexity in treating the subject matter. Higher levels of information overload as it arises from conceptual complexity are likely to hinder the achievement of such educational objectives as knowledge, understandability, and application of the subject matter. Conceptual complexity is a function of the number of new concepts and the conceptual and operational definitions of each new concept that students must learn. The more scientific the language or technical jargon that is used to illustrate the concept, the higher the conceptual complexity. While one's tolerance for technical jargon and sentence structure is also a function of one's reading ability and familiarity level with the subject matter (e.g., concepts, topics, and industry practices) as well as business acumen in relating it to the changing world of business, when conceptual complexity reaches a certain level, students experience conceptual overload, a point where ability to learn is impaired due to lack of familiarity with or comprehension of the topic under study (e.g., Kintsch 1975; Santa and Burstyn 1977; Chacon 1992). Inability to process or comprehend fully the meaning, implications, or significance of the concepts and practices can be frustrating. It can hinder students from completing reading assignments efficiently and progressing effectively through the hierarchy of learning goals on their own. Consequently, the lack of student preparation and/or attention in the class may force the instructor to conduct the lectures or learning activities at a merely conceptual or theoretical level.

The issue of conceptual complexity is especially relevant and important, as it is likely to be present in business-to-business marketing textbooks. Both the quantity and the sophistication of the relevant published research findings (Reid et al. 2000) as well as information technology-related business-to-business marketing concepts, business models, and practices have increased sharply. Perhaps no other field is characterized by such rapid growth and diversity. Furthermore, business-to-business marketing has a vast body of its own as well as having been enriched by several other disciplines, including organizational behavior, management science, economics, accounting, information technology systems, and a broad spectrum of marketing disciplines. Both of these factors increase the potential for conceptual complexity. Furthermore, an increase in the sheer number of concepts or topics compounds the problem. Impetus to include topics and research findings comes from faculty members who look for more and more coverage of traditional, new, and emerging business-to-business marketing themes, practices, and concepts in a business-to-business marketing textbook. Employers in business-to-business marketing firms also prefer the textbook to cover a broad range of business-to-business marketing themes, concepts, and practices. At the same time, they want the textbook to have provided enough insights on how to apply the concepts and processes in making marketing decisions in various contextual situations; how to implement major business-to-business marketing tasks and activities, such as developing sales forecasts and determining personal selling strategies unique to each organization; how to implement closer/collaborative working relationships with business partners; and how to effectively utilize the potential of business-to-business marketing technology. A mere cataloging of newer business-to-business marketing concepts, technology, and research findings with scientific conceptual/operational definitions, therefore, may not achieve the effective transfer-of-knowledge goal. The very notion of understanding implies that the student has the ability and knowledge of how to apply the standard formal knowledge as well as how to vary it from one situation to another. It is the integration and illustration of marketing significance and implications of the current concepts and major research findings that when presented in a simple and coherent writing style from a practitioner point of view, would allow the student to gain mastery of the subject matter as well as permit wider coverage of course material per unit of study time. The basic proposition is that, in order for the student to move beyond the theoretical domain of learning, the newer concepts and practices need to be relatively easy to read and easily digested.

The authors' efforts in operationalizing the knowledge, understanding, and application criteria, therefore, are commendable. While the books' formal structure index (e.g., number of characters per line and number of lines per page), the readability level index (e.g., LIX), the visualization levels, and the number of themes covered in a passage are the first steps in the assessment process of the knowledge and application criteria, they may not reflect the extent of the conceptual complexity problem that may be present. The assessment process, therefore, should be supplemented by qualitative review, including the use of an expert judgment method and involvement of a sample of potential business-to-business marketing students in the process, to gain firsthand insights on the problem. Subjective judgment is also required to select appropriate topics or concepts in addition to a random sample of topics for examining the conceptual complexity and student information overload issue.

For those teaching the next generation of business-to-business marketers, as well as the business-to-business marketing textbook authors, reducing conceptual complexity will be more important than ever before, given the rapid pace of change and the emergence of relatively new and more complex business-to-business marketing processes and models. But once students have developed a solid foundation for newer concepts, processes, or schemes of business models, it is less difficult to incorporate them into their mental representations. In addressing the problem, therefore, business-to-business marketing textbook authors must confront several key questions:

1. How many and what mix of current and relatively new or emerging business-to-business marketing topics need to be covered in the book?
2. How much emphasis needs to be put on the relatively new topics as well as the traditional topics or practices that do not add much incremental value to the book and are becoming less relevant to current business-to-business models and practices?

This is an important issue, as it would affect overall length of business-to-business textbooks, which influences faculty members' business-to-business marketing textbook selection. It is preferable to maintain the length at a reasonable level. Until some of the older, less relevant or prevalent topics and material, which add little incremental value to the book in terms of their usefulness to students or business-to-business marketing practices, are deleted or deemphasized, the potential problem of student information overload will exist. Consequently, we need to rethink how much attention and coverage should be devoted to the traditional topics (e.g., differences between consumer and business marketing, global marketing issues, ethical marketing dilemmas, performance measurement, or transaction versus commodity approaches) and the emerging business-to-business marketing themes and practices (e.g., value creation framework/processes, relationship-marketing strategies/tactics, managing close working relationships with business partners/network organizations, or marketing of IT, e-commerce, and Internet products). Another important issue is how to treat these topics. Should they be treated in separate chapters, integrated with other topics, deleted, or covered through case studies?

3. How can the newer business-to-business marketing themes and topics be treated pedagogically in the text, and to which level of Bloom's (1956) hierarchy of educational objectives should the text aspire? Should a concept be merely introduced and described? Illustrated for applications and marketing implications? Discussed for its managerial significance? Analyzed for assessing potential solutions to business-to-business marketing issues and decisions? Or should all of these aspects be included?

The importance and the growing acceptance of each topic or concept in question would certainly provide answers to many of these questions. However, the specific pedagogical orientation and approaches might vary from topic to topic in their treatment in the textbook. Again this has to be in concert with the textbook's positioning focus (e.g., value creation-based focus in the Anderson and Narus 1999 text), the specific overall orientation in treating the subject matter (e.g., managerial, research, descriptive), and the pedagogy (e.g., short case, diagrams, illustrations) that the textbook authors select as an executional strategy for the entire textbook.

The textbook orientation and pedagogy can go a long way in facilitating the achievement of higher-level learning goals in the taxonomy. The case method is certainly instrumental to establishing the theory-practice link as well as integrating several business-to-business marketing decision variables. Designing, developing, or obtaining case studies with a decision focus, whether comprehensive or concise, would be a formidable task, especially if the cases involved current marketing situations and buying behavior issues involving buyers and sellers of IT, e-commerce, or Internet products, and incorporating maturing philosophies of building closer and more durable marketing relationships. However, it will enhance the value of the book for students as well as faculty members. Consequently, a quantitative assessment regarding whether the textbook contains cases or how many should be supplemented by a qualitative review of the currentness and the importance of marketing situations that are represented in those cases.

Another pedagogical tool that is likely to address the conceptual complexity problem and assist in achieving higher-level learning goals in the taxonomy is a glossary of terms. Generally, textbooks append glossaries at the end of the books, or list key terms at the end of the chapters, and/or provide a subject index. However, a glossary of terms (concepts, practices) as it pertains to each chapter, if prominently featured at the beginning of each chapter, perhaps following the chapter behavioral objectives, might be more productive. It would provide explanations of the concepts up-front along with behavioral objectives, which should facilitate a high level of comprehension for their application, and their relationship with other concepts in the chapter.

Last, appropriateness (or suitability) of the textbooks to graduate or undergraduate levels, although not directly considered in the textbook assessment process, does come out in the analysis stage by the authors as an important criterion for positioning the business-to-business marketing textbook. An interrelated issue relates to the focus of the book, i.e., whether the business-to-business marketing book should emphasize mainly core or fundamentals of business-to-business marketing concepts and practices, or to present a specialized focus, such as the one pursued by Anderson and Narus (1999). The textbook at the undergraduate level perhaps would be more useful and consistent with preferences (or requirements) of business-to-business marketing employers if it focused more on the fundamentals and core practices, in terms of preparing students for entry to mid-level positions. Students need that resource, know-how, and repertoire of skills to enter a business-to-business marketing career effectively. On the other hand, graduate students, who would have more than likely completed the entire curriculum of business and marketing courses at the undergraduate level, have had some industry experience, and possess an understanding of current marketing and business practices, might benefit a lot more from a book that adopts a specialized focus or philosophical marketing perspective of growing importance and acceptance by industry practitioners. The challenge of creating a book with such a specialized focus, e.g., value creation and relationship marketing, would be how to adopt the core processes and marketing fundamentals covered in the previous editions of the textbook to best implement the specialized focus.

CONCLUDING SUMMARY

The main purpose of this commentary is to reinforce the need to expand upon the textbook criteria and assessment process as suggested by the authors of the previous chapters. Based upon my own personal experience and observations associated with teaching and selecting textbooks for business-to-business marketing courses, I have indicated how the evaluative criteria and assessment process and, consequently, the operationalization of Bloom's (1956) taxonomy of learning goals can be enhanced. In the process, I have identified several issues for further scrutiny in the areas of topical coverage, textbook pedagogy and orientation, length of the textbook, and positioning of the textbook for graduate and undergraduate levels. These issues are linked to conceptual complexity and student information overload problems that a business-to-business marketing textbook may present, and how or why that might impede the student's effective progression through the hierarchy of learning goals in Bloom's (1956) taxonomy. Furthermore, consistent with the authors' direction for future work in this area, I do echo that the assessment process and methodology should be supplemented by the use of subjective and expert judgment methods for selecting a sample of topics and material (e.g., case studies, diagrams) for evaluating the textbook on the taxonomy of learning goals. The commentary also raises several challenges and implications, therefore, for business-to-business marketing textbook writers.

REFERENCES

Anderson, James and James A. Narus (1999). "Business Market Management: Understanding, Creating, and Delivering Value." Upper Saddle River, NJ: Prentice-Hall.

Anderson, Lorin W. (1999). "Rethinking Bloom's Taxonomy: Implications for Testing and Assessment." ERIC No. ED435630.

Bloom, Benjamin S. (1956). *Taxonomy of Educational Objectives, Handbook 1: Cognitive Domain.* New York: Longmans.

Bower, G. H. (1981). *Theories of Learning.* Englewood Cliffs, NJ: Prentice-Hall.

Chacon, F. (1992). "A Taxonomy of Computer Media in Distance Education." *Open Learning* (February).

Clabaugh Maurice G. Jr., Leslie L. Forbes, and Jason P. Clabaugh (1995). "Bloom's Cognitive Domain Theory: A Basis for Developing Higher Levels of Critical Thinking Skills in Restructuring a Professional Selling Course." *Journal of Marketing Education.* 17(3), 25-34.

Kintsch, Walter (1975). "Comprehension and Recall of Text As a Function of Content Variables." *Journal of Verbal Learning and Verbal Behavior.* 14(1), 196-214.

Reid, David A. and Richard E. Plank (2000). "Business Marketing Comes of Age As a Comparative Review of Literature." *Journal of Business-to-Business Marketing.* 7(2/3), 136-214.

Santa, Carol and Joan Burstyn (1977). "Complexity As an Impediment to Learning: A Study of Changes in Selected College Textbooks." *Journal of Higher Education* (September/October).

Comparative Review of Business-to-Business Marketing Textbooks: A Commentary

Michael D. Hutt
Thomas W. Speh

Drawing on Bloom's (1956) taxonomy of educational objectives, in Chapter 16, Backhaus, Muehlfeld, and Okoye provide a comparative analysis of business-to-business marketing textbooks, including our volume (Hutt and Speh 1998), and offer some interesting and provocative observations. As an outgrowth of their analysis, they suggest that content and coverage gaps evident in existing offerings might be filled by structuring a textbook around an explicit typology of business relationships or transaction types. Issuing from the commodity school (Sheth, Gardner, and Garrett 1988), they argue that the transaction-types approach addresses the extreme heterogeneity of marketing processes in the business market. Moreover, they contend that such an approach provides a base for considering the differentiated development of marketing strategies tailored to particular types of customer relationships.

Rather than exploring the appropriateness of Bloom's (1956) framework to the topic at hand or considering findings related to particular criteria (e.g., comprehensibility) we chose instead to center our commentary on the core recommendations that issue from the authors' analysis. In particular, we center attention on the knowledge areas that provide the foundation for a relationship marketing perspective as well as those which define the domain of a business marketing course. We believe that a text built around a transaction-types perspective is likely to suffer on some of the criteria that the authors use in evaluating existing volumes, most notably on the dimensions of breadth, the coverage of current topics (for example, supply chain management), and depth of treatment. Before we begin, we will offer some brief observations on the comparative analysis.

THE POSITIONING OF THE TEXTS

The comparative analysis of business marketing texts presented in Chapter 16 required a significant investment of time and we commend the authors for their effort and systematic approach. The textbooks were evaluated on numerous dimensions and some decisive recommendations are offered for consideration. Moreover, the discussion serves to highlight the complexity of organizing the content of business marketing and unfolding it in a way that squarely responds to the needs of both the student reader and the instructor.

While we are pleased with the overall assessment that the authors provide of our volume, we feel compelled to address some positioning issues that emerge in the analysis of competing volumes. In particular, we believe the authors err by classifying Anderson and Narus (1999) and Webster (1995) as undergraduate texts. While, no doubt, both can be used effectively at the undergraduate level, we believe the analysis overlooks the way in which the volumes are used. Anderson and Narus (1999) provide a very timely and innovative discussion of the value creation process for business markets. By adopting a clear focus and exploring the value creation process in a systematic and comprehensive way, they provide an important contribution to the business marketing literature. Rather than an undergraduate text, the volume—augmented with Harvard cases—would seem to be best suited to the graduate level. The stated goal of the volume is to provide an integrated treatment of value creation strategies in the business market and, in our view, they deliver on that promise. In turn, Webster (1995), supported with a selection of cases, has likely been used more at the graduate or executive program level than at the undergraduate level. On balance, then, the distinct merits of both volumes become more apparent when positioned at the graduate level and used by an instructor who emphasizes a case format. We will now turn our attention to the authors' recommendation that a transaction-types perspective may provide the most appropriate organizing framework for a business marketing text.

BUILDING A FOUNDATION

The design of a textbook should mirror the organization of a course, particularly at the undergraduate level. Because students enter the course with limited exposure to the business market, the early chapters of a text must engage the student-reader and provide an important foundation for understanding how buyer-seller relationships operate in the business market. Before the proposed transaction-types framework could be adequately grasped and understood by the reader, important content must be established in at least three areas: (1) the distinguishing characteristics of the business market; (2) the structure and orientation of the purchasing organization; and (3) the organizational buying process.

Business Market Characteristics

To instill a focus on organizations (rather than households) as the unit of analysis, special attention must be given to the similarities and differences between consumer goods marketing and business marketing, the types of customers that comprise the business market, and the forces that drive business market demand.

The Purchasing Organization

As leading-edge organizations such as General Electric, Dell, and Honda adopt more sophisticated purchasing approaches, business marketers must respond with well-conceived and timely strategies. In turn, the business marketing course should reflect the forces that are reshaping the purchasing function and how organizations buy goods and services. For example, purchasing managers are giving increased attention to the *total cost of ownership,* which "considers both supplier and buyer activities and costs over a product's or service's complete life cycle" (Laseter 1998, p. 224). Moreover, purchasing managers continue to utilize value analysis and complexity management that seeks cost reductions by simplifying the design of products.

Leading procurement organizations are also giving increased attention to segmenting their total purchases into distinct categories and sharpening their focus on those purchases which have the greatest impact on revenue generation or present the greatest risk to corporate performance. Such a trend has profound implications on relationship-marketing strategies. To illustrate, business marketers should define where their offerings are positioned in the portfolio of purchases that a particular organization makes. Of course, this will vary by firm and by industry sector. The profit potential is greatest in those purchasing organizations which view the purchase as strategic. By understanding how customers segment their purchases, business marketers are better equipped to develop customized strategies and target profitable segments. Compared to more traditional buyers, recent research also suggests that more strategically oriented purchasing managers are (1) more receptive to information and draw it from a wide variety of sources, (2) more sensitive to the importance of longer-term supplier relationships and questions of price in relation to performance, and (3) more concerned with the distinctive competencies of suppliers in evaluating alternative firms (Spekman, Stewart, and Johnson 1995).

Organizational Buying Behavior

Each decision a business marketer makes is based on the probable response of organizational buying. At a fundamental level, we believe that students should be exposed to the rich research tradition that has emerged in the marketing literature. Understanding the dynamics of organizational buying is a prerequisite for identifying profitable segments of the organizational market, for locating the buying influences within these segments, and for reaching these organizational buyers efficiently and effectively with a relationship marketing strategy.

Hurdles for a Transaction-Types Perspective

Bloom's taxonomy (1956) includes basic capabilities (knowledge and understanding) and skills (application, analysis, synthesis, and evaluation). One of the complexities of organizing a text around a transaction-types framework is the need to provide the student-reader with a strong foundation of knowledge related to the defining characteristics of the business market. Before relationship marketing strategies can be explored beyond the descriptive level, the student must develop an understanding of the distinguishing characteristics of business markets, the perspectives and tools of analysis that purchasing managers employ, and the nature of organizational buying behavior. A central challenge in the undergraduate business marketing course is to unfold the content in a way that moves from knowledge fundamentals and application to analysis and evaluation. Before a transaction-types perspective can be fully grasped, appreciated, and applied by the student, these fundamental knowledge areas must be established.

DEVELOPING A RELATIONSHIP MARKETING PERSPECTIVE

Backhaus et al. (2002) suggest that a business marketing text might start with a general derivation of transaction types and then, in subsequent chapters, explore particular types of relationships using a marketing management or alternative perspective. We agree that relationship marketing constitutes the heart of business marketing but, of course, adopt an alternative structure in exploring the area. In fact, the seventh edition of our text (Hutt and Speh 2001) clearly demonstrates the significant importance that we assign to the area. Part II of the text, *Managing Relationships in Business Marketing,* is comprised of three chapters—"Relationship Strategies for Business Markets," "E-Commerce Strategies for Business Markets," and "Supply Chain Management." (To provide an objective comparison, we understand the authors' decision to use our sixth edition in the analysis, thereby centering attention on volumes published in the 1990s.)

Relationship Strategies

The goal of our relationship marketing chapter is to examine

- the patterns of buyer-seller relationships in the business market, including the types of customer relationships;
- the relationship connectors that are used in different types of buyer-seller relationships (Cannon and Perreault 1999);
- a procedure for designing effective relationship marketing strategies; and
- the critical determinants of success in managing strategic alliances.

E-Commerce Tools

Because the Internet provides a powerful medium for developing a one-to-one relationship with customers in the business market, e-commerce strategies are explored in conjunction with our treatment of relationship marketing. Leading-edge companies, such as General Electric and IBM, are using the Internet to convey information, conduct transactions, deliver a host of new services, and forge closer customer relationships. E-commerce strategies likewise pose a host of relationship challenges with channel members as well as with the firm's sales organization.

Supply Chain Management

Supply chain management is crucial in the execution of relationship marketing strategies. Supply chain management assures that product, information, services, and financial resources all flow through the entire value creation process in an effective and efficient manner (Cooper, Lambert, and Pagh 1997). Organizational buyers assign great importance to supply chain processes that reduce cost and eliminate the uncertainty of product delivery. Likewise, business marketers invest considerable financial and human resources in creating supply chain connections to serve the needs and special requirements of customers. For these reasons, we elected to give chapter-length attention to supply chain management in the seventh edition in order to provide a more comprehensive examination of buyer-seller relationships in the business market.

Hurdles for a Transaction-Types Perspective

As supply chain management and a host of e-commerce tools are transforming buyer-seller as well as channel relationships, students are introduced to a new set of theories and concepts that illuminate how business marketers can synchronize activities with suppliers and customers and forge tighter connections with both. In designing a text around customer relationship types, a key hurdle will concern the treatment of these important areas. For example, should the concept of supply chain management be treated in an integrated way before tackling various types of customer relationships or should the treatment be spread across the volume? In the end, the choice, once again, may come down to identifying the core topics that provide the reader with the proper foundation for grasping, understanding, and applying a transaction-types perspective. These are the types of questions that make text writing both interesting and challenging.

CAPTURING STRATEGIC MARKETING CONTENT

Strategic management theorists criticize the marketing literature for its dominant focus on competition in clearly defined, existing markets. For example, Prahalad (1995, p. v) notes:

> It is imperative that researchers consider not only served markets, but also evolving markets; not only existing benefits to customers, but also newer (potential) benefits to customers. Existing conceptions of "served markets" are not a good basis for understanding competitiveness in industries that are evolving.

Clearly, high-technology industries, featuring rapidly changing customer requirements and fast-paced changes in the field of competitors, fall squarely into the business marketing domain. Indeed, high-tech markets represent a rapidly growing and dynamic sector of the world economy but yet often receive only modest attention in the traditional marketing curriculum. The business marketing course provides an ideal vehicle for examining the special features of high-technology markets and for isolating the unique challenges that confront the marketing strategist in this arena.

Hurdles for a Transaction-Types Perspective

To meet the challenges of new competitors, to respond to the changing needs of existing customers, or to carve out enticing new market opportunities, a range of strategic processes are involved at the product market, business unit, and corporate levels. A text built around the management of various types of customer relationships must be supported by frameworks that explore strategic decision processes and the innovation management process. Without this strategic perspective, the discussion will be confined to the served market, overlooking many themes that capture the interests and attention of students.

CONCLUSIONS

Since the first edition of our text was introduced two decades ago, we have found the marketing management perspective to be an effective organizing framework for incorporating new content into a subject area that is growing and developing. Responding to changes in practice, a growing body of research in the business marketing domain, and new theoretical perspectives, some new chapters were added, others were consolidated, and all were thoroughly updated. During this time, increased emphasis on theory and practice has been given to value-based strategies and customer satisfaction, customer relationship management and customer retention, business-to-business services, innovation management, e-commerce, high-technology marketing, and supply chain management. Indeed, many new terms and concepts have entered the vocabulary of the practicing manager. Over time, however, our goal and central focus has remained the same: to provide the student-reader with a foundation of knowledge on the core concepts that informed business marketing managers need to know and to provide them with tools and conceptual frameworks for enhancing their decision-making capabilities in the field.

The proposal by Backhaus, Muehlfeld, and Okoye to design a volume around a transaction-types perspective is intriguing and particularly useful in sparking a debate on the issue of what should actually be taught in the business marketing course, particularly at the undergraduate level. However, as our commentary suggests, we believe that the approach may increase the attention given to relationship marketing, but do so by sacrificing coverage of core content that students and informed business marketing managers need to know. In the end, we opt for a comprehensive approach in exploring strategy making for the business market while Backhaus and colleagues chart a narrower and more specialized path.

REFERENCES

Anderson, James and James A. Narus (1999). *Business Market Management: Understanding, Creating, and Delivering Value.* Upper Saddle River, NJ: Prentice-Hall.

Anderson, Matthew G. and Paul B. Katz (1998). "Strategic Sourcing." *The International Journal of Logistics Management,* 9(1), 1-13.

Bloom, Benjamin S. et al. (1956). *Taxonomy of Educational Objectives, Handbook I: Cognitive Domain.* New York: Longmans.

Cannon, Joseph P. and William D. Perreault Jr. (1999). "Buyer-Seller Relationships in Business Markets." *Journal of Marketing Research* 36(November), 439-460.

Cooper, Martha C., Douglas M. Lambert, and James D. Pagh (1997). "Supply Chain Management: More than a New Name for Logistics." *The International Journal of Logistics Management,* 8(1) (Winter), 1-12.

Hutt, Michael D. and Thomas W. Speh (1998). *Business Marketing Management,* Sixth Edition. Fort Worth: Harcourt.

_____ and _____(2001). *Business Marketing Management,* Seventh Edition. Fort Worth: Harcourt.

Laseter, Timothy W. (1998). *Balanced Sourcing: Cooperation and Competition in Supplier Relationships.* San Francisco: Jossey-Bass Publishing.

Prahalad, C. K. (1995). "Weak Signals Versus Strong Paradigms." *Journal of Marketing Research* 27(August), iii-vi.

Sheth, Jagdish, David M. Gardner, and Dennis E. Garrett (1988). *Marketing Theory: Evolution and Evaluation.* New York: Wiley.

Spekman, Robert E., David W. Stewart, and Wesley J. Johnston (1995). "An Empirical Investigation of the Organizational Buyer's Strategic and Tactical Roles." *Journal of Business-to-Business Marketing* 2(4), 37-63.

Webster, Frederick (1995). *Industrial Marketing Strategy,* Third Edition. New York: Wiley.

Comparative Review of Business-to-Business Marketing Textbooks: A Commentary

James A. Narus

I want to begin by discussing my own experiences with textbook writing, addressing a number of critical issues overlooked in the paper by Backhaus, Muehlfeld, and Okoye. Later on, I will reflect on the research of Professor Backhaus and his colleagues.

CRAFTING A BUSINESS MARKETING TEXTBOOK

A good place to begin is with a question that many instructors will initially assume that they can answer: "What is a management textbook?" To resolve it, I telephoned representatives of the AACSB International, the American Marketing Association (AMA), and our publisher, Prentice-Hall. Officials at the AACSB International, the premier accreditation organization for academic management schools worldwide, informed me that there are "no formal and universally accepted standards as to what constitutes a management textbook." At the AMA, the leading professional marketing association in the United States, representatives similarly responded that the AMA does not have any formal standards concerning the makeup of a marketing textbook. A manager at Prentice-Hall provided the answer that the business book publishing industry appears to use: "A textbook is a book that an author and a publisher mutually agree to market as a textbook." Thus, potential authors have broad latitude as to how to structure a textbook and what materials to include and/or exclude.

Given the absence of formal standards for a management textbook, one might now ask, "What subjects should be covered in a business marketing textbook?" Self-confident instructors might quickly respond that it should address the "common body of knowledge" for business marketing. However, representatives of the AMA have assured me that that organization has no formally agreed-upon statement of the common body of knowledge for business marketing. And, according to AACSB International officials, when their evaluation teams inspect university courses such as business marketing during a program accreditation review, they do not assess whether or not assigned textbooks address the common body of knowledge for those subjects. Instead, they examine the "total collection of materials an instructor uses" in relation to the course objectives that the individual instructor and the institution have jointly specified.

In the book *Taxonomy of Educational Objectives* (Bloom et al. 1956), which Professor Backhaus and his colleagues purportedly use as the foundation of their paper, Bloom and his colleagues state that in determining the amount and kind of knowledge to be covered in a curriculum or course of study individual instructors must strike a balance between attempting to be exhaustive, including all knowledge known about a subject, and focusing exclusively on knowledge that is most germane to the subject. Furthermore, this decision must be tempered with an understanding of how much knowledge a student can reasonably digest and retain within the time frame of the course. Thus, when selecting a textbook for inclusion along with other educational materials used in a course, the individual instructor can legitimately select from books along a continuum from "encyclopedic" (i.e., containing all knowledge) to "focused" (i.e., containing only the most germane). According to the AACSB International, the ultimate decision should be a function of the objectives that the individual instructor hopes to achieve and the total collection of materials to be used in a given course.

With such an extensive range of possibilities, a reader might ask, "So, how did you and Jim Anderson determine how to structure your textbook and what topics to address?" As the reader hopefully knows, our book, *Business Market Management: Understanding, Creating, and Delivering Value* (1999), does not follow the traditional "four P's with industrial examples" approach. Rather, we sought to provide a more progressive approach for business markets. Among our key goals for the project were the following:

1. We wanted *value* to be the cornerstone of the book. As we see it, *Business Market Management* is the process of understanding, creating, and delivering value to targeted business markets and customers. For doing so, a supplier firm is entitled to an equitable share of that value. We intended that all aspects of the book would ultimately relate to the provision and sharing of value.

2. We wanted to demonstrate that business market management decisions are based on rigorous value assessment and data gathered from the marketplace.

3. We wanted to meld emerging and proven management concepts and approaches such as *business processes, doing business across borders,* and *working relationships* and *networks.* These along with value serve as the guiding principles of our book. They enable us to integrate all materials across each chapter. At the same time, they demand that we be cross-functional in our approach rather than focusing exclusively on marketing issues.

4. As we targeted the book for master's-level students, we wanted to write in a managerial style, providing practical approaches to business market management and furnishing abundant examples from global businesses.

5. Most important, we wanted our textbook to be part of a customized solution that an instructor offered to his or her students. Center stage in this solution would be the instructor and his or her unique perspective on business marketing. To enable an instructor to deliver a course tailored to the unique requirements of his or her students, institution, and geographic area, we would provide a focused textbook plus an instructor's manual in which we recommend discussion cases, exercises, simulation games, and supplemental readings along with detailed lesson plans, chapter summaries, student preparation questions, and useful information sources and Internet Web sites.

With a prospectus in mind, we met with representatives of all the major publishers of business marketing textbooks in the United States. We quickly learned that textbook publishing (as contrasted with academic journal publishing) is primarily profit-driven. Not only would our textbook have to be academically sound, it would have to be commercially successful. Furthermore, the top-selling marketing textbooks fall in three mainstream categories: marketing management, marketing research, and consumer behavior. With total annual sales falling well below those in the three mainstream categories, business marketing textbooks constitute a small niche.

As a result of limited profit potential, publishers severely constrain the resources committed to a business marketing textbook project. For example, to most publishers the ideal length of a business marketing textbook is between 400 and 500 pages. Why? Because as page length increases so do production costs. To maintain a reasonable profit margin, the publisher would have to correspondingly increase book price, an increasingly unpalatable option in the highly competitive textbook market. You may have noticed that most business marketing textbooks appear in black and white or have one or two colors. Why? Additional colors dramatically increase costs. The same can be said about illustrations and photographs, particularly those which are copyrighted and require royalty fees for reproduction. To keep costs low, publishers provide niche textbook writers with scant funds to develop support materials such as an instructor's manual, discussion cases, test banks, and presentation slides. Last, niche textbooks are likely to be placed on a three- or four-year revision schedule (as contrasted to a two- or three-year cycle for mainstream textbooks). Thus, how current a textbook's content is will be a function of where it is in the revision cycle at the point of evaluation.

I emphasize these points for several important reasons. First, authors who write niche textbooks such as business marketing are doing so primarily to contribute to the discipline. Second, the constraints on number of pages, colors, and illustrations that publishers impose force authors to agonize over what topics "not to include" in the textbook. Presenting all knowledge from a discipline is becoming increasingly untenable. As one publisher's representative told me, "The market requires only one encyclopedia of marketing. And that spot is competently dominated by Kotler's *Marketing Management* (2000)." Third, any evaluations of textbook content, pages, illustrations, and colors that do not include economic considerations come across as overly simplistic and naive.

To select content for our textbook, we began with a comprehensive review of the academic, popular management, and trade literatures. Then, Jim and I conducted focus groups and surveyed business marketing instructors, students, and business managers. We discovered that the preferences of these latter three constituencies had many similarities.

What have we learned from business marketing instructors? To begin with, instructors, particularly at the master's level, want to be able to clearly differentiate their course content from other marketing electives as well as from business marketing courses offered at the undergraduate level. Increasingly, administrators are calling upon instructors to justify the continued presence of a business marketing course in their school's curriculum. Instructors need to be able to demonstrate that their course is unique, covering materials not found in other electives. We firmly believe that a course designed around our approach to business market management enables them to do so. And, we routinely work with instructors to help them develop and distinguish their courses in business marketing, offering guidance on session topics, discussion cases, exercises, and projects.

As is common in master's-level programs, instructors want to be able to customize their courses to the local requirements of their students by selecting their own discussion cases and supplemental readings that address current topics of interest. To accommodate them, we do not include discussion cases within the textbook. Instead, we recommend a handful of Harvard Business School, University of Western Ontario, or IMEDE discussion cases that instructors can use along with each chapter and provide summaries of those discussion cases in our instructor's manual. In addition, we furnish at "no charge" to adopters of our textbook a number of proprietary discussion cases that we have written for instructors to reproduce and use. By doing these things, we help to hold the textbook's price in check while freeing up space to discuss other contemporary topics such as e-procurement, outsourcing, and network management in greater detail. Last, instructors want a textbook with between 400 and 450 pages that has a reasonable price tag for students.

What have we learned from business marketing students? Most important, they do not want a long book. Ideally, they would like ten to fifteen chapters with not more than twenty-five pages of text per chapter. Of course, they expect the text to be supplemented with numerous charts, illustrations, and break-out boxes. As with publishers and instructors, students believe that a book with a total of 400 to 500 pages is reasonable. Clearly, students would prefer reading a textbook that discusses fewer, critical topics in greater detail to one that provides superficial treatment of a myriad of seemingly unrelated and unimportant topics. As one student complained to me, "Studying marketing entails memorizing a large number of lists." In response to this observation, we have made a deliberate attempt to avoid the "marketing list syndrome" (i.e., covering a broad range of issues superficially). Instead, we focus on what we believe to be the most germane topics and attempt to integrate them across the book via our guiding principles.

Students said they prefer a managerial orientation to a theoretical one and want examples from business practice that illustrate concepts, frameworks, and strategies described in the text. In response, Jim and I conducted extensive field research at major U.S., European, and Asian companies over a three-year period and devised fifty-seven mini case studies to improve student understanding of important concepts. These fifty-seven minicases appear as break-out boxes throughout the text. Simultaneously, we summarized our findings in three management practice articles for the *Harvard Business Review.*

Finally, students want reasonably priced textbooks. We feel that one way to keep price in check is to eschew the "more is better" syndrome. To do so, we carefully scrutinize every potential topic, avoid rehashing subjects that are covered thoroughly in introductory marketing textbooks such as Kotler's *Marketing Management,* and limit ourselves to those topics which we believe deliver the greatest practical value to students.

Ultimately, the purpose of management education is to prepare students for careers in business. For this reason, Jim and I felt that it was critical that our textbook be relevant to business managers. To ensure that it was, we sought out topics from, brainstormed with, and reviewed materials repeatedly with senior executives from major corporations across a variety of industries. These corporations included ABN-AMRO Bank, Arthur D. Little, Asea Brown Boveri (ABB), Allegiance Healthcare, Dresner Klienwort Benson, DuPont, GLS, Grainger, Heineken, Microsoft, and Sonoco Products. The directors of Institute for the Study of Business Markets (ISBM) and managers from select sponsoring corporations also assisted us in grounding our book in reality. When we completed rough drafts of our chapters, Jim and I sent copies to these executives and asked them along with their colleagues to review the content and writing style for relevance and comprehensibility. And their contributions have paid off in that to the best of my knowledge about 20 percent of our textbook sales come from corporations. Our publisher tells us that this rate is unusually high for a textbook and reflects the relevance of our subject matter and approach to business managers.

CRITICISMS OF THE RESEARCH

Although Professor Backhaus and his colleagues may be well intentioned, this is not sound academic research. Let me raise a few "reasonable doubts" about their procedures and conclusions.

Where Are the Validity Test Results?

Professor Backhaus and his colleagues indeed undertake ambitious research. Standards for research in the behavioral sciences call for validity tests in such instances. Yet, the authors neither discuss validity nor provide appropriate supporting validity test results in their chapter. Here are a few instances where validity tests are clearly needed.

The Adaptation of the Bloom et al. (1956) Taxonomy. As the following quotes from the book indicate, Bloom and his associates had specific applications in mind for their taxonomy:

> Teachers building a curriculum should find here a range of possible educational goals or outcomes in the cognitive area . . . (pp. 1-2)

> It should be noted that we are not attempting to classify the instructional methods used by teachers, the ways in which teachers relate themselves to students, or the different kinds of instructional materials they use. We are not attempting to classify the particular subject matter or content. What we are classifying is the *intended behavior* of students—the ways in which individuals are to act, think, or feel as the result of participating in some unit of instruction. . . . The emphasis in the Handbook is on obtaining evidence on the extent to which desired and intended behaviors have been learned by the student. (pp. 12-13)

Bloom and his associates intended that the taxonomy be used to evaluate a curriculum or course of study, not a textbook. Individual teachers set the educational objectives for their courses, not academic researchers. Teachers are under no obligation to pursue every educational objective in every course. All six specified educational objectives are concerned with the cognitive domain of learning, not just the last five, as Table 22 implies. To evaluate the degree to which educational objectives have been met, teachers and/or administrations must assess students after they have completed the course, not by counting words, pages, topics, and illustrations in a textbook. Clearly, Professor Backhaus and his colleagues have applied the Bloom taxonomy out of its intended context in a way not originally planned. Without validity tests, there is no way for the reader to determine whether or not Professor Backhaus and his colleagues' adaptation is appropriate and meaningful.

The Development of Indicators for Educational Objectives. As Professor Backhaus and his colleagues state, "no conclusive and general operationalization of Bloom's six fundamental cognitive abilities as educational activities has yet been undertaken." Thus, their overriding task in this research is to develop and test indicators of Bloom's educational objectives. Yet, Professor Backhaus and his colleagues do not follow standard procedures for measurement development, reliability testing, or validity testing (APA 1985). Without validity tests results, how can you know, for example, whether or not "knowledge conveyed" is in fact a function of net page area, number of lines, depth of subdivisions, and the use of various structuring models? After all, an unread textbook achieves no educational objectives!

Professor Backhaus and his colleagues merely declare that their proposed indicators measure corresponding educational objectives. Several of these unsubstantiated indicators are highly questionable. For example, they rely upon pricing discussions to indicate "depth of coverage," the extent to which ten arbitrarily selected market segmentation approaches are covered to indicate the "theory-practice connection," and the presence of case studies to indicate "more complex capabilities." Again, without validity test results, how do we know this is so?

Perhaps the most specious procedure for measurement development that they employ is the LIX index. For starters, Professor Backhaus and his colleagues offer a confusing explanation as to the connection between LIX and the underlying educational objective.

Bloom et al. (1956) define their second educational objective as "comprehension." For no apparent reason and without explanation, Professor Backhaus and his colleagues change this to "understanding." Then they argue that "readability" is a criterion for the "transfer of knowledge," without explaining how this relates to understanding. They state that the LIX index measures readability and then assert, "LIX represents comprehensibility quite adequately." In simple terms, what does this all mean?

Readers who have successfully modeled behavioral phenomena know that a latent construct has multiple facets. To capture each of its dimensions, researchers must develop several measures or indicators. LIX, which is calculated as the sum of the average number of words per sentence and the percentage of words with seven or more letters in sample passages, is but a single measure of readability. And, there are a number of critical limitations to this measure. Most notably, there is the assumption that words with fewer than seven letters are more readily comprehended than longer words. However, consider the following list of paired synonyms: important-basal, express-indite, eliminate-exsect, boundary-bower, and posterior-caudal. The first synonym in each pair has seven letters or more while the second synonym has fewer than seven. Which of these word pairs do you think your students would find easier to read? Of course, to answer that question you would have to survey students and not just count words and sentence length in textbooks.

There are a number of other unanswered questions concerning measure development in this article. Bloom et al. (1956) specify six educational objectives. With no explanation, Professor Backhaus and his colleagues combine the last three—analysis, synthesis, and evaluation—into a single objective. Furthermore, Professor Backhaus and his colleagues devise three indicators of knowledge, two indicators of understanding, one of application, and one for combined objectives. Are not readers entitled to know how and why these operations were performed?

The Specification of Business Marketing Topics. As mentioned earlier, AMA representatives state that there is no formal and universally accepted statement of the "common body of knowledge" in business marketing. Thus, Professor Backhaus and his colleagues' listing of business marketing topics and subsequent evaluation of textbook content is based solely on their own opinions and preferences. They provide no evidence whatsoever that their opinions and preferences are better or worse than anyone else's. In fact, had any other researcher conducted this evaluation, they would likely come out with significantly different results!

Let me give you but one example. Professor Backhaus and his colleagues state, "The Anderson and Narus book presents market segmentation criteria, but no particular approach." In fact, our approach is embedded in "market sensing," a contemporary and progressive process that Professor George Day of Wharton has developed (Day 1994). And, we advocate value-based segmentation that is driven off of value assessment (see Dowling et al., 2000 for a recent treatment). As neither Day's market sensing nor value-based segmentation appear on the Backhaus et al. list of "preferred" segmentation approaches in Table 27, we receive no credit for covering market segmentation. Had another researcher who acknowledges market sensing and value-based segmentation as legitimate approaches conducted this evaluation, we would have received credit for covering market segmentation.

To assemble a list of their "preferred" topics, Professor Backhaus and his colleagues turn to Reid and Plank (2000) and Narus and Anderson (1998) for the academic perspective. However, the Reid and Plank article is a "positive" (i.e., descriptive) literature review that catalogs academic marketing research over a twenty-year period and is not intended to provide "normative" guidance on which topics to address in a business marketing textbook. In fact, a book designed around the Reid and Plank article would probably be better suited for a PhD seminar on academic marketing theory and research than an undergraduate or master's-level course. Furthermore, the Reid and Plank article is structured around the traditional four P's of marketing and would likely lead to a bias favoring textbooks organized around the four P's. Similarly, the Narus and Anderson (1998) article reports on topics that business marketing professors currently teach and not those which they should teach.

Perhaps even more curious is their selection of the Plank (1982) article as the source of the practical perspective. The Plank article is about twenty years old. To put this in perspective, Professor Plank wrote the article three years prior to the widespread acceptance of the personal computer and ten years before the adoption of the Internet as business tools. Based on the research presented in this article, there is no way for the reader to determine whether or not the topics listed in the Plank article capture the current thinking of managers. In fact, I would argue that many of the managers Plank surveyed in 1982 have long since retired.

What Methodology Did the Authors Actually Use?

Although Professor Backhaus and his colleagues claim to have been systematic, the manuscript does not provide sufficient detail to allow the reader to make such a judgment. In fact, it is not really clear what procedures the authors followed. For example, they neither describe the sampling approach (e.g., quota, convenience, random) they used to select the ten passages for the LIX evaluation nor how the textbooks were sorted into three groups (e.g., discriminant analysis, cluster analysis). Here are other major gaps in the description of their methodology.

Selection of Textbooks. Professor Backhaus and his colleagues state that they gathered the names of business marketing textbooks from the *Marketing Education Review* (1999), the *Industrial Marketing Practitioner* (1999), and the study of Narus and Anderson (1998). *The Marketing Education Review* Web site lists eleven textbooks. Why did the authors choose to review only seven? Conspicuous in its absence is *Business Marketing: Connecting Strategy, Relationships, and Learning* by F. Robert Dwyer and John F. Tanner Jr. (2001), which is now in its second edition. Given that Professor Dwyer is an eminent scholar in business marketing and marketing channels, the exclusion of his textbook merits a full explanation. Equally questionable is their inclusion of *Industrial Marketing Strategy* by Frederick E. Webster (1995). At the 2001 AMA Summer Educators' Conference in Washington, DC, a representative of John Wiley and Sons, Inc., informed me that his firm no longer actively promotes the Webster book. And, it was not even on display in the exhibition hall. If the publisher no longer promotes it, why did Professor Backhaus and his colleagues evaluate it?

Coverage of Business Topics. To assess the educational objective of "knowledge," Professor Backhaus and his colleagues go to great length to report on the level of coverage that each of the seven textbooks provides to the listing of business topics based on their opinions and preferences. Curiously, they never provide an operational definition of the word "coverage." And they alternate its use with other undefined terms, including handle, portrayal, treat, isolated treatment, and integrated in overall treatment. What are the distinctions among these various terms and are they important? Furthermore, they never explain how a textbook merits the rating of "covered" for a given topic or what procedures were followed when the textbooks were evaluated. To top it all off, Professor Backhaus and his colleagues provide no reliability test results for their coverage measures. As a result, there is no way to know whether or not other researchers can replicate the results of this study. Let me give you but a few examples from their assessment of our textbook.

When referring to our textbook, the authors state, "Consequently, the instrument 'price' is considered, with the focus on value-based pricing, and channel management as a component of the instrument 'distribution.' All other aspects of the marketing mix [product and promotion] are consequently ignored." In fact, we address "product," which has been subsumed into the more relevant and contemporary notion of market offerings or total solutions in two separate chapters—"Managing Market Offerings" (pp. 161-199) and "New Offering Realization" (pp. 200-249). Promotion, on the other hand, is part of the chapter "Gaining Customers" (e.g., integrated marketing communications are discussed beginning on p. 302, and personal selling beginning on p. 306).

They similarly claim that we ignore organizational purchasing behavior. In fact, this topic is addressed in our chapter "Understanding Firms As Customers." For example, we discuss the variety of purchasing orientations that firms adopt and their implications for buying behavior from pages 84 to 104. We examine how purchasing professionals interact with other functional areas as part of the resource acquisition process from pages 105 to 113. We describe how actual purchase decisions are made and evaluated from pages 113 to 121.

In another passage they state, "Apart from the consideration of individual pricing strategies, all other areas are excluded." As we mention in our preface, we have adopted a process approach. Instead of grouping all discussions of pricing into a chapter on pricing, we introduce them throughout the book whenever a given process requires that they be considered. Here are some of the pricing topics we address: price analysis (p. 86), target pricing (p. 88), the Lopez Approach (p. 88), target costing (p. 95), trading higher price for lower total costs (p. 95), value-in-use price (p. 99), the SPI Index (p. 117), operational excellence strategy (p. 130), commodity pricing trap (p. 164), flexible market offerings approach to pricing (beginning on p. 167), augmenting service pricing (p. 173), cost-plus pricing (pp. 186-187), competition-based pricing (p. 187), pricing across borders (pp. 194-196), initial use discounts (pp. 244-246), reseller discounts (p. 280), negotiating initial price (pp. 326-327), revenue management (pp. 330-331), constructing a reseller pricing sheet (pp. 346-348), cooperative pricing (p. 381), pricing as a function of customer relationship offerings (pp. 380-381), base-loading (p. 382), collaborative risk-sharing and gain-sharing agreements (p. 401), transaction pricing (pp. 403 to 404), loyalty programs (p. 404), and price defections (p. 410), among others.

In fact, I could provide page numbers in our text where most of the "themes" listed in Tables 20 and 21 are discussed. Why then is there a discrepancy between my evaluation and theirs? A reader simply cannot answer the question because Professor Backhaus and his colleagues do not describe their assessment process in sufficient detail.

Moreover, passages within this paper hint that the methodology described is not the one they actually utilized. For example, in the Criteria and Methodology section, the authors state that they will compare the seven textbooks based on the characteristics of the "instrumentally oriented approach" (i.e., the four P's) and the "marketing-management approach" (i.e., analysis, planning, implementation, and control). Later on in the Results section, they say that in addition to the instrumentally oriented approach and the marketing management approach, "we analyzed the extent to which other approaches were used in all the textbooks considered." They conclude with this statement: "This confirms the statement made by Backhaus (1998) that no English-language textbook really uses a transaction-types approach for structuring." The reader must wonder, "Which approaches did Professor Backhaus and his colleagues actually study and what is the true purpose of this article?"

Do the Research, Data, and Findings Support Their Conclusions?

Other than the LIX index, all of the data that Professor Backhaus and his colleagues collect is "nominal" and they report no statistical "tests of differences." Yet, Professor Backhaus and his colleagues do not hesitate to draw many profound and far-reaching conclusions. Let's examine a few.

> . . . the books of Anderson and Narus and Webster do not offer either case studies or test questions. Therefore, it is doubtful that, on their own, they contribute much toward developing complex skills.

To begin with, Professor Backhaus and his colleagues never provide an operational definition of case studies. I can cite four types. A "minicase" or "caseette" is a short (i.e., one or two pages) illustration of an approach, strategy, or tactic a company has used. These typically appear as break-out boxes in textbooks and management practice magazines. They are used to demonstrate a concept or approach. For example, we provide fifty-seven minicases in our textbook. A "research case study" provides a compendium of findings from a qualitative research project. A "consulting case study" recounts the entire set of activities from design, data collection, analysis, and recommendations that a team from a management consulting firm completes for a client. A "class discussion case study" is a pedagogical tool instructors often use to teach management concepts and frameworks in a class setting. To which of these types of cases does Professor Backhaus and his colleagues refer?

More important, they provide no data, validity tests, or statistical tests that enable them to link the presence or absence of case studies (whichever variety they mean) to the development of complex skills. To do so, they would have to conduct a survey or controlled experiments among students who have used these books.

> No English-language textbook uses a transaction-types approach for structuring.

The research conducted and data reported in this manuscript do not support this conclusion. Apparently, Professor Backhaus and his colleagues are unaware of the fact that in the United States instructors often use the transaction-types approach to structure marketing electives courses titled Relationship Marketing or Strategic Account Management. In the field of operations, the approach is similarly used to structure Supply Chain Management courses. According to the search engine of Amazon.com, there are some seventy-five books on relationship management and ninety on supply chain management on the market. Some of these are used as textbooks. Before Professor Backhaus and his colleagues can draw this conclusion, they need to thoroughly evaluate these 165 books. They do not do so in this manuscript.

> Although the authors frequently acknowledge that the various transactions in business-to-business markets are particularly heterogeneous, and that this requires differentiated marketing strategies, the actual approach followed in the books is undifferentiated. A possible solution to this could . . . be found in structuring a textbook according to an explicit typology of transactions.

As Professor Backhaus has advocated a transaction-types approach to marketing in previous works (e.g., Backhaus 1998), I am not at all surprised that he comes to this conclusion. In fact, over 50 percent of both the Conclusions and Limitations and Directions for Future Research sections of this paper deal with the transaction-types approach. Yet, neither the research procedures described in the Criteria and Methodology section nor the nominal data reported in the Results section of this paper lend any credence to this claim. Furthermore, until the authors reach the end of the paper, they never mention differentiated versus undifferentiated marketing strategies at all. When they do, they do not bother to provide and then use standard academic definitions of those constructs.

Having reflected upon and reviewed this paper, I wonder if the true purpose of its content is to promote the transaction-types approach, and in particular the Backhaus version (Backhaus 1998), as a structure for a business marketing textbook. If so, the authors should have stated it clearly in the introduction and designed research to demonstrate its utility. Professor Backhaus and his colleagues may be convinced of the superiority of the transaction-types approach; however, this research neither supports nor discredits that view.

REFERENCES

Anderson, J.C. and J.A. Narus (1999). *Business Market Management: Understanding, Creating, and Delivering Value.* Upper Saddle River, NJ: Prentice-Hall, Inc.

APA (1985). *Standards for Educational and Psychological Testing.* Washington, DC: American Psychological Association, Inc.

Backhaus, K. (1988). "Industrial Marketing: A German View." *Thexis* 15(4), 2-6.

A Committee of College and University Examiners (1956). *Taxonomy of Educational Objectives,* B. Bloom, M.D. Engelhart, E.J. Furst, W.H. Hill, and D.R. Krathwohl (eds.). New York: David McKay Company, Inc. [*Note:* I refer to this as Bloom et al. 1956 in this commentary].

Day, G.S. (1994). "The Capabilities of Market-Driven Organizations." *Journal of Marketing* (October), 37-52.

Dowling, G., G.L. Lilien, A. Rangaswamy, and R.J. Thomas (2000). *Harvesting Customer Value: Understanding and Applying Customer-Value Based Segmentation.* University Park, PA: Institute for the Study of Business Markets.

Dwyer, F.R. and J.F. Tanner Jr. (2001). *Business Marketing: Connecting Strategy, Relationships, and Learning,* Second Edition. Boston: Irwin McGraw-Hill.

Industrial Marketing Practitioner (1999). Industrial Marketing Library, <http://www.practitioner.com/library1.htm>.

Kotler, P. (2000). *Marketing Management,* The Millennium Edition. Upper Saddle River, NJ: Prentice-Hall, Inc.

Marketing Education Review (1999). Business Marketing Textbooks, Case Books, Readers, Trade Books, and Simulation Games. <http://cbpa.Louisville.edu/mer/business_textbooks.htm>.

Narus, J.A. and J.C. Anderson (1998). "Master's Level Education in Business Marketing: *Quo Vadis?" Journal of Business-to-Business Marketing* 5(1/2), 75-93.

Plank, R.E. (1982). "Industrial Marketing Education: Practitioner's Views." *Industrial Marketing Management* 11, 311-315.

Reid, D.A. and R.E. Plank (2000). "Business Marketing Comes of Age: A Comprehensive Review of the Literature," *Journal of Business-to-Business Marketing* 7(2/3), 9-185.

Webster, F.E. Jr. (1995). *Industrial Marketing Strategy,* Third Edition. New York: John Wiley and Sons.

Comparative Review of Business-to-Business Marketing Textbooks: A Commentary

Richard E. Plank

Professor Backhaus and his colleagues have done an excellent job in examining textbooks currently available, primarily in the United States, for use as tools in both graduate and undergraduate instruction in business marketing. The authors note the importance of the book as a teaching tool and make a major contribution by applying Bloom's *Taxonomy* (1956) of learning outcome types to the examination of the textbook as a teaching tool. Arguably, this taxonomy is the major theoretical underpinning in the education research field, and as noted by the authors, its relevance is clear in terms of its continued usage in developing educational programs and in research. The authors group the seven textbooks into three groups of five, one, and one, respectively. They note that all books provide content, the first group of five books having the most comprehensive content. Also all books provide the instructor with some assistance in the development of higher-level cognitive skills. They also provide some very interesting descriptive comments on the ability of the books to provide specific themes of knowledge. They do note that no book provides all the educational criteria. Finally, they suggest that there may be room for a text that is structured along the lines of transaction or relationship types, rather then the standard marketing management approach that all seven books basically employ. We will come back to that suggestion later.

The purpose of this commentary is not to criticize or debate the presentation but to start extending the authors work by taking it to another level. This author appreciates the contribution that Professor Backhaus and his colleagues have made and seeks to extend their work and to engender some debate. The critical contribution seems to me to be the application of Bloom's *Taxonomy* (1956) and the application of those types or levels of learning to the textbook and the ability of the textbook to support those types or levels of learning. The extension I hope to convince readers I am making is to realize that education is a process, not much different from many other processes undertaken by people, such as assembling an automobile, writing up a purchase order, or millions of other processes consisting of sets of activities that are somehow linked into what we define as a process. Therefore, as in all other processes this author is familiar with, the development of the textbook for a course needs to start with the vision of the learning process, not just for that course, but for education in general. Since a course such as business marketing can be included in many different learning situations, undergraduate degree programs, graduate degree programs, and continuing education of various types, I will focus my comments on the undergraduate situation. I recognize that the position I am taking is controversial, but what I hope to do is to stimulate further debate among our colleagues, and while many may not agree with all my assertions, and my position may ultimately prove to be nonfavored by most of my colleagues, I think that the debate it might stimulate will ultimately improve both course development and textbook development.

Industrial or business marketing has always been something of a stepchild. Even though early textbooks date back to the 1930s, the existence of business marketing as a field of study has come under attack in the past (Fern and Brown 1984) and continues to occupy what appears to be a very minor place in most marketing curricula. In schools that offer business marketing at the undergraduate level as an elective it is mostly a single elective course, with few exceptions. For example, Lichtenthal and Butaney (1991) estimate that fully one-half of all business school graduates begin their careers with business marketing firms, yet less than 2 percent of them had business marketing in their curriculum. Discussion of undergraduate curriculum issues in business marketing in the marketing literature is also not deemed very important as only a few authors have talked about content, the most complete discussion being the aforementioned piece by Lichtenthal and Butaney. These authors do a thorough job of discussing what they believe the course should consist of, what concepts need to be applied, what skills need to be learned, and what pedagogical tools can be used.

The past ten to fifteen years have seen some real changes in business practices. The continuing information technology advances, the continuing shrinking of the globe, and movements such as increasing quality, integrating functional activities, and the notion of the supply-value chain have had dramatic impacts on how organizations do business. Anderson (2000), for one, suggests how these activities are changing how business is done, what skills are needed, and even the potential role of business school education in dealing with these changes.

Perhaps one of the major changes in the past ten to fifteen years has been the increasing focus on business processes and their improvement. Not that this is exactly a new idea; it started off as time and motion studies, was called short-interval scheduling in the 1970s, and has since been broadened in focus and called business process re-engineering. In all cases the focus is to understand some process at some level of abstraction and to use that information to improve that process. While a number of contributions have been made over the years, a major recent contributor is Eli Goldratt (Goldratt and Cox 1992). His classic book, *The Goal,* outlines his theory of constraints in a business novel, including the trials and tribulations of one Alex Rogo and his team of manufacturing personnel who use the principles of the theory of constraints to turn an unprofitable plant into one that makes money. The general focus is on throughput with the efforts made to decrease inventory and operating expenses.

The theory of constraints is grounded in systems theory and has a number of perspectives. For example, Cooper and Loe (2000) have used the specific problem-solving methodology of the theory as a teaching tool to get students to identify the core problem and work into solutions. It has seen substantial debate in the accounting literature (Ruhl 1997; Kee 1995; Fritzch 1997-1998), especially as theory of constraints relates to activity-based costing, and has many other applications in virtually every functional area of business as well as in general management areas such as managing projects (Steyn 2001). I would not argue that the theory of constraints is necessarily widespread and ubiquitous, or well understood, but it has been explored in many contexts.

The fundamental point of the theory of constraints is simply that each and every process has a constraint in it that limits the ability of that process to reach the goal. For example, in the book *The Goal* the problems are defined in terms of cycle time, the time it takes to complete the process and the cost to produce the product. The firm had just completed the installation of robotics in one part of the process but was not seeing throughput; that is, the total cycle time and costs were not dropping. The lesson to the reader is simply that the expenditures were made on a part of the process, which did not lead to improvements of the total process and therefore were ineffective. As the reader progresses through the book he or she learns how to identify where the constraints are and how to deal with them. The reader also learns that dealing with one constraint only means that some other constraint exists, so that process improvement is typically a journey, not something with finite beginning and ending points. The reader also quickly learns the problems with defining process problems narrowly, as in the robotics example, and recognizes that while it is useful to break up a process into manageable pieces, one must always examine the big picture to assess true benefits.

My fundamental argument that I am asking the reader to consider is that education is a process. As such, the notion of process improvement and the use of theory of constraints have application in our endeavors as well. Perhaps the first issue is to examine how education as a process is similar and different from other processes, such as putting an automobile together on the assembly line. One piece of the education process is a business marketing course; one piece of assembling an automobile is attaching the starter motor to the engine. Both consist of a set of activities linked together. Both are pieces of an overall larger system or process. It seems to me that the primary difference is in the people involved. By that I mean in the automobile assembly operation the value is created by an assembler who connects one inanimate object, a starter, to another, an engine. In the educational example we have a person, a professor who is trying to impart knowledge, skills, and attitudes to a student, who clearly is not an inanimate object.

Process improvement has two very important constructs that drive it. One is synchronization and the other is standardization. In the automotive example it is important to put the starter in at the correct time in the process and to synchronize it with other parts of the overall process. Put it in too early and you may have to take it back out to put something else in. One of the basic rules of processes is that if law does not require it, or the customer is not willing to pay for it, why are you doing it? Standardization is also an important construct. Quality has many definitions and examples, but a simple way of looking at it is to consider design quality and build quality. In the automotive example we can design quality both in terms of the materials used and the processes used to assemble those materials. But we still have to execute those processes. If, for example, the starter is required to be torqued to a particular spec and the assembler ignores that, you the buyer of that new car may find, three days after taking delivery, that your starter is dragging on the highway making an awful noise. That is a build quality defect caused by the assembler not following procedures regarding putting in the starter. For that particular example, the standardized process was not followed and resulted in a quality defect.

What I am arguing is that education, as a process, also needs to consider standardization and synchronization. And it needs to consider this from both the perspective of the individual course and major and the overall process of education.

Let us begin by asking some basic questions about the overall role of education at the undergraduate level. Without getting into the debate about the role of education, which has been going on as long as formal education has existed, we first need to consider as concretely as possible the overall goals of education, how our specific program will meet those goals, and, of course, how we will measure them. All AACSB business schools in the United States are mission driven and have thus gone through this thinking process. Part of that process is the development and ongoing improvement of the structure of the curriculum that defines in concrete terms the nature of the knowledge skills and attitudes/values that should be the outcome of the process. At a macro level, the activities of this process of delivering the curriculum are the courses, and important questions that need to be resolved are simply how we synchronize and standardize them. I am sure most of my colleagues have gone through the standardization debate at some level of abstraction, for example, the use of the same textbook or not for the marketing principles course. At Western Michigan University we have a standard syllabus, which defines the core knowledge areas and to a lesser extent, skills and attitudes/values, and our expectation is that instructors will at least deliver in some form the core knowledge areas. However, there are no measures. My perception is that most marketing departments have had similar debates and there is a wide range of standardization being practiced, from none to much more structured environments. My perception is that in other parts of the world, there is on average more structure.

I believe that synchronization is an issue that is much less considered. Our colleagues in accounting consider this issue extensively, as much of accounting builds on previous knowledge. However, in the marketing discipline, I believe, and I am not aware of any empirically based knowledge, that this is considered rarely by most faculties and, when it is, it is superficial. In fact, I would argue that many faculty members might not even be aware of what their colleagues are teaching, even in the same course.

At the business marketing course level, the concepts of synchronization and standardization are equally important. Standardization comes into play whenever there is more than one section, and given the lack of popularity of business marketing as a discipline and a course, this is probably not much of an issue in most institutions that offer the course. However, synchronization is much more of an issue. For most institutions that offer the course, it needs to be thought through in terms of how the course contributes to the outcome goals at various levels and, given that, how it should be designed and delivered. Not just with other marketing courses, but the core courses in other disciplines, notably accounting and finance, which, arguably, constitute the language of business.

The textbook is a tool. As you will recall, Professor Backhaus and his colleagues suggested that a transaction or relationship focus might be a better or at least alternative focus for the textbook. The reader familiar with Reid and Plank (2000) would probably suggest that this author would agree with that suggestion. My own argument is simply that the two most important constructs in any business marketing course are how business customers value purchases, and thus make decisions, and how they want to relate to the company, as well as personal relationships with supplier company personnel. I would argue that the crux of business marketing revolves around those two issues, and, therefore, any book that through its focus provided the student with the knowledge, skills, and attitudes corresponding with those goals I would be in favor of. However, those colleagues who define the goals of the course differently and the linkages with the other parts of the educational process differently are going to come to different conclusions. The key point is that we go through the process, not necessarily that each university who offers a program or course agrees.

In developing a textbook we have to consider synchronization not only within our discipline but also from the perspective of other disciplines. While it is my perception that all of the business marketing texts have given some consideration to this, all could be much more explicit. As instructors I wonder if the reader is as frustrated as I am with having to teach some basic accounting or financial concepts, for example, because the student either has not had them or does not remember them. The former is caused by lack of standardization and the latter by the fact that students are not inanimate objects and learn differently as well as more or less than their fellow students. By being more explicitly synchronous or integrative a textbook could provide an important service to all of us teaching the business marketing course.

One final note: I think it is important to consider how one would implement this kind of thinking and to recognize the "sacred cow" it attacks. In the United States we have this concept called academic freedom. While an official definition is published and available, the interpretation and understanding of that concept is almost as varied as there are faculty. When you formally and objectively examine education as a process with the goal to standardize and synchronize the process, given the limits of our students, you effectively suggest that our notion of academic freedom is somewhat narrow. You agree as a group of faculty to pursue certain goals, to standardize certain aspects of the curriculum and to synchronize the process, and to develop and use measures to judge how well you are doing. To faculty who define academic freedom very broadly this is, in a word, repugnant. And, there are risks. As has been argued by Plank, Minton, and Blackshear (1997), in a sales process improvement context, one does not want to standardize or synchronize out the creativity that is so important in delivering a high quality education experience.

In conclusion, I hope the preceding discussion generates some further discussion and further thinking. I firmly believe that education is a process and would argue that the discussion needs to revolve around similarities and differences of the process we are involved with versus others that have been successful and continuously improved. What is in question is not the issue that education is a process, or that processes need to be improved, but rather how what we have learned in other contexts about processes and improvement applies or does not apply to our context. The key to get answers is to ask the right questions, and while these may not be the right questions, we need to explore them and then continue on to answer these or other more relevant questions.

REFERENCES

Anderson, Shirley (2000). "The Globally Competitive Firm: Functional Integration, Value Chain Logistics, Global Marketing, and Business College Strategic Support." *Competitiveness Review* 10(2), 33-45.

Bloom, Benjamin S. (ed.) (1956). *Taxonomy of Education Objectives: The Classification of Educational Goals.* New York: D. McKay Co.

Cooper, Marjorie J. and Terry W. Loe (2000). "Using the Theory of Constraints Thinking Process to Improve Problem-Solving Skills in Marketing." *Journal of Marketing Education* 22(5), 137-146.

Fern, Edward F. and James R. Brown (1984). "The Industrial/Consumer Marketing Dichotomy: A Case of Insufficient Justification." *Journal of Marketing* 48(2), 68-77.

Fritsch, Ralph B. (1997-1998). "Activity Based Costing and the Theory of Constraints: Using Time Horizons to Resolve Two Alternative Concepts of Product Cost." *Journal of Applied Business Research* 14(Winter), 83-90.

Goldratt, Eliyahu M. and Jeff Cox (1992). *The Goal: A Process of Ongoing Improvement.* New York: North River Press Publishing Corporation.

Kee, Robert (1995). "Integrating Activity-Based Costing with the Theory of Constraints to Enhance Production-Related Decision Making." *Accounting Horizons* 9(December), 48-61.

Lichtenthal, J. David, and Gul Butaney (1991). "Undergraduate Industrial Marketing: Content and Methods." *Industrial Marketing Management* 20(3), 231-240.

Plank, Richard E., Ann P. Minton, and Thomas Blackshear (1997). "Standardizing the Sales Process: Applying TQM to the Selling Process." *American Business Review* 10(2), 52-58.

Reid, David A. and Richard E. Plank (2000). "Business Marketing: A Twenty-Year Review." *Journal of Business-to-Business Marketing* 7(2-3), 9-185.

Ruhl, John M. (1997). "Managing Constraints." *The CPA Journal* 67(1), 60-63.

Steyn, Herman (2001). "An Investigation into the Fundamentals of Critical Chain Project Scheduling." *International Journal of Project Management* 19(6), 363-369.

Business-to-Business Marketing Textbooks: Replies to Commentaries

Klaus Backhaus
Katrin Muehlfeld
Diana Okoye

INTRODUCTION

In conducting our comparative analysis, our main objective was to gain insight into the strengths and weaknesses of various English-speaking textbooks on business-to-business marketing. While attempting to derive results as systematically as possible, we did not try to establish an objective "rating" of the selected books as their suitability hinges on the underlying, context-specific teaching objectives. Despite this subjective element, we were nevertheless hoping to be able to share our results with other business marketing scholars and practitioners, for they, too, may have been confronted with the problem of textbook selection in the past and might find our analysis helpful in the future—either in terms of the results or the methodology. The thoughtful commentaries by Professors Butaney, Hutt and Speh, Narus, and Plank, to whom we are very thankful for their much appreciated efforts, add important and interesting perspectives, some taking a broader, more visionary view, others discussing our analysis itself in greater detail.

This English version was edited by Brian Bloch. The authors are grateful to Dr. Bloch for his comments and suggestions relating to the clarity and precision of the text.

REPLY TO PROFESSOR BUTANEY'S COMMENTS

Professor Butaney very constructively discusses our application of Bloom's taxonomy (1956) and the challenge of what topics should be included in a business marketing textbook in order to ensure an effective progression of students through that hierarchy. The latter issue concerns mainly aspects of conceptual complexity and student information overload, as well as suggestions for enhancing the procedures for comparing and evaluating textbooks. First, with respect to the enhancement of the criteria, Professor Butaney convincingly argues in favor of broadening the knowledge criteria in order to additionally analyze conceptual complexity. The problem, though, in our view, lies with the measurement of the relevant, i.e., the *perceived* complexity. As he points out, the perceived conceptual complexity depends largely on the reader, on the level of knowledge and skills he or she has already acquired in the field. We strongly support that this is a factor of prime importance. However, we feel that a sound assessment in this regard could not be included in our analysis but has to be undertaken by the teacher of a particular class, just as, for example, a qualitative evaluation of the importance of marketing situations presented in a book's case studies. Professor Butaney then expresses concerns that business marketing might be especially prone to excessive conceptual complexity in terms of the number of new concepts. He thus poses the question as to whether a reduction in complexity could be achieved by decreasing the attention devoted to traditional topics such as differences between consumer and business marketing. This is a difficult question to answer. Our position would probably be that traditional topics do not necessarily become less relevant to current business-to-business problems (e.g., auction theory and e-auctions), although they may need some complements. A textbook that provides students with fundamental, theoretically grounded, and flexible-to-use "equipment" demonstrates applications of these concepts in current business contexts, and thus allows students to tackle a large variety of problems that they will encounter in their later work experience, would be our preferred solution.

REPLY TO THE COMMENTS
OF PROFESSORS HUTT AND SPEH

Professors Hutt and Speh focus on our proposition that in addition to the prevailing approaches in business-to-business marketing, a transaction (or business)-types approach might offer an interesting extension to the conceptual spectrum of textbook structuring. Although this idea was originally intended to figure only as a supplement, we nevertheless appreciate the interesting discussion by Professors Hutt and Speh and agree that the questions they pose relate precisely to those aspects which contribute to the challenge of textbook writing. Our first remark, however, concerns their conclusion, that we had classified the books by Anderson and Narus and by Webster as undergraduate texts. While we are well aware of their classification as graduate texts by the *Marketing Education Review* Web site, we nonetheless chose to abstain from an a priori classification for the reasons explained.

Regarding the discussion on building a foundation for conveying business marketing knowledge, we very much support the view expressed by Professors Hutt and Speh, that a text (also one built around a business-types perspective) would have to start with a general section, dealing with topics such as specific characteristics of business markets and organizational buying behavior. However, apart from this requirement, we do not think that breadth, coverage of current issues, and depth of treatment would necessarily suffer from a structure centered around business types. For example, the discussion of the impacts a purchasing organization exerts by segmenting their purchases addresses an important topic that has gained even more attention due to the increasing use of EDI- and Internet-based technologies in procurement during the past couple of years. Understanding customers' classification of purchased goods is surely an area of prime importance to seller companies. Yet, we maintain that this issue could well be addressed according to different (business) types (e.g., standardized versus customized products or products creating a customer lock-in versus no customer lock-in), because we would expect different classifications to be associated with these types.

The second area where Professors Hutt and Speh see hurdles for organizing a textbook around business types is the integrative development of a relationship marketing perspective, particularly with regard to such topics as electronic commerce and supply chain management. The reason why we do not share these doubts is that for each business type, we expect distinct features of the buyer-seller relationship to prevail, in general, but also with respect to the specific use of different modes of electronic commerce (information, communication, and transaction; private and public marketplaces; different models of auctions; etc.) and different forms of supply chain management. And while these issues present a variety of challenges to companies, we are not convinced that overcoming them will require a completely new set of theories. The emergence of e-auctions may serve as an example: undoubtedly, e-auctions are characterized by a couple of features setting them clearly apart from real-world auctions, due to reductions in information and transaction costs: asynchronous bidding, frequently a large number of geographically dispersed participants, fixed closing times for certain types of auctions (Lucking-Reiley 2000), and greater opportunity of acquiring additional information during the course of the auction. Consequently, through the mechanism of e-auctions, the auction model has been extended to a large variety of goods previously not auctioned due, for instance, to their low value. Nonetheless, the key elements of traditional auction theory still constitute a solid starting point, if not an appropriate framework, for complete analysis of transaction processes via e-auctions (Lucking-Reiley 2000). Finally, Professors Hutt and Speh present some considerations on the need to capture strategic marketing content. In this respect, we again agree on the importance of the topic, yet maintain that a business-types approach, particularly from a dynamic perspective including strategically motivated changes between different business types (e.g., the development of Application Service Providing[1]), may address the issue quite adequately. So, while we are still convinced that a business-types approach might represent a suitable framework for organizing a business marketing text, we see it as an additional perspective within a range of concepts (marketing management perspective, value approach, etc.), each of which has its legitimation regarding different purposes.

REPLY TO PROFESSOR NARUS'S COMMENTS

After sharing his own experiences with textbook writing, Professor Narus provides a detailed discussion of a variety of aspects he regards as particularly critical to our comparison. His main concerns are the validity of our results, the methodology applied, and the support for the conclusions. Having stimulated such a personal response and remarkably intensive analysis of our paper as the one provided by Professor Narus confirms our belief in the necessity of discussing the subject and our hopes of encouraging the debate on future developments of business-to-business textbooks. In terms of enabling us to follow his argument, the introductory description of his experiences with the process of textbook writing, the Anderson and Narus book *Business Market Management,* proves very helpful. Not all parts (e.g., the discussion on economic constraints, a phenomenon all those familiar with textbook publishing will already have encountered) being directly related to our core research question, they nonetheless supplement it very well for everyone interested in the background of textbook crafting.

For those confronted with the problem of choosing a textbook on business marketing suitable for their purposes, it is precisely the absence of formal standards for management textbooks, as Professor Narus notes, that makes the decision so difficult. Hence, the lack of standards is, in our opinion, rather than an obstacle *to* a reason *for* conducting a comparison of business-to-business marketing textbooks. Given a certain set of books available, we conducted the analysis from a teaching perspective, referring to one of the most established theories in the field of research on education and its assessment, Bloom's (1956) taxonomy of educational objectives. The neglect of economic constraints on the process of *publishing* textbooks from this perspective seems to us legitimate, if not necessary. Hinting explicitly at the students' perspective is another great merit of Professor Narus's comments and in line with current psychological theories (e.g., Confrey 1990). Stating that "students would prefer reading a textbook that discusses fewer, critical topics in greater detail to one that provides superficial treatment of a myriad of seemingly unrelated and unimportant topics," however, comes as no big surprise: who would not? The challenge in textbook writing precisely is to cover a certain amount of material in relating the individual topics to one another and to a broader context. Particularly regarding the latter aspect, it is not obvious per se that a managerial orientation ensures this better than a theoretical one—nor that they need necessarily be mutually exclusive.

Following his considerations on the process of textbook publishing, Professor Narus raises some reasonable doubts about the procedures and conclusions of our analysis. He poses important questions, which all academic research has to withstand: questions of validity, methodology, and legitimacy of inferences. When examining our research with respect to these issues, he expresses considerable unease. In this, we can only guess, but an important contributing factor might have been an unfortunate misunderstanding about the intentions of our research and its envisaged contribution to the field. With respect to an issue that has hardly gained any attention in the literature, we have tried to establish a first, maybe provisional basis for a systematic, theoretically guided approach. This claim, however, does not imply ignoring the remaining subjective factor, nor were we intending to conduct empirical research in the sense of using formal statistical methods. Rather, due to the subjectivity in evaluation of criteria as "link between theory and practice," we decided a qualitatively dominated approach with some quantitative elements (e.g., LIX) to be appropriate.

Looking in detail at some of Professor Narus's concerns, we will begin with his criticism of using Bloom's taxonomy (1956) as a theoretic basis for our comparison, because here, obviously, some misunderstanding is present. By no means did we imply with our Table 22 that only Bloom's higher five educational objectives are concerned with the cognitive domain. What is implied by the first and second columns, and might have caused the misunderstanding, is a link between the objectives of a textbook, as stated by Berry (1993) or Lichtenthal and Butaney (1991), and the six elements of the taxonomy. The combination of three elements of the taxonomy (analysis, synthesis, and evaluation) that he criticizes is not unusual in the relevant literature (e.g., Dyrud and Worley 1998). They are referred to as "higher-order" thinking skills, because all three ask from the subjects extension of their minds beyond purely information-related processes. With respect to Professor Narus's claim that we applied the taxonomy out of its originally intended context, we surely must concede that this is the case. Our legitimation we see, though, in the close relatedness of the context and the lack of a specific framework for textbook comparison. Modifications, particularly concerning operationalization of and empirical support for our indicators, and, as suggested by Professor Narus, validity testing, are likely to be needed. We strongly hope that future research will address these issues.

Professor Narus's criticism of one of our indicators, the LIX, we would like to consider in some detail. *Comprehension,* as developed by Bloom et al. (1956), refers to grasping a material's meaning, that is, classifying, describing, discussing, and summarizing. These activities in our opinion belong in the category of *understanding* a material's meaning. While, by itself, the term *understanding* is closer cognated to the construct of *understandability* that is commonly used in measuring the effectiveness of communication as distinct from *readability* (Patel and Day 1996),[2] we regret the confusion and admit that sticking to the original term might have prevented this. Why then did we choose to measure readability instead of understandability? The answer is that although understandability is admittedly the more extensive construct, readability as independent from the reading subjects themselves seemed more appropriate in our case, as we intended to evaluate the books as such, independent from particular (groups of) readers.

Concerning Professor Narus's doubts as to whether counting words and sentence length is a suitable indicator for readability, there is empirical support that these admittedly simple measures may actually represent fairly good indicators: A very thorough analysis of assessing readability was conducted by Klare as early as the 1970s (1974). He found that counting word length and sentence length (as, e.g., in LIX; for application of this measure see, e.g., Anderson 1983), two rather simple measures of the formal structure of a text, allow for relatively good predictions of readability.

Professor Narus's final point regarding validity is our specification of business marketing topics. We share his critical perspective on the subjectivity of selecting a number of topics in the field. Nonetheless, we still see no practicable alternative in attempting to conduct a systematic comparison of business marketing textbooks than to rely on a range of more or less established topics. In the case of the cited market-sensing approach to market segmentation, for instance, future research, in our view, still has to relate this capabilities/resource-theory-based concept (Day 1994) more explicitly to "traditional" rather than market-based segmentation approaches. It is necessary to elaborate in detail how market-sensing processes that "are likely to be fragmented, obscured by the dispersal of critical activities throughout the organization, and woven into other processes" (Day 1994) may figure on their own as a market segmentation approach.

Of the many concerns voiced by Professor Narus regarding our methodology, we will focus on some prominent examples. He first expresses unease with respect to our method for grouping the textbooks and also to the sampling approach for the LIX. In first responding to the more fundamental issue, we would like to stress that we do not claim the use of any statistical tool for grouping as in, for instance, any kind of formal cluster analysis (for detailed discussion of different methods see, e.g., Backhaus et al. 2000). As to our sampling approach for the LIX, we acknowledge that we should possibly have described it in detail.[3] However, due to the limited space, we still regard this omission as acceptable. The same argument applies essentially to Professor Narus's criticisms regarding the examination of coverage of business topics. For those interested in having a closer look at how we derived at our results, we provide detailed tables (http://www.wiwi.uni-muenster.de/ias). These results provide no support for Professor Narus's suggestion that we claimed the Anderson and Narus book ignored organizational buying behavior. The contrary is the case and we assume that the description of our findings unfortunately was not sufficiently clear: When comparing coverage of pricing and organizational buying behavior, we were intending to emphasize the common focus on value in both areas.

The value-based approach, in our view, represents a recent, yet highly interesting and important perspective on business marketing. Taking into consideration the variety of teaching objectives, learning purposes and types, we appreciate the existence of a variety of different approaches in the field. Transaction-types approaches—as, for example, outlined in the concluding part of our paper—constitute another concept within this variety. While this kind of approach is quite common in, for instance, the German literature (e.g., Backhaus 1999; Plinke 1992 and 1997; Kaas 1995; Schade and Schott 1993; for an English-speaking review, see Kleinaltenkamp and Jacob 2001), it has not yet been treated extensively in the English-speaking literature on business marketing.[4] This may have been the reason why one of our anonymous reviewers requested a more detailed outline of the approach than presented in the first version of our paper. Consequently, we included a lengthier description, aimed at offering just one additional perspective. Unfortunately, this seems to have created the impression that, in our analysis, we did not follow the previously presented methodology. We regret this and would like to assure Professor Narus that the purposes of our analysis were just the ones stated in our paper.

One last point should be made regarding Professor Narus's concerns as to whether our conclusions are supported by our study. While we feel that we have already addressed sufficiently his criticism of the presentation of a transaction-types approach, the "case study" question remains open. In our study, we refer only to Professor Narus's category of "class discussion case studies"; i.e., we did not include purely descriptive material that required no problem solving. Yet, we should probably have stated this more explicitly. Our position that such case studies are linked to the development of higher-order thinking skills, we still believe to be substantiated by the literature (e.g., Miller 1990).

In retrospect, we acknowledge that we should probably have outlined aspects of validity and methodology of our research more clearly and explicitly. Still, we maintain that the comparison could prove helpful for teachers and practitioners in their choice of a textbook and promote debate on the future of business marketing textbooks.

REPLY TO PROFESSOR PLANK'S COMMENTS

Professor Plank takes up our idea to stimulate debate on business marketing education. Drawing on continuous improvement process thinking and the theory of constraints, he provides a visionary discussion of education as a process, with standardization and synchronization as critical factors in improving this process. His argument is intriguing and may hold for a large number of educational processes, especially those involving undergraduates. Following his main idea and extending it to other types of learning situations, there may, however, be processes in education with opposite requirements: as an analogy, one may consider the process of designing and producing, not a mass-market product such as a car, but a highly customized product such as a power station that is constructed for one specific customer, e.g., regarding climatic and geographic conditions. This kind of process might for instance be prominent when working with students who have learning difficulties or in highly specialized education such as with doctoral students. The importance of Professor Plank's emphasis on education as a process is reflected in growing concerns voiced in the literature, and also by public institutions such as the European Commission, about aspects of "lifelong learning,"[5] calling for a more process-oriented perspective on education. Increasing numbers of adults returning to college (James and Sonner 2001) or entering (online) distance learning programs (Evans 2001) are just some indicators for this phenomenon. Taking up Professor Plank's idea, lifelong learning could be interpreted as a metaprocess of education, composed of a number of subprocesses (ranging from elementary schooling to distance learning), each being characterized by distinct properties to be addressed by those involved in their design.

SOME THOUGHTS ON FUTURE DEVELOPMENTS OF BUSINESS-TO-BUSINESS MARKETING TEXTBOOKS

With the advances in new information and communication media, we observe changing modes of acquisition of data, information, and finally knowledge and competence (for categorization see, e.g., Davenport and Prusak 1998). Education faces the challenge of keeping up. Imparting knowledge in this rapidly changing environment has to tackle a variety of problems. To name just a few, there is an increase in the total amount of data and information and in the amount available at a nonprohibitive cost (w.a. 2000; Tanner 1999). Thus, in the same time, ceteris paribus, a smaller proportion of a field's body of knowledge can be conveyed by a course, textbook, or other means of education. This results in higher degrees of specialization and fragmentation. Hence, the proportion of basic, common sense knowledge to highly specialized knowledge decreases. With the discovery of new knowledge, we need to consider if the same amount of knowledge of the same complexity and the same relevance simultaneously becomes obsolete. Otherwise, shortage of (course) time and (textbook) space becomes relatively more prominent. And even if that condition was fulfilled, the increasing "turnover rate" of knowledge would cause problems. Thus, the question of *what* should be conveyed in the scarce time and space at hand becomes harder to solve. A second issue, related to new information and communication media, is the changes in teaching techniques, that is, the evolution from traditional teaching to technology-based education (Evans 2001): *How* can we best use the different teaching materials available in increasing quantities?

In our view, these phenomena hold, not only for education in general, but also for education in business marketing (Vlosky and Wilson 1998). If one agrees with this, how then do they impact the long-term future development of business marketing textbooks? In an attempt to answer this, we distinguish a textbook's *functional* features from its *physical* properties. We expect the *physical* properties of business marketing textbooks to stay in line with the developments of books in general. While traditional books still continue to dominate, media such as electronic books or electronic paper can be expected to gain share once a convincing quality has been achieved at acceptable prices. Arguably, this could be even more pronounced for nonfictional reading: aspects associated with the sensory feeling of paper-style books might be less important here, with purchase and consumption being motivated more rationally. Moreover, electronic media could offer additional advantages by facilitating updates and enhancing possibilities for modular design of textbooks.

We expect the *functional features* or objectives of business marketing textbooks, essentially, to last. What might change, however, is the focus: An increasing emphasis on imparting knowledge, i.e., on the lower levels of the taxonomy, with the higher-order thinking skills being supported by online tutorials, computer simulations, Internet-based games, etc. (Rodriguez 1998; Strauss and Frost 1999; Vlosky and Wilson 1998), seems a viable option. Concerning content, that is, the question of what topics should be included, we believe that, due to an increase in spectrum of contexts in which people will use books on business-to-business marketing, aspects of lifelong learning will open up space for an even greater variety of approaches. In any case, our expectation is that the question of identifying those parts of the body of knowledge which apply to a large variety of contexts (e.g., auction theory for real-world and e-auctions) becomes even more crucial.

Our view on the further developments may not be shared by everyone, and only the future will tell. But in the meantime, we hope that our research, complemented thoughtfully by the commentaries of Professors Butaney, Hutt and Speh, Narus, and Plank, may contribute some interesting arguments to the debate on business marketing textbooks.

NOTES

1. Under the umbrella of Application Service Providing (ASP), a large variety of different contractual and product/service-related features is offered (e.g., <http://www.allaboutasp.org>, the ASP Industry Consortium Web site). ASP generally addresses issues of hiring software instead of buying it.

2. While readability relates only to the complexity of the content itself, understandability takes into account the capacity of readers to grasp the relevant message of a text (Patel and Day 1996).

3. In order to cover large parts of the textbooks in our analysis, we chose the following sampling approach: We started at page 10, conducting first a 100-word-analysis at the top of the page, followed by a sentence analysis of the directly following ten sentences. We continued with this procedure, choosing sections every forty pages (starting from p. 10). The size of the page gaps (forty pages) was due to considerations about the minimum length of a textbook (ca. 400 pages).

4. Distantly related classifications, though often not grounded in New Institutional Economics, can mainly be found in the literature on relationship marketing, e.g., Coviello, Brodie, and Munro 1997.

5. On November 21, 2001, the European Commission adopted "Communication on Making a European Area of Lifelong Learning a Reality." It defines lifelong learning as "all learning activity undertaken throughout life, with the aim of improving knowledge, skills and competence, within a personal, civic, social and/or employment-related perspective" (http://europa.eu.int/comm/education/life/; 01-10-2002).

REFERENCES

Anderson, James C. and James A. Narus (1999). *Business Market Management: Understanding, Creating, and Delivering Value.* Upper Saddle River, NJ: Prentice-Hall.

Anderson, Jonathan (1983). "LIX and RIX: Variations on a little-known readability index." *Journal of Reading* (March), 490-496.

Backhaus, Klaus (1999). *Industriegütermarketing* [Industrial goods marketing], Sixth Edition. München: Vahlen.

Backhaus, Klaus et al. (2000). *Multivariate Analysemethoden: eine anwendungsorientierte Einführung* [Multivariate analysis: An application-oriented introduction], Ninth Edition. Berlin: Springer.

Berry, Leonard L. (1993). "Our Roles As Educators: Present and Future." *Journal of Marketing Education* 15(3), 3-8.

Bloom, Benjamin S. et al. (1956). *Taxonomy of Educational Objectives, Handbook 1: Cognitive Domain.* New York: Longmans.

Confrey, Jere (1990). "A Review of the Research on Student Conceptions in Mathematics, Science, and Programming. Cazden, Courtney (ed.), *Review of Research in Education, American Educational Research Association* 16, 3-56.

Coviello, Nicole E., Roderick J. Brodie and Hugh J. Munro (1997). "Understanding Contemporary Marketing: Development of a Classification Scheme." *Journal of Marketing Management* 13(6), 501-522.

Davenport, Thomas H. and Laurence Prusak (1998). *Working Knowledge: How Organizations Manage What They Know.* Boston, MA: Harvard Business School Press.

Dyrud, Marilyn A. and Rebecca B. Worley (1998). "Critical Thinking." *Business Communication Quarterly* 61(3), 62-78.

Evans, Joel R. (2001). "The Emerging Role of the Internet in Marketing Education: From Traditional Teaching to Technology-Based Education." *Marketing Education Review* 11 (Fall) <http://cbpa.louisville.edu/mer/elecarticles.htm>. Retrieved: January 12.

James, William L. and Brenda S. Sonner (2001). "Just Say No to Traditional Student Samples." *Journal of Advertising Research* 41(5), 63-71.

Kaas, Klaus Peter (1995). "*Marketing zwischen Markt und Hierarchie* [Marketing between markets and hierarchies]." In *Kontrakte, Geschäftsbeziehungen, Netzwerke: Marketing und neue Institutionenökonomie* [Contracts, business relationships, networks: Marketing and new institutional economics], Kaas, Klaus Peter (ed.), *ZfBf* (Special Edition) 35, 19-42.

Klare, George R. (1974). "Assessing Readability." *Reading Research Quarterly* 10(1), 255-264.

Kleinaltenkamp, Michael and Frank Jacob (2002). "German Approaches to Business-to-Business Marketing Theory: Origins and Structure." *Journal of Business Research* 55, 149-155.

Lichtenthal, J. David and Gul Butaney (1991). "Undergraduate Industrial Marketing: Content and Methods." *Industrial Marketing Management* 20, 231-239.

Lucking-Reiley, David (2000). "Auctions on the Internet: What's Being Auctioned, and How?" *The Journal of Industrial Economics* 48(3), 227-252.

Miller, Charles (1990). "Higher-Order Thinking—An Integrated Approach for Your Classroom." *Vocational Education Journal* 65(6), 26-27, 69.

Patel, Chris and Ron Day (1996). "The Influence of Cognitive Style on the Understandability of a Professional Accounting Pronouncement by Accounting Students." *British Accounting Review* 28(2), 139-154.

Plinke, Wulf (1992). "Ausprägungen der Marktorientierung im Investitionsgütermarketing" [Different forms of market-orientation in industrial goods marketing]. *Schmalenbachs Zeitschrift für betriebswirtschaftliche* Vol. 44, (9), 830-846.

Plinke, Wulf (1997). "Grundlagen des Geschäftsbeziehungsmanagements" [Principles of business relationship management]. Plinke, Wulf and Michael

Kleinaltenkamp (eds.), *Geschäftsbeziehungsmanagement* [Business relationship management]. Berlin, 113-159.

Rodriguez, Carlos M. (1998). "Commentary on: 'Technology in the Classroom: Teaching Business Marketing in the 21st Century,' by Richard P. Vlosky and David T. Wilson." *Journal of Business-to-Business Marketing,* 5(1/2), 157-160.

Schade, Christian and E. Schott (1993). "Instrumente des Kontraktgütermarketing" [Design of marketing-instruments depending on different contraction modes]. *DBW,* 53(4), 491-511.

Strauss, Judy and Raymond D. Frost (1999). "Selecting Instructional Technology Media for the Marketing Classroom." *Marketing Education Review* 9(1), <http://cbpa.louisville.edu/mer/abst1999.htm>. Retrieved: January 12.

Tanner, Jeff (1999). "Key Issues in Marketing Education." *Marketing Education Review* 9(1), <http://cbpa.louisville.edu/mer/abst1999.htm >. Retrieved: January 12.

Vlosky, Richard P. and David T. Wilson (1998). "Essay: Technology in the Classroom: Teaching Business Marketing in the 21st Century." *Journal of Business-to-Business Marketing* 5(1/2), 145-156.

w.a. (2000). "Survey: The New Economy (Untangling E-Conomics, and: Elementary, My Dear Watson)." *The Economist* (September 23), 5-11.

PART VII:
BOOK REVIEW

Review of *Cabell's Directory of Publishing Opportunities in Marketing*
(Eighth Edition).

David E. Cabell and Deborah L. English, editors; Brooke S. Abernethy, Assistant editor. *Beaumont, TX: Cabell Publishing Company, 2001.*

J. David Lichtenthal

Presenting the latest descriptive compilation of published journals in marketing, this directory helps authors select journals likely to consider publishing their manuscript based on the topic. This volume provides a "first glance assessment" of the kind of commitment required in time and effort based on the detail of the review procedures and process. If given by the editor, the *Directory* also provides the complete set of manuscript guidelines.

Within the industrial marketing area per se, full coverage is given to the *Journal of Business-to-Business Marketing, Industrial Marketing Management,* and the *Journal of Business and Industrial Marketing.* This coverage is placed in the topical area "Marketing Theory and Applications." There are also more than twenty journals listed under the heading of "Purchasing and Materials Management," with more than thirty in the area "Transportation and Physical Distribution." Many journal titles are listed more than once, which can have a positive effect if actively managed. This overlap allows for maximizing the likelihood of finding more outlets while forcing the consideration of more journals that will also be deemed superfluous. As well, many journals are inherently interdisciplinary. Finally, many journal titles, although not nominally or inherently business-to-business, have coverage of marketing mix and behavioral issues. Given the growing demand for business-to-business literature, perhaps the time has come for Cabell's to add this topic to its list.

This directory, formerly in three volumes (the management area is now separate), is a standard reference for any department of marketing. It provides a comprehensive collection detailing publication-related information covering more than 160 journals appearing alphabetically. This directory characterizes each journal entry by approximately twenty-five attributes. This "manual" would help would-be authors seeking publication outlets as well as subscribers needing professional literature to keep abreast of their fields of interest.

Cabell's Directory lists the following information, if given (information supplied voluntarily by either the journal editor or publisher) for each publication in this typical order:

Of assistance to both aspiring authors and subscribers:
- Journal name
- Editor name(s), address, phone and fax(s), e-mail and WWW (if given)
- Circulation data: frequency of issue, copies per issue, subscription price, and sponsorship
- Manuscript topics
- Mission of the journal
- Subscription price

Of assistance primarily to aspiring authors for manuscript preparation and perspective during the review process:
- Publication guidelines
- Manuscript length
- Manuscript style
- Manuscript preparation
- Number of required copies
- Disk submission and format
- Type of review
- Number of external and internal reviewers
- An acceptance rate
- Time required for a review
- Reviewers' comments (if any)
- Fees charged (if any) to review or publish
- Percentage of invited articles
- Rules regarding reprints and copyrights

To help in selecting those journals which are most likely to publish your manuscripts, the index classifies journal titles into twenty-five different topic areas. In addition, the directory provides information on the journal's review process characteristics. To further assist you in organizing and preparing your manuscripts, the directory includes extensive information on style and format of most journals. If a journal has its own set of guidelines, a copy is published in the directory. Also, each entry indicates the use of a standard set of publication guidelines, such as *Chicago Manual of Style* or *Publication Manual of the American Psychological Association.*

The directory can also help scholars scan for journals in cognate disciplines of management/strategy, applied behavioral sciences, decision sciences, public policy, as well as applied statistical sciences. A summary index in the back provides in summary form multiple listings for many journals sorted by topic: Advertising and Promotion Management; Business Education; Business Information Systems; Business Law, Public Responsibility and Ethics; Direct Marketing; Global Business; Health Care Administration; Labor Relations and Human Resource Management; Marketing Research; Marketing Theory and Applications; Nonprofit Organizations; Office Administration and Management; Operations Research and Statistics; Organizational Behavior and Theory; Productions/Operations; Public Administration; Purchasing and Materials Management; Sales and Selling; Services; Small Business Entrepreneurship; Strategic Management Policy; Technology/Innovation; Transportation/Physical Distribution.

This directory focuses on journals in the specialized area of marketing, while other directories focus on management, accounting, economics, and finance. The decision to place journals in the respective directory is based on manuscript topics selected by the editors as well as the journal's guidelines for authors. The most current information can be found at <www.cabells.com>. There is a log-on in registration procedure.

Cabell's Directory of Publishing Opportunities in Marketing is required reading for junior faculty members and doctoral/masters students concerned with finding suitable publication outlets for their work. Veterans will find it useful for refreshing their perspective and learning about the newest entrants to the discipline. There is a narrative section, "How the Directory Helps You Publish," that contains helpful hints for choosing a journal by exploring the relationships between theme, readership, methodology, acceptance rate, manuscript topics, review process, submission, and reviewer comments. A section titled "What Is a Refereed Article?" emphasizes the blind review process and the use of external reviewers. Seasoned faculty members will find it useful for expanding their publication base options both within the discipline and in allied areas. Business professionals may also use this volume to shop for quality sources of information regarding an ever-expanding base of broad and focused periodicals within and related to marketing. The mere increase in the incidence of sources is testimony to the ever-growing intellectual diversity and expanding boundaries of the field.

Index

AACSB (American Assembly of Collegiate Schools of Business), 10-12, 136
AACSB International, 243, 244
Abernethy, Brooke S., 283-286
Academic freedom, 265
Accomodators, 172
Account management, 116-117
Accreditation, undergraduate programs, 136
Action learning
  EMBA, 78-79
  executive education, 60-63
  project cycle, 61-62, 63
Admission criteria, survey, 19, 21-22
Advertising agency jobs, 110
After-marketing, 143
Alexander, Shirley, 159
Alliance agreements, 121-122, 144
Alternative technologies, classroom teaching, 159-168
Alutto, Joseph A., 13
AMA (American Marketing Association), 243, 244, 251
Amazon.com textbooks, 257
American Assembly of Collegiate Schools of Business (AACSB), 10-12, 136
American Marketing Association (AMA), 243, 244, 251
Analysis
  cognitive ability, 185, 194, 195
  conjoint, 78, 82
  tradeoff, 78
Anderson, James C., 3-4, 87, 109-112.
  See also Textbooks, comparative review
Anomaly detection, 68-70

Application, cognitive ability, 185, 193, 195
Applied research, 43-44
Asian schools, 88
Assimilators, 172
AT&T's Leadership Development Program, 61-62
Ausubel, David, 176

B2B Marketing Exchange, 111
B2B SIG, 89, 102, 111
B2B SIG (Business-to-Business Special Interest Group), 89, 102, 111
Background, 1-5
Backhaus, Klaus
  executive education, 267-278
  manuscript methodology, 253-257
  relationship marketing, 237
  research criticisms, 249-252
  textbook comparative review, 181
Balanced scorecard approach, 132-133
Barath, Robert M., 171
Baxter International, Inc., 143
Beckert, Beverly, 146
Benassi, Ken, 145
Bingham, Frank G. *See* Textbooks, comparative review
Bloom, Benjamin S., taxonomy
  applications, 249-250
  background, 224
  criteria and methodology, 184-194
  criticism of use, 272-273
  textbook applications, 223, 244, 259-260
  transaction-types perspective, 236

BMC (business-to-business marketing course), 139-148
Boettcher, Judith V., 168
Bose Corporation, JIT II, 76
Bozman, Carl S., 172
Brierty, Edward G. *See* Textbooks, comparative review
Browsers, 165
Buckles, Tom A., 171
Budgets for training, 51
Bulletin board, Internet, 108
Burgelman, R. A., 124
Business Education Forum Policy Statement Number 53, 168
Business Market Management, 244-245
Business marketing
   characteristics, 235
   executive education, 75-79, 81-82
Business school, historical development, 10-13
Business Week
   executive education costs, 51
   master's-level education, 88
Business-to-business marketing, financial value, 9
Business-to-business marketing course (BMC), 139-148
Business-to-Business Special Interest Group (B2B SIG), 89, 102, 111
Butaney, Gul, 4
   lack of undergraduate programs, 260
   relationship marketing, 152-154
   reply to commentary, 151, 268
   textbook commentary, 223-230
   textbook criteria and methodology, 183
   undergraduate curriculum commentary, 139-148
Buying behavior, 129–130, 236
Byrt, William, 10

Cabell, David E., 283-286
Cabell's Directory of Publishing Opportunities in Marketing, 283-286
Canadian schools, 87, 97
Capabilities, 185
Case discussions
   buying-selling operations, 141-142
   class discussions, 275
   contribution to education, 111
   live cases, 135
   shortage of materials, 100-102
   strategic alliances, 122
   textbook, 209-210, 256
   as tools, 70
   two-course sequence, 134-135
Case Research Journal, 101
Category managers, 110
CBI (computer-based instruction), 159-161
CD-ROM in multimedia learning environment, 162-163
Cespedes, Frank V., 121, 122, 152
Challenges, doctoral program, 41-45
Characteristics
   business market, 235
   program, 17-19, 20, 28-31
   undergraduate programs, 129
Chrysler procurement trends, 119-120
CIF (customer information file), 143
Clark, R. E., 159
Classification of educational objectives, 184-194
Classroom technology, 159-160, 168
   advanced technology, 162-163
   challenges and success, 167-168
   commentary, 171-173
   Indiana University example, 162
   integrated software, 163
   Internet use, 164-165
   purpose of, 160-161
   reply to commentary, 175-177
   virtual classrooms, 160-161
   World Wide Web, 165-167
Climate, educational, 176

Cognitive abilities
  analysis, 185, 194, 195
  application, 185, 193, 195
  basic capabilities, 185
  development of, 214
  evaluation, 186, 194, 195
  knowledge, 185, 186-190, 195, 210, 213-214
  skills, 185-186
  synthesis, 185, 194, 195
  understanding, 185, 190-193, 195, 273
Collaborative advantage, 118
Coloring and understandability of text, 192
Comprehensibility, textbook, 203-205
Comprehension, defined, 273
Compression product development strategy, 128, 146
Computer-based instruction (CBI), 159-161
Computers, speed of product development, 128
Conceptual complexity, 225-230
Conceptual structure, 52-57
Concurrent marketing, 121
Conjoint analysis, 78, 82
Conservatives, 123-124
Consulting jobs, 109-110
Content, book, 2-5
Convergers, 172
Cooper, Marjorie J., 261
Costs
  higher education, 159
  reference in textbook, 254
  textbook production, 246, 248
  training, 51
Courses, required, 22-26, 27
Coverage, 253-254
Coye, Ray W., 161
Creativity research, 66
Cross-functional integration, 147-148, 153-154

Cross-functional working relationships
  trends, 118, 125-127
  undergraduate programs, 116, 131-132
Cross-sectional data, 42
Crossing the chasm, 124
Cultural change, 65-66
Curriculum, 175
Custom education elements, 63
Customer information file (CIF), 143
Customer-linking process, 116-117
Customized executive education, 59-60
Cycle time, 261-262

The Dallas Conference (1992), 12
Danneels, Erwin, 2-3
  doctoral programs, 9, 42, 44
  program of action, 47-48
Data collection
  cross-sectional, 42
  for evaluating market opportunities, 130
  surveys, 13-17, 89-93
Day, George, 252
Design principles, executive education, 64-70
Desktop publishing, 163
Dhebar, Anirudh, 65
Diagrams, defined, 192
Directory of publishing opportunities, 283-286
Discovery tools, metaphors, 67
Distance learning
  advantages, 164-165
  history, 161
  role of technology, 63-64
Divergers, 172
Doctoral programs, 37-38
  admission criteria, 19, 21-22
  background, 9-10
  business school recommendations, 36
  challenges, 41-45
  characteristics, 17-19, 20, 28-31

Doctoral programs *(continued)*
  commentary, 41-45
  courses, 22-26, 27
  faculty deficiencies, 31-32
  PhD, 10-13, 37
  placements, 32-33, 34
  preparation for teaching, 26-28
  program of action, 47-48
  relevance, 26-28
  reply to commentary, 47-48
  survey data collection, 13-17
Dowling, Grahame R., 3, 41-45, 47-48
Dulek, Ronald E., 12-13

E-auctions, 270
EC (electronic commerce), 145
Eckles, Robert W. *See* Textbooks,
  comparative review
Ecole des Hautes Etudes Commerciales
  (HEC), 10
E-commerce tools, 238
ECR (efficient customer response), 142
EDI (electronic data interchange), 141,
  142, 152
Education. *See* Executive education
Educational Resources Information
  Center (ERIC), 184
Educators
  classroom teaching materials, 106
  deficiencies, 31-32
  experience of, 106, 107
  marketing textbooks, 247
  role in action learning, 60-61
  role in customized executive
    education, 60
  role in executive education, 65
  role in the classroom, 175
Efficient customer response (ECR), 142
Eisenhardt, K. M., 127-128
Electronic commerce (EC), 145
Electronic data interchange (EDI), 141,
  142, 152
Ellis, Richard S., 160, 168
E-mail, use in marketing education, 164

EMBA (executive MBA), 78-79
Employment
  PhD industry employment, 37
  trends, 109-110
English, Deborah L., 283-286
Environment, impact of products,
  146-147
ERIC (Educational Resources
  Information Center), 184
European schools, 87-88, 97
Evaluation, cognitive ability, 186,
  194, 195
Evans, Mary Ann, 192
Exchange relationships, 41-42
Executive education, 51-52
  action learning, 60-63
  business marketing, 75-79, 81-82
  case discussions, 70
  changes in emphasis, 55
  commentary, 75-79
  customized, 59-60
  design principles, 64-70
  lectures, 70
  reply to commentary, 81-82
  role of technology, 63-64
  simulations, 71-72
  structure, 52-57
  traditional programs, 57-59
  trends, 57, 58
Experiential product development
  strategy, 128
Explicit knowledge, 68

Faculty, applicant deficiencies, 31-32
Fielden, John S., 12-13
Flaherty, Teresa B., 145
Focused programs, 57-58
Foundation discipline, 25

General education elements, 63
General Electric (GE)
  action learning format, 62
  service marketing strategy, 117
  Work Out program, 64

General programs, 57-58
Gilbert, Steven W., 160
Global sourcing, 140-141
Globalization, 54, 57
Glossary of terms, 229
GMAT score, 19, 21, 22
The Goal, 261-262
Goldratt, Eli, 261, 262
Gordon, Robert A., 11
Gowin, D. Bob, 175
Graduate programs
    masters. *See* Master's-level
        education
    textbooks, 234
    undergraduate. *See* Undergraduate
        programs
Green, Kenneth C., 160
Gronlund, Norman E., 185
Grove, A. S., 124

Haas, Robert W. *See* Textbooks,
    comparative review
Harvard Business Review (HBR), 44
Hautes Etudes Commerciales (HEC),
    10
HEC (Hautes Etudes Commerciales),
    10
High-technology markets
    in business marketing practice, 118
    overview, 123-125
    undergraduate programs, 144-145,
        153
Historical development
    business school, 10-13
    business-to-business marketing
        education, 1-5
    conceptual structure, 52-57
    industrial or business marketing,
        260-261
Home Depot, environmental impact,
    147
Honeycutt, Earl D.
    commentary, 105-107

Honeycutt, Earl D. *(continued)*
    educational needs, 4
    reply to commentary, 109-112
    Web technology study, 145
Hoskinson, Ronald A., 168
Howard, Shea and Chan Asset
        Management case, 101
Howell, James E., 11
Hunt, C. Steven, 187
Hutt, Michael D., 4
    reply to commentary, 151-154,
        269-270
    textbook review commentary,
        233-240
    textbooks. *See* Textbooks,
        comparative review
    themes in marketing courses, 188
    undergraduate curriculum, 115

IBM Corporation, environmental
        issues, 147
Impact measurement, 48
Implicit knowledge, 68
Indiana University multimedia learning
        application, 162
INDUSTRAT, 71
Industrial Marketing Management, 101
Industrial marketing strategy, 53, 181,
        260-261
Industry analysis projects, 133-134
Industry linkages, 43
Industry sponsors, 27
Information highway, 166
Information technology, 159
In-plant supplier representatives, 76
Inserted text, 192, 205
Inside the Tornado, 123
Institute for the Study of Business
        Markets (ISBM)
    crafting of textbook, 248
    networking, 102
    purpose of, 9, 48
    survey data collection, 14
Instructional technology, 159

Instructors. *See* Educators
Internet. *See also* Web sites
    bulletin board clearinghouse, 108
    distance learning. *See* Distance
        learning
    e-commerce, 238
    instructional activities, 164, 166
    use in marketing education, 164-165
Internship recommendations, 36
Introduction of Microsoft's Product
        Support Network case, 101
Inventory management, just-in-time,
        143
ISBM. *See* Institute for the Study of
        Business Markets

Japan
    business marketing education, 54
    master's-level education, 88
JBBM *(Journal of Business-to-Business
        Marketing)*, 88
JIT II, 76
*Journal of Business-to-Business
        Marketing* (JBBM), 88
Journals
    applied, 44
    top five, 43-44
Just-in-time inventory management,
        143

Kill, Bernie, 146
Klein, Lisa R., 153
Knowledge
    cognitive ability, 185, 186-190, 195,
        210, 213-214
    explicit and implicit, 68
Kozma, R. B., 160
Krishnan, H. Shanker, 79

Larréché, Jean-Claude, 71
Lateral learning, 58-59

Leadership Development Program,
        AT&T, 61-62
Learners
    roles of, 175
    types, 172
Learning
    action, 60-63, 78-79
    distance, 63-64, 161, 164-165
    lateral, 58-59
    meaningful, 176
Leavitt, Harold, 12
Lectures as tools, 70
Lichtenberg, James, 164
Lichtenthal, J. David
    industrial marketing stepchild, 260
    review of *Cabell's Directory*,
        283-286
    textbook criteria and methodology,
        183
    twenty-first century education, 1-5
Lifelong learning, 276
Lilien, Gary L., 2-3
    doctoral programs, 9, 42, 44
    program of action, 47-48
Little, John, 42-43, 47
LIX readability index
    use by Backhaus, 250-251, 273, 274
    overview, 190-191
    textbooks, 203
Loe, Terry W., 261
Longitudinal research methodology, 42
Lotus Freelance Plus, 163
Lotus SmartSuite, 163

Madansky, Albert, 13
Majchrzak, A., 125
Management Science, 42
Manager
    cross-functional connections and,
        126
    industrial firm, 116
    training, 56, 58
"Managing Customers for Profit"
        simulation, 71

Mangold, W. Glynn, 161
Manji, James, 146
Marketing, defined, 9
Marketing concept, 53
Marketing list syndrome, 248
Marketing manager, role of, 116
Marshall, Leon, 10
Master's-level education, 87-89, 103
    commentary, 105–108
    promoting growth in education, 97,
        100
    reply to commentary, 109-112
    research analyses, 93-94
    research procedure, 89-93
    survey results, 94-97
    teaching materials shortage,
        100-102
Materials shortage, 100-102
May, Robert G., 13
McKenna, Regis, 55, 76
McKibben, Lawrence E., 11-12, 34-35
Measurement and reward, 48
Meister, Jeanne C., 51
Menter, John T., 79
Metaphors as discovery tools, 67
Methodological skills, 35
Methods discipline, 25
Microsoft Office, 163
Microsoft PowerPoint, 163
Microsoft Publisher, 163
Miller, Fred, 161
Modular programs, 87-88
Moon, Mark A., 79
Moore, Geoffrey A., 123, 124
Muehlfeld, Katrin, 181, 267-278
Multimedia
    benefits of classroom technology,
        172
    educational instruction, 162-163,
        171
    virtual classrooms, 160-161

NAICS (North American Industrial
    Classification System), 130
Narayandas, Narkesari, 3, 51, 81-82

Narus, James A., 3-4
    commentary, 243-257
    master's-level education, 87,
        109-112
    reply to commentary, 271-275
    textbooks. *See* Textbooks,
        comparative review
National Science Foundation, 127
Nayak, P. Ranganathan, 146
Networking, 102
North American Industrial
    Classification System
    (NAICS), 130
Novak, Joseph D., 175

OBB (organization buying behavior),
    53
Off-campus applications, 63-64
Okoye, Diana, 181, 267-278
On-campus applications, 63-64
On-the-job training, 57
Operationalization of knowledge, 225,
    226-227
Organization buying behavior (OBB),
    53
Organizational buying behavior,
    129-130, 236

Paradox, current knowledge, 66-67
Partnering recommendations, 37
Patel, Chris, 186
Perry, James, 171
PhD programs. *See also* Doctoral
    programs
    history, 10-13
    purpose of, 9
    recommendations, 37
Pierson, F. C., 11
Placements, graduate, 32-33, 34
Plank, Richard A.
    reply to commentary, 275-276
    research criticisms, 252-253
    textbook commentary, 259-266

Population sampling for survey, 14
Porter, Lyman W., 11-12, 34-35
Porter-McKibben report, 11-12, 34-35
Porter, Thomas W., 79
Postdoc recommendations, 36
Powell, Judith D., 188
Powers, Thomas L., 188
Pragmatists and high-technology
     markets, 123-124
Prahalad, C. K., 239
Prentice-Hall, management textbook,
     defined, 243
Presentation software, 163
Pricing policies, 202, 254–255
Princeton Review Student Advantage,
     88
Process improvement, 262-263
Procurement process. *See* Purchasing
Product development
     fast-cycle, 146-147, 153
     impact of technology revolution, 54
     time to market, 54, 118, 127-129
Professors. *See* Educators
Program of action, doctoral programs,
     47-48
Project cycle, action learning, 61-62, 63
Purchasing
     trends, 118-121, 140-142, 151-152,
          235-236
     trends, in textbooks, 235-236
Purdue University pilot study, 164
Purpose of book, 2-5

Quelch, John A., 153

Rangan, V. Kasturi, 3, 51, 81-82
Ray, Charles M., 187
Readability, 190-191, 273
Ready, Douglas A., 51
Recommendations
     business schools, 36
     prospective PhDs, 37
     recruiting, 36

Recruiting recommendations, 36
Reeder, Robert R. *See* Textbooks,
     comparative review
Reid, David A., 252
Reisman, Sorel, 161
Reizenstein, Richard C., 79
Relationship marketing
     defined, 142
     executive education, 81
     goal of, 143-144
     in textbooks, 237–239
     undergraduate programs, 121-123,
          130, 142-144, 152
Relationships, exchange, 41-42
Relevance, program
     academic research, 34
     doctoral programs, 42
     preparation for teaching, 26-28
     rigor versus, 47
Reliability testing, 250
Research
     analyses, 93-94
     applied, 43-44
     creativity, 66
     doctoral, 41-42
     improving methodology, 106-107
     master's-level education, 89-94
     schooling emphasis, 19
     textbooks, 249-257
Reward systems and measurements, 36,
     48
Rich, D. Layne, 188
Rigor, 34, 42, 47
Robicheaux, Robert, 161
Rodriguez, Carlos M., 4, 171-173, 175
Ronchetto, John R., 171
Rugimbana, Robert, 186

Sabbatical recommendations, 36
Sales function, 52-53
Sampling for survey, 14
SCANS (Secretary of Labo''s
          Commission on Achieving
          Necessary Skills), 160-161

Schmidt, B. J., 160
Schools, responses to survey, 14-16.
    See also Business school;
    Doctoral programs;
    Undergraduate programs
Scientific Certification System, 147
Sears, Roebuck & Company,
    environmental issues, 147
Secretary of Labor's Commission on
    Achieving Necessary Skills
    (SCANS), 160-161
Segmentation, 53, 252
Service support strategy, 117
Sharma, Arun, 142
Sheth, Jagdish N., 142
SIC (standard industrial classification),
    130
Simulations as tools, 71-72
Skeptics and high-technology markets,
    124
Skill development, undergraduate
    programs, 133-134
Skills, cognitive ability, 185-186
Socialization, 61
Software programs
    desktop publishing, 163
    INDUSTRAT, 71
    integrated for classrooms, 163
    presentation, 163
Special interest group, 89, 102, 111
Speh, Thomas W., 4
    marketing course themes, 188
    reply to commentary, 151-154,
        269-270
    textbook review commentary,
        233-240
    textbooks. *See* Textbooks,
        comparative review
    undergraduate curriculum, 115
Stallard, John J., 187
Stallkamp, Thomas, 119
Standard industrial classification (SIC),
    130
Standardization, 262-265
Stonebraker, Peter W., 161
Strategic alliances, 121-122, 144

Strategic marketing, 239
Strategy variables, 132-133
Structure, conceptual, 52–57
Students
    textbook preferences, 247-248
    training, 1-2
Studies
    educational technology, 167
    ISBM. *See* Institute for the Study of
        Business Markets
Substance discipline, 25
Supply chain management
    purchasing trends, 118-121
    in textbooks, 238
    undergraduate programs, 140-142
Survey data collection, 13-17, 89-93
Synchronization, 262-265
Synthesis, cognitive ability, 185, 194,
    195

Tables, defined, 192
Tabrizi, B. N., 127-128
Tacit knowledge, 68
Task force, 61
Taxonomy. *See* Bloom, Benjamin S.,
    taxonomy
Teachers. *See* Educators
Teaching
    preparation for, 26–28
    schooling emphasis, 19, 35
    shortage of materials, 100-102
    use of textbooks, 106, 108, 111
    user-friendly teaching materials,
        111-112
Technology
    adoption life cycle, 123
    classroom. *See* Classroom
        technology
    enthusiasts, 123
    information, 159
    revolution, 53-54
    role in executive education, 63-64
Textbooks
    comparisons. *See* Textbooks,
        comparative review

Textbooks *(continued)*
    design of, 235-237
    functional features, 277
    future developments, 276-278
    instructor preferences, 247
    physical properties, 277
    production costs, 246, 248
    student preferences, 247-248
    use of. *See* Textbooks used in
        teaching
Textbooks, comparative review,
        181-182, 240
    analysis, 185, 194, 195
    application, 185, 193, 195
    approach, 196-199
    assessment criteria and application,
        225-230
    basic capabilities, 185
    Bloom's taxonomy, 184-194, 223,
        224
    cognitive abilities. *See* Cognitive
        abilities
    commentary, Butaney, 223-230
    commentary, Hutt and Speh,
        233-240
    commentary, Narus, 243-257
    commentary, Plank, 259-266
    comprehensibility, 203-205
    coverage, 253-254
    crafting, 243-249
    criteria and methodology, 183-194
    developing complex capabilities,
        208-210
    evaluation, 186, 194, 195
    formal structure, 194-196
    future research, 214-215
    knowledge, 185, 186–190, 195, 210,
        213-214
    objectives, 183-184
    positioning of texts, 234
    relationship marketing perspective,
        237-239
    reply to commentary, 267-278
    research criticisms, 249-257
    selection for comparison, 182-183
    skills, 185-186

Textbooks, comparative review
        (continued)
    strategic marketing, 239
    summary of results, 211-212
    synthesis, 185, 194, 195
    thematic treatment, 202
    themes, 189-190, 199-202
    theory and practice link, 205,
        207-208
    understanding, 185, 190-193, 195,
        273
    visual comprehensibility, 191-193,
        203-205, 206
Textbooks used in teaching
    CD-ROM versus, 162-163
    graduate texts and high-quality
        instruction, 108
    inexperienced instructors and, 106,
        111
Themes and knowledge areas
    business market characteristics, 129
    cross-functional relationships,
        131-132
    market opportunity evaluation, 130
    organizational buying behavior,
        129-130
    relationship marketing, 130
    strategy variables, 132-133
    textbooks, 189-190, 199-202
Theory of constraints, 261-262
Thomas, Kenneth W., 148
Thomas Register, 145
"Time to market", 54, 118, 127-129
Tools
    discovery, 67
    executive education, 70-72
Topic areas, 95, 96, 98-100
Tornado, technology adoption life
        cycle, 124
Tracks, program, 22-26, 27
Tradeoff analysis, 78
Traditional executive programs, 57-59
Trainer. *See* Educator
Transaction-types perspective,
        236-237, 238-239, 274-275

Trends
  business marketing executive
    education, 75-76
  cross-functional working
    relationships, 118, 125-127
  employment, 109-110
  executive education, 57, 58
  purchasing, 118-121, 140-142,
    151-152, 235-236
Turnover rate of knowledge, 276-277
Two-course sequence, undergraduate
  program, 134-135

Undergraduate programs, 115, 135-136
  business market characteristics, 129
  business marketing course, 116-117
  central themes and knowledge,
    129-133
  commentary, 139-148
  course design, 133-135
  cross-functional connection trends,
    118, 125-127
  cross-functional connections, 116,
    131-132
  cross-functional integration,
    147-148, 153-154
  directions in business marketing
    practice, 117-129
  evaluating market opportunity, 130
  fast-paced product development,
    118, 127-129, 146-147, 153
  high-technology markets, 118,
    123-125
  high-technology product marketing,
    144-145, 153
  organizational buying behavior,
    129-130
  purchasing trends, 118-121,
    140-142, 151-152
  relationship marketing, 118,
    121-123, 130, 142-144, 152
  reply to commentary, 151-154

Undergraduate programs *(continued)*
  role of education, 263-264
  skill development, 133-134
  strategy variables, 132-133
  textbooks, 229-230, 234
  trends in purchasing and supplier
    relations management,
    140-142
  two-course sequence, 134-135
Understanding, cognitive ability, 185,
    190-193, 195, 273
"Using technology", defined, 160

Validity testing, 250, 273
Value analysis, supplier selection, 141
Value-based approach, 274
Value-based segmentation, 252
Van Winkle, Barrik, 163
Vendor selection, 141
Vicere, Albert A., 51
Virtual classroom, 160-161
Visionaries and high-technology
    markets, 123
Visualization and understandability,
    191-193, 203-205, 206
Vlosky, Richard P., 4-5, 159-168,
    175-177

Wang, Q., 125
Watson, Cathrine, 192
Web. *See* World Wide Web
Web sites
  B2B Marketing Exchange, 111
  electronic commerce, 145
  LIX sampling results, 274
  textbook criteria, 199
  textbook thematic treatment, 202
Webster, Frederick, E., Jr., 147. *See
    also* Textbooks, comparative
    review

Weimer, George, 146
Weinstein, David, 71
Welch, Jack, 64, 117
West, Richard W., 12
White, Alan F., 51
Willows, Dale M., 192
Wilson, David T., 4-5, 159-168,
        175-177
Wilson, Elizabeth J., 3, 75-79
Woodruff, Robert B., 79

World Wide Web (WWW). *See also*
        Internet; Web sites
    classroom use, 165-167
    research and data collection, 161
Wynd, William R., 172

Zaltman, Gerald, 3, 51, 81-82